RED FLAGS

RED

How to Spot Frenemies, Underminers, and Toxic People in Your Life

FLAGS

Wendy L. Patrick, Ph.D.

St. Martin's Press

New York

www.stmartins.com

Library of Congress Cataloging-in-Publication Data

Patrick, Wendy L., 1968–
    Red flags : how to spot frenemies, underminers, and toxic people in your life / Wendy L.
    Patrick, PhD.—First Edition.
        Pages cm
    ISBN 978-1-250-05292-6 (hardcover)
    ISBN 978-1-4668-6971-4 (e-book)
    1. Interpersonal attraction.   2. Physical-appearance-based bias.   3. Influence (Psychology)   I. Title.
    HM1151.P36 2015   302—dc23

St. Martin's Press books may be purchased for educational, business, or promotional use. For information on bulk purchases, please contact Macmillan Corporate and Premium Sales Department at 1-800-221-7945, extension 5442, or write specialmarkets@macmillan.com.

First Edition: May 2015

10 9 8 7 6 5 4 3 2 1

This book is dedicated to all the upstanding men and women I have been privileged to work with over the course of my career, and all the victims-turned-survivors on whose behalf I continue to engage in the relentless pursuit of justice. It is also dedicated to the two women in my life who are the ultimate examples of when what looks good really is: my mother, Elizabeth Patrick, and my sister, Jennifer Patrick.

Contents

Acknowledgments

I would like to thank a small, special group of people for their selfless contributions to this work. These people include fellow prosecutors Summer Stephan, Gary Schons, Kate Flaherty, and Bryn Kirvin, dear friends Don Cole and Craig and Linda Barkacs, and in particular, my sister, Jennifer Patrick and my mother, Elizabeth Patrick—from whom the best ideas come.

On the Front Lines

I don't just play a lawyer on TV; I am in court every day. Unlike legal commentators sitting on the sidelines watching the action, I have spent the last two decades in the game. It is my privilege to share what I learned on the battlefield, as a playbook to help you successfully navigate the minefield of relationships in your life. The game changing strategies in this book are designed to help you declare victory.

The fact patterns in this book are illustrations of the specific ways that I have seen people fall for manipulators who look good. Many of the facts are taken from real cases I have handled, which are all a matter of public record. Nonetheless, these case examples were deliberately modified to maintain the anonymity of the individuals involved.

RED FLAGS

Why Bad Looks Good

We have all met them. Smooth-talking, attentive admirers. They boost our self-esteem and make us feel loved, valued, and respected. People like this seem too good to be true. And in some cases, looking back . . . we see that they were.

They were manipulators who broke our hearts, exploited our resources, talked us into doing something we later regretted, or left us emotionally or physically damaged. Afterward we ask ourselves—how did they get away with that? How could someone so bad look so good? Why didn't we see the red flags?

This book will explain why we miss the warning signs, and how to improve our ability to see more clearly. Incorporating real experience with manipulative criminals and their victims over the course of my twenty-year career, corroborated with abundant empirical research, this book will enhance your ability to see other people clearly, both personally and professionally.

As co-author of the revised version of the *New York Times* bestseller *Reading People*,[1] I offer my new book: *Red Flags*. While *Reading People* discussed how to perceive information about other people by looking and listening, *Red Flags* goes much further—recognizing that appearances can be deceiving. It reveals the deeper reasons that we are attracted to certain people who satisfy us emotionally, and why we miss warning signs signaling that they are not as good as they look.

Even when we detect signs of deception or danger, if we are enjoying a relationship, we often downplay the significance of troubling information, muting what should sound like the ringing of alarm bells to the pleasant tinkling of wind chimes.

How Perceptive Are You?

This book is designed to help you distinguish between good people and bad people by enhancing your tools of perception. So let us begin by determining how perceptive you are already. Consider how many of the following questions you can answer:

Your day care provider: how many children does she have and what are their genders and ages?

Your partner: what radio stations are pre-set in his or her car?

Your next-door neighbor: what magazine subscriptions are delivered to his home?

The employee with the office next to you: can you name five books on her shelf?

Your teenage daughter: which social media sites (in addition to Facebook—where she surprisingly accepted your Friend request) is she on?

The lifeguard at your community pool: how much sleep does she get a night? Does she take any drugs or medications?

Your doctor: to what professional associations does he belong? Does he have any specializations and if so, how long has he had them?

Your pastor: what television programs does he watch?

Your boss: how and with whom does she spend her lunch hour?

Your new cyberspace love interest: where does he go after work? What does he do on weekends?

The security guard in your office building: how much time during his shift does he spend on Facebook?

Your accountant: does he gamble? If so, how often, and what type of gambling does he prefer?

Your therapist: how would you characterize her relationship with her office staff? Does she practice the same active listening skills that she suggests you do with your partner?

Your mechanic: what type of car does he drive? How about his wife and children?

The person who parks next to you at your apartment complex: what do they do for a living? Who do they live with?

If you were able to answer five or more, congratulations. You are paying attention to people around you who play a significant role in your life. The information in this book will augment the skills of perception you are already using by enhancing your ability to read below the surface, in order to more accurately determine the significance of the facts and behaviors you perceive.

If you were able to answer less than five, you are going to be very glad you picked up this book.

I Read Red Flags for a Living

As a deputy district attorney and team leader in the Sex Crimes and Human Trafficking Division of the San Diego County District Attorney's Office, I am committed to our mission of protecting the innocent and vigorously prosecuting the guilty. However, we have a saying around the office: It takes a good prosecutor to win a case; it takes a great prosecutor to prevent a crime. We are dedicated to being great prosecutors.

Great prosecutors are never off duty. In order to prevent crime and protect the community, I read red flags for a living—around the clock. Detecting criminals is more challenging than many people think, because clever, intelligent lawbreakers have mastered the art of skillfully flying under the radar. They don't exhibit the external warning signs that many FBI profilers and other experts on criminal behavior are trained to look for. To the contrary—not only do crafty manipulators fail to arouse suspicion, they often generate trust through their cleverly cultivated appearance, demeanor, and personality.

Having worked as both a prosecutor and a criminal defense attorney, I am extremely familiar with the strategies manipulative people use to divert suspicion, and the alluring interpersonal dynamics that distort perspective, causing people to miss signs of deception and danger. I wrote this book to share with you the wisdom learned through these experiences.

My goal in writing *Red Flags* is to use the practical knowledge I have gained over the course of my career to help you understand why bad people often look good. When you are able to separate the dangerous from the desirable, you will be better able to protect yourself and your loved ones, and enhance relationships in every aspect of your life.

Trading Rose-Colored Glasses for Reading Glasses

There are plenty of books designed to help you spot when bad looks bad. Written by law enforcement agents and criminal profilers, these books discuss outwardly observable characteristics such as clothing, body language, micro-expressions, furtive movements, and other signs of suspicious activity.

However, being wary of vagrants in oversized clothing loitering outside public restrooms won't help you gauge the intentions of your handsome new boss or your son's friendly preschool teacher. And knowing to avoid a shifty-eyed, sweating stranger in an alley won't help you interpret the intentions of your new Internet love interest, who has thus far only revealed his basic information and handsome avatar (if that really is his picture).

There are also books designed to help you identify people who *behave* in ways that can make your life miserable. Your visceral response to toxic individuals who make you feel *bad* can help you determine who you need to remove from your life, if possible.

This book, by contrast, is designed to be used with people who do *not* look dangerous and make you feel *good*. These people are able to infiltrate your life more easily. In fact, in many cases, *you invite them in*.

In order to determine whether someone is really as good as they look, this book proposes an examination of people in four areas that, over the course of my career, I have found to be most likely to reveal a person's true colors *when they look good*. They are organized into an easy-to-remember mnemonic spelling FLAG:

Focus: What captures the person's attention? Do they focus on themselves or others?

Lifestyle: How does the person spend their time? What are their hobbies and interests?

Associations: What sort of company do they keep? To what organizations do they belong?

Goals: What are their priorities? Are their ambitions selfish or selfless?

While no method of detection is foolproof, particularly with a practiced manipulator, these four areas can provide a glimpse below the surface, in order to shed light on the motivation behind the moves.

The ability to see through the illusion of good in order to perceive a person's true colors is enhanced through understanding the psychology of attraction.

The Psychology of Attraction:
Lessons from the Dark Side

My background in psychology includes a bachelor's degree in psychology from UCLA with honors, and a doctoral dissertation on the psychology of attraction—focusing on lessons learned through studying the dark side of relationships, including the strategies sexual predators and other criminals use to seduce their victims.[2]

My practical experience in the field of psychology, however, has come from both prosecuting and defending some of the most charming manipulators you have ever met. I have prosecuted murderers who were both handsome and educated, intelligent stalkers who used chillingly disturbing methods of tracking their victims, human traffickers who were white-collar executives by day, and sexually violent predators who seduced *hundreds* of victims while escaping detection for years.

The emotional appeal of these polished, savvy criminals follows them into the courtroom, where they are often perceived as likable and credible in front of a jury. Their cleverly cultivated veneer allows them to draw jurors, judges, and even the lawyers themselves into a false sense of security. We begin to smile and say good morning to the defendant, as we are *ourselves* manipulated by his charm.

These charismatic lawbreakers ingratiate themselves with members of court staff as well—sometimes becoming the most popular person in the courtroom by the end of the trial, often making a better impression on the jury than either of the lawyers trying the case.

When these defendants are referred for psychological evaluations, many of the psychologists share with me afterward that despite their recognition of the offender's obvious manipulative tactics, they find themselves during the examination thinking, *hey, this guy really isn't so bad* . . .

My experience with the psychology of attraction also comes from years of working with victims of crimes that were facilitated through relationship building. These crimes have included everything from child molestation, human trafficking, domestic violence, and stalking, to elder abuse, property crime, economic crime, fraud, and more.

What these cases have in common is the strategies of seduction used by the perpetrators, whom the victims found to be physically, socially, and emotionally appealing. That is why these criminals are so successful. And so dangerous. These wolves in sheep's clothing exploit human vulnerabilities and get away with murder—sometimes literally.

I have assisted expert witnesses in throwing red paint on white boards around the courtroom to explain the blood pattern found at the crime scene, and wrestled with a mannequin on a table in front of the jury to demonstrate how the defendant raped the victim. But what the jury also wants to know, is how the victim came to the crime scene to begin with. In many cases, the answer is *willingly*.

Having completed over one hundred and fifty trials including several co-defendant cases tried to two jury panels simultaneously, I can attest that the most shocking stories about the psychology of attraction come from the witness stand, not the therapist's couch. For the last two decades, I have been the one asking the questions. This book is about the answers.

Under the Influence:
Bad Looks Good When You Feel Good

As a prosecutor I try to avoid discussing intoxication in a positive sense. But here, the shoe fits. Attraction creates a euphoric buzz that infuses our world with exhilaration and feelings of pleasure. Whether we are receiving love, attention, or admiration, we bask in the glow of emotional fulfillment, and can't get enough of people who provide this satisfaction.[3]

We describe people who make us feel this way in glowing terms when they become part of our lives. We gush about our wonderful new love interest. Or the charming neighbor we met at the park. We brag about the new employee we just hired and how lucky we were to snap her up.

In many cases, however, once we sober up, we can see that our reactions to these people do not reflect objective assessments of them—but of ourselves, and how they make us feel. Sometimes we learn the hard way that not everyone who makes us *feel* good, *is* good.

When we are enjoying a relationship over time, soft spots can become blind spots. These emotional blinders prevent us from perceiving or processing negative information that would threaten the positive image we hold of another person, or threaten the stability of the relationship we are enjoying so much. As a result, just as alcohol intoxication can cause us to miss traffic signals such as red lights, emotional intoxication can cause us to miss interpersonal signals such as red flags.

In order to maintain the relationship, we trade in our reading glasses for rose-colored glasses and toxic traits become pleasantly obscured, or misperceived. Aggressiveness becomes assertiveness. Risk taking is interpreted as adventure seeking. Moodiness is viewed as contemplation. Flirtatiousness is downplayed as friendliness.

And finally, sometimes even when we see the warning signs, we still have a hard time extricating ourselves from people who deliver the goods that fuel our emotional addictions—even when we know they are bad for us. We are willing to overlook whatever we have to in order to continue to experience the pleasure.

The Wolf in Sheep's Clothing:
Attraction to the Wrong People for the Right Reasons

What makes another person attractive? Sometimes it is physical beauty, which is often in the eye of the beholder. Some people like women with long hair; others prefer short and curly. Some like women who are slight of build; others prefer curves.

What looks good on the guys? Some people like broad shoulders; others prefer chiseled features. Some love thick hair; others believe that bald is beautiful. And then there are cultural preferences, manner of dress, style, and so on.

When it comes to what is *emotionally* attractive, however, there is far more agreement. Emotionally, we are often attracted to people who make us feel good about ourselves. We find people emotionally attractive when they make us feel loved, respected, valued, admired, accepted, attractive, and the list goes on. These emotions are wholesome, healthy, self-affirming reasons we are drawn to other people. The problem is that both good and bad people satisfy these emotional needs.

The Wolf in Wolf's Clothing:
Attraction to the Wrong People for the Wrong Reasons

Sometimes attraction is counterintuitive. Some people look good *because* they look bad. Distinguished from cases where people are attracted to individuals *despite* the other person's faults, sometimes unsuitability is part of the allure.

What I refer to as the seeking-the-wolf phenomenon is something I have become familiar with through the cases I have handled over the course of my career. This destructive desire causes people to pursue relationships that are stimulating and emotionally arousing, but also unhealthy, dangerous, and sometimes against the law.

This area is explored in order to gain perspective into *why* some people intentionally veer off the path in order to walk on the dark side. It will examine when and why bad looks are appealing, how people rationalize the detour, and how to spot the warning signs sooner rather than later in order to navigate back onto the right path.

The Sheep in Wolf's Clothing:
When Good Looks Bad

We all know wholesome, honest, hardworking people who can look pretty scary on the street. Like the neurosurgeon down the block who presents a foreboding, shadowy figure in the dark at 4:00 AM in his bulky jogging suit and bandana. Or the tattooed, motorcycle-riding, bearded Christian evangelist who drives through downtown neighborhoods at night, passing out food to the homeless.

By the same token, we know people with hearts of gold who come across as aloof and arrogant in public, because they are terribly insecure in social settings. And regarding actions, sometimes seemingly suspicious behavior means nothing. This is why the FLAGs cover four broad areas of examination and not just one. It is not the intention of this book to infect personal relationships with unnecessary distrust or paranoia. To the contrary, it aims to equip the reader with the tools necessary to detect danger or deception in order to avoid or disentangle yourself from unhealthy relationships—leaving you with more time to enjoy healthy ones.

It is also true that good people have character flaws. Nobody is perfect. In addition, some individuals to whom you are attracted are not bad people, but might be bad choices for *you*. A gregarious flirt is not a good match for a person who is insecure. A couch potato is not a healthy choice for a fitness fanatic. When relational mismatches fizzle, it doesn't necessarily mean you chose a bad person; it seems more likely that you made a bad *choice* in selecting a partner.

APPEARANCES CAN BE DECEIVING

- The wolf in sheep's clothing looks good *although* he is bad.
- The wolf in wolf's clothing looks good *because* he is bad.
- The sheep in wolf's clothing looks bad although he is *good*.

Ten Reasons Bad People Can Look Good

Research and popular wisdom identify an exhaustive list of qualities people find to be attractive. In the cases I have handled over the course of my career, I have condensed that list to highlight ten sources of attraction that *consistently* draw people in like magnets. These ten sources are not based solely on the way a person looks, what they have, or how they behave. They are based on the *way they make us feel*.

In the chapters that follow, these ten areas are explained in detail, and their appeal is corroborated with scientific research. These categories range from the delusion that *beautiful is always good*, to the trendy notion that *bad is the new good*. Here they are. Bad people can look good because they are:

Attractive
Powerful
Credible
Attentive
Affirming
Similar
Familiar
Exciting
Forbidden
Dangerous

Wait a minute, you might be thinking, this list sounds like the qualities that describe my ideal partner. I agree. It would be a dream come true to become involved with a *good* person who has all of these traits. Because even the last two, under the right circumstances (i.e., not forbidden in the legal sense or personally dangerous to *you*), can be incredibly arousing. But if you had that kind of luck, where everyone you met who looked good really was, you probably wouldn't have picked up this book. Most of us have not been that fortunate.

As you also may have noticed, these ten areas of attraction are not mutually exclusive. Most people, whether good, bad, or somewhere in the middle, have varying degrees of the qualities on this list. And some of these qualities are particularly potent when used in combination.

For example, attractive admirers can be double trouble. Some manipulators use the combination of good looks and positive attention as a one-two punch to knock out our defense mechanisms in order to get what they want. Consider the handsome golf instructor who uses flattery and attentiveness to seduce middle-aged, wealthy women by making them feel young and beautiful.

On the other hand, there is the talented, professional basketball player who uses a combination of power and credibility to encourage and mentor troubled youths who have a passion for sports and view him as a role model.

You will meet both of these examples in this book, as well as many others. But for now, let us examine each of the ten areas in more detail.

The Power of Attraction

We tend to believe that beautiful is good. Physically attractive people are not only "easy on the eyes," but prompt positive judgments in other areas. When we find someone physically attractive, we believe they have other positive traits—which is not always the case. The challenge is being able to determine when what looks good on the outside is also good on the inside.

The Attraction of Power

Whether attained through fame, money, or prestige, power is magnetic. People are drawn to power like moths to a flame. Whether in politics, corporate business, or show business, many believe that people in power deserve what they have, and filter negative information through a lens of reverence and respect.

However, like other forms of attraction, power can be used both benevolently and malevolently. What is most telling is how a person acquired power, and how they use the power they have.

The Comfort of Credibility

We want to have confidence in the services we seek and on which we depend—from our doctor to our local sheriff to our political representatives. We therefore often choose to believe that people with the appropriate credentials, training, and expertise can deliver the goods and services we need.

Sometimes we are correct; other times we learn the hard way that credentials do not necessarily translate into character. The veneer of credibility that accompanies an impressive façade sometimes provides the perfect cover for unscrupulous activity.

The Pleasure of Positive Attention

People love attention—especially positive attention. Receiving attention causes many people to fall head over heels in love with the attention giver—particularly if they are receiving it for the first time. Selective attention is particularly seductive.

But when someone's attention is focused on you, the most important question is *why*. Consider whether they are genuinely captivated with *you*, something you have access to, or something you can do for them.

The Allure of Affirmation

We all want to be accepted, respected, validated, and approved. Someone who is affirming makes us feel good about ourselves, boosts our self-esteem, and gives us the satisfaction of knowing we are important and valuable.

Some people who shower us with compliments mean every word they say. Others don't. A more in-depth examination of the motives of the praise-giver will help to tell the difference.

The Seduction of Similarity

Similarity is seductive. We gravitate toward people who look like us, talk like us, or share the same rank or position. We view these people as safe, approachable, and trustworthy. Bonding through identification, we gain a sense of connectedness, security, and belonging.

Some people who appear to be similar are kindred spirits; others are manipulative chameleons who aren't really similar to us at all.

Familiarity Breeds Contentment

In most cases, familiarity breeds contentment not contempt. We tend to view people we see frequently as "safe," regardless of how well we know them. Sometimes we are horribly mistaken.

We see these cases on the news, when the next-door neighbor, described as "such a nice guy," turns out to be an ax murderer. Or a terrorist. Cases like this prove that true familiarity requires more than mere recognition through repeated exposure or proximity.

The Call of the Wild

Many people who live "normal" lives are fascinated by those who don't. Craving excitement, some sensation seekers gravitate toward daredevils who can spice things up through the exhilaration of novelty and adventure.

Unfortunately, some people who are stimulating are neither safe nor sincere. Reckless thrill seekers are not soul mates—just playmates. Responsible like-minded enthusiasts, on the other hand, are ready to ride into the sunset (wearing helmets), on a motorcycle built for two.

The Temptation of Taboo

Some people find individuals who are "off limits" to be particularly attractive—despite their better judgment. Scandalous behavior is often driven by the urge to indulge in activity that is prohibited—sometimes for that reason alone.

Some relationships are illegal, such as having an underage girlfriend. Some people are off-limits because of the relational status of one or both parties. Other people are considered to be taboo due to social and conventional norms.

However, some people who are initially off-limits can become perfectly acceptable over time. Relational breakups, job transfers, and other changed circumstances can transform what might otherwise have been an inappropriate relationship into an inspirational pairing.

When Dangerous Is Desirable

Some individuals are drawn to people who are dangerous, finding them both stimulating and arousing. Who are the main characters in the wildly popular television shows *Twilight*, *Dexter*, and *Breaking Bad*? That's right: a vampire, a serial killer, and a drug dealer. And let us not forget the notorious secret agent James Bond, who was employed how? As an assassin.

Some people attracted to dangerous characters seek out dark personalities in real life. Prison groupies and women who fall in love with serial killers demonstrate the unfortunate extent of the phenomenon that even *really bad* can look good.

On the other hand, many good people are dangerous too—but their mission is to protect others. For these people, being dangerous is not a vice, but a virtue.

Different Shades of Red:
You Can't Avoid What You Don't See

Clearly, there are varying degrees of bad. On one end of the spectrum is the type of client I sometimes represented as a public defender—the homeless man who recklessly dines and dashes in the dead of winter in the hopes of landing himself a warm bed in jail for the holidays, to avoid having to sleep on the street in freezing temperatures. He knows that committing a felony would gain him a longer sentence, but he is not willing to commit a more serious crime.

On the other end of the spectrum is the white collar criminal who rolls up to the office valet parking stand in a high-end Lexus, who is strategically infiltrating his company by ingratiating himself with all the right people in order to gather the information he needs to facilitate an economic heist.

A simple video surveillance system will identify the homeless diner and dasher, if management or other patrons don't catch him first. The white collar con artist is far more dangerous, much more attractive, and can cause his company exponentially more economic loss because he is more likely to get away with his crime.

Some criminals commit the same crime using very different techniques. One type of rapist breaks into a home, hides in a closet, and leaps out at night to sexually assault a woman in her bedroom. A good home alarm system and a few pitbulls might keep this man out.

But consider the handsome rapist who is charismatic and clever enough to prompt a woman at a bar to *ask him* for a ride home, only to pull over in a remote area, rape her, then steal her phone and her clothes in order to give himself enough time to make a getaway.

Sophisticated manipulators like the white collar criminal and the handsome rapist are extremely dangerous because not everyone takes the right precautions to keep them at bay. Although they might be as bad as they come, the darkness is veiled behind a mask of good.

Reading in the Dark:
The Dark Triad Personality

Reckless criminals and toxic individuals who are abusive, egotistical, intolerant, volatile, selfish, or condescending are often easily identifiable—and thus avoidable. Many people with darker traits are not. In fact, some of the most dangerous individuals display one or more of the ten qualities of attraction, which camouflage the darkness beneath the surface. Many of these people share another dangerous trait in common: they are smart enough to pull off the disguise. Meet the Dark Triad personality.[4]

The Dark Triad is made up of narcissism, Machiavellianism, and psychopathy.[5] This notorious trio of negative personality traits, dubbed a "James Bond psychology,"[6] is often distinguished from other character flaws by its ability to present a very attractive façade. While men tend to score higher in Dark Triad traits than women,[7] there are Bond Girls as well, because Dark Triad traits are shared by both genders.[8]

What are Dark Triad personalities really like behind the mask? Narcissists have an entitlement mentality and a "grandiose self view," Machiavellians are extraverted, insincere, and "interpersonally duplicitous," and psychopaths are heartless, lacking in empathy, and behave in a fashion that is erratic and antisocial.[9] In addition, the Dark Triad traits are linked by dishonesty, aggressiveness, and short-term mating practices,[10] as well as callous manipulation.[11]

These people sound awful, you might be thinking. They are. But *you* might not think so, because you might not see any of their dark traits until it is too late. These people avoid detection through employing unique tactics of influence, geared toward the specific situation.[12]

With polished impression-management abilities, excellent reading-people skills, and enhanced attention to detail, they often fly under the radar.[13] This is why they are successful at committing crimes, soliciting resources, and taking advantage of people.[14] The scope of their deception stretches from the boardroom to the bedroom, as they can be toxic employees who manipulate coworkers, as well as manipulative lovers.[15]

Each of the three Dark Triad personality subtypes presents a distinctive profile. Let us examine them individually.

The Appeal of the Narcissist

Of the three Dark Triad personality traits, narcissists are perceived as most attractive.[16] Narcissistic Personality Disorder is described in the Diagnostic and Statistical Manual of Mental Disorders-5 as "A pervasive pattern of grandiosity (in fantasy or behavior), need for admiration, and lack of empathy."[17] While this clinical description may not sound attractive, narcissists themselves often are.[18]

Narcissists are popular at first sight due to their flashy appearance, superficial charm, and self-assuredness.[19] This is particularly true with narcissists who have an entitlement mentality, are manipulative, and seek to exploit others.[20] And believe it or not, narcissists are liked at first sight despite being accurately perceived as narcissistic.[21]

The Charm of the Psychopath

In *Without Conscience*, Dr. Robert Hare defines psychopaths as "social predators who charm, manipulate, and ruthlessly plow their way through life, leaving a broad trail of broken hearts, shattered expectations, and empty wallets." [22] They selfishly take what they want without feeling any regret or guilt.[23]

I have met a steady stream of psychopaths throughout the course of my career, once they have finally been arrested for their often sophisticated crimes. But not all psychopaths make it into the courtroom, or shall I say, at least not into the defendant's chair.

They can also be found in the corporate boardroom, the office break room, and possibly, in your bedroom. The challenge is picking them out. Because despite the visceral reaction to the clinical title, these smooth operators do not look like deranged, soulless crazies. They look just like everyone else. In fact, they often look *better*.

As Hervey Cleckley discusses in his seminal work *The Mask of Sanity*, a psychopath's "poisonous mix of traits" include not only callousness and a lack of remorse, but also self-assuredness, alertness, and charm.[24] They can be witty, clever, amusing, entertaining, and likable.[25]

But before you start pointing fingers at people you know (yourself?) who have some of the characteristics described, Dr. Hare warns that psychopathy is a clinical diagnosis to be made by a trained professional, and that there are plenty of non-psychopaths who share some of the same attributes.[26]

In addition, while psychopaths make up only one percent of the general population,[27] many people possess psychopathic *traits*, which we are cautioned not to confuse with the full-blown disorder.[28] Famous television characters with psychopathic traits include Alan Shore from *Boston Legal*, and J. R. Ewing from *Dallas*.[29]

Meet the Machiavellian

People high in Machiavellianism are perceived as more intelligent and attractive than other people, even though Machiavellianism is not linked with intelligence or evidence of success such as status or income.[30] It is linked with something far more dangerous: manipulation.

Named after the writings of Niccolo Machiavelli, Machiavellianism is expressed through a manipulative, insincere, cold personality and cynical view of the world.[31] You might hear a Machiavellian use the phrase "screw them before they screw you," because they live by this philosophy and behave accordingly, considering it better to manipulate others before they are manipulated.[32]

Machiavellianism is manifest through interpersonal strategic behavior in pursuit of self-interest, often using both manipulation and deception.[33] Machiavellianists use others in a goal-driven fashion as a means to an end.[34] While they are emotionally cunning in order to promote their own interests, they are generally low in the ability to read the emotions of other people.[35]

> **DETECTING THE DARK TRIAD**
>
> **Focus:** Self-focused, not other-focused.
>
> **Lifestyle:** Pattern of exploitation and manipulation.
>
> **Associations:** Relationships characterized by shallowness instead of warmth.
>
> **Goals:** Selfish, not altruistic.

The Myth of Invulnerability

I am having coffee with one of my good friends in law enforcement. He is telling me about a woman he is dating, who is recently divorced. She assures him that she is no longer seeing her ex-husband, but he is not convinced. Oblivious to the irony, with a concerned expression he asks me, "Do you think she is telling me the truth?"

What do you think this man does for a living? You won't believe it. Polygrapher. With twenty-five years of experience. That's right, a man who detects lies for a living can't tell if his new girlfriend is lying. What hope is there for the rest of us?

Plenty. That is where the FLAGs come in. This is simply a classic example of how regardless of how perceptive we are in other areas of our lives, we are all vulnerable to losing objectivity when we become emotionally involved.

And if you think that you are immune from being unduly influenced because you are self-confident, attractive, and successful, think again. Everyone has a crack in the armor. Having spent my career working with crime victims and their families, I have seen time and again that the belief that only the underprivileged and the weak become victimized is delusional and dangerous.

In fact, one of the most sobering truths about manipulative people is their astonishing success in seducing intelligent, accomplished, successful individuals who do not fit within any preconceived "victim" profile. This is because people with dark personalities target *everyone*, perceiving all people to be weak and vulnerable to exploitation.[36] Whether this is due to a perception of emotion as weakness or a propensity to evaluate everyone negatively,[37] this observation may help explain their quest for victim quantity over quality.[38]

Identifying Emotional Needs

One of the most disturbing aspects of the bad-looks-good phenomenon is the fact that the class of people who are deceived is not limited to lonely, unintelligent people with unfulfilling lives. Successful people with prestigious jobs, loving families, and financial stability are lured off the right path and into the weeds every day by smooth-talking manipulators. Here is how it happens.

Everyone has emotional needs and desires they depend on others to fulfill. Ironically, many relationships fail because neither partner has a clue what they are. People are often oblivious about their own emotional needs, much less dialed in to the emotional needs of others.

Practiced manipulators, on the other hand, know what you need before you do. Psychopaths are good at reading people and uncovering areas of weakness and vulnerability.[39] This allows them to function as "social chameleons," able to wear different masks and turn many colors in order to appeal to a wide range of individuals.[40] They flatter the narcissist with attention, and reassure the anxious with a nonthreatening style.[41]

Psychopaths prey on areas of weakness, as buttons that can be pushed.[42] They can even fool professionals trained to deal with psychological disorders.[43] How do they know what our emotional needs are? For starters, by observing our relational preferences, and relational status.

Chasing the Right Kind of High

Emotional needs are often revealed through examining the types of people to whom we are drawn. People who are insecure with their physical appearance often seek partners who provide consistent validation of their physical attractiveness. People who suffer from intellectual insecurity seek partners who provide encouragement and affirmation of their cognitive abilities.

Someone seeking romance might happily overlook red flags in exchange for attention and affection. Someone who is *not* looking for romance may be better able to recognize signs of dishonesty and deception, even in an attentive, affectionate, potential suitor.

A new employee seeking professional respect might be manipulated by someone who provides job-related recognition, while a person at the top of the corporate ladder may view such attention as cheap flattery. However, although the person at the top of the company food chain may be confident in the boardroom, he or she may be insecure in the bedroom—and may therefore have married a partner who provides reassurance and encouragement in that arena.

Shopping While You Are Hungry

For someone who is single and hoping to partner up, relationship shopping presents some of the same dangers as grocery shopping. These include exercising bad judgment in choosing what to buy, and pursuing what will make them feel good the fastest.

If you go to the grocery store while you are hungry, your cart will likely include items that look really good, although you know they are bad for you. That is why candy and soda are displayed right next to the register. People who relationship-shop out of desperation are prone to making the same bad choices.

This can happen because the fear of being single causes people to lower their standards and settle for less, believing that any relationship is better than being alone.[44] Once involved, the fear of being single causes people to lower their standards within relationships in order to maintain them.[45] And after a breakup, many people seek to re-partner quickly.[46]

With observation, practiced manipulators can detect a person's emotional soft spots and relational desires, and capitalize on areas of vulnerability.

When Appearances Are Reality:
When Good Looks Good

Before you wave a white flag of defeat in your search for the right relationship, remember that much of the time, what looks good really is. The world is filled with wonderful, authentic people, who are attractive, kind, and genuinely care about you. They brighten your day and make you feel valued and loved.

To illustrate this point, I will share an observation that surprises most people. After a career of dealing with literally the worst of the worst in society, I have reached the heartening conclusion that most people are *good*. For every child that is abducted, there are scores of volunteers who jump into search and rescue mode looking for clues. For every family that loses their house due to an arsonist, there are hundreds of people who donate their time and money to helping the victims rebuild.

Similarly, for every manipulative individual who malevolently seeks to exploit human vulnerabilities, there are millions of people who benevolently seek to fulfill human needs. In other words, the good far outnumber the bad.

Celebrating this realty, this book ends on a high note. The final chapter is filled with examples of how in all ten areas, frequently, what looks good *really is*.

From Red Flags to Green Lights

This book illustrates, through practical examples, the wide range of emotional influence generated by the ten sources of attraction, and how to use the four FLAG areas to distinguish red flags from green lights. Each chapter contains vignettes in both personal and professional contexts, demonstrating how each of the ten characteristics has the potential to color our perspective through evoking positive emotion.

While some of the examples are heartbreaking, others are heartwarming—reflecting the reality that each source of attraction presents both a warning and an opportunity. When you are aware of your own emotional needs, you are better able to spot manipulators before you become emotionally addicted.

When you can detect and authentically fulfill the emotional needs and desires of other people, *you* become the narcotic. Genuinely enhancing the lives of others in this fashion will improve the satisfaction of all your relationships. You will strengthen your marriage, empower your children with the self-esteem they need to flourish, and build stronger friendships and relationships in every aspect of your life.

Sound good? Let's get started.

Reading Red FLAGs

Four Ways to Separate the Dangerous from the Desirable

S ome of you may remember those 3D images that became popular in the 1990s—where at first glance they appeared to be a senseless mix of colors and designs, but if you relaxed your eyes and looked long enough, a very different picture would emerge.

Similar to clarifying optical illusions, reading red flags requires a combination of attention and patience. If you think you can always spot a dangerous person just by looking, think again. All you can see in most cases is what is on the outside.

We don't need to be told to avoid a shadowy figure in a dark alley, or a person who arrives at work with the butt of a gun sticking out of his waistband. And at a social event, we won't accept a ride home with someone who is stumbling around and reeks of alcohol.

We might, however, accept a ride from a handsome man in a suit and tie wearing an expensive watch. We might do this even if we knew he had a glass of wine. Surely, based on his professional image, he is responsible enough to know when he is able to drive safely . . . right?

Wrong. Sometimes—dead wrong. I have both prosecuted and defended vehicular homicide cases where the drivers were clean-cut professionals. Some drunk drivers are sporting thousand-dollar suits in their mug shots—proving that there is no correlation between a polished appearance and safe driving. Sadly, there is no correlation in other areas either. Identity thieves, insider traders, and manipulators of every kind are often attractive, poised, and well spoken.

Misperception touches our lives personally as well as professionally. The handsome, muscular man in the online profile may not be the same guy who walks through the door of the restaurant on your first date. And what you see in a job interview may not be what you get on the job, due to the self-presentation tactics used by interviewees.[1]

We need a better way to analyze people than just looking and listening because we jump to conclusions quickly—forming impressions of someone within a tenth of a second.[2] Not only is that enough time to form trait inferences, but those judgments are enduring.[3] How much do we need to see? We determine whether to approach or avoid potential romantic suitors based on our perception of just their face.[4] Once introduced, we might decide on how positive a future relationship with someone will be after only three to ten minutes of conversation.[5]

Our impressions of a situation are also fueled by what we hear. An illustration of this phenomenon comes from my public defender days, conducting video arraignments from the local jail. During the course of one afternoon, the judge, who could only see me and one client at a time on the television screen, became seriously alarmed when I suddenly darted off camera to the sound of twenty grown men screaming. I still remember the look of relief on his face when I returned a few seconds later, explaining that I had to kill a spider that was crawling towards the bench where they were sitting, unable to escape.

Despite the speed with which we judge people and situations, experience demonstrates that we cannot always trust what we see, hear, or otherwise perceive. Let's look at some examples.

When Appearances Are Deceiving

When I was a criminal defense attorney, I represented clients charged with everything from homicide to throwing peanuts at a policeman at a

ball game. Some of these people were innocent; most were not. My role
as a zealous advocate, however, included ensuring that a jury did not
convict them based on their appearance alone.

Some of my clients came to court looking like a million bucks.
Other might as well have carried a sign that read "Guilty as Charged."
In fact, some of them dressed in a fashion that made them look as if
they were guilty of crimes *much worse* than those with which they were
charged.

There is nothing quite like the challenge of connecting with a jury when
you are sitting next to a man who looks like he just walked out of central
casting ready to audition for a role as a gangster. While thankfully, the
colored bandanas and chains some of these young men brought to court
were usually confiscated by the bailiff before the jury arrived, the inappropriate slogans on their T-shirts were often still visible even after the
court directed that they be worn inside out.

Because my job was to provide the best possible defense, in cases like
these where my clients and I were working at cross-purposes, my only
hope was to connect with the jury in a fashion that would divert their
attention away from my client and onto me. Attempting to radiate a spirit
of springtime and innocence through my pastel-colored suits and pearls,
I hoped the jury would fail to notice my client sitting beside me doodling
gang monikers on a notepad.

Now as a veteran prosecutor, many of the defendants I prosecute look
nothing like the clients I represented as a defense attorney. To the contrary, they often show up in court looking more professional than most
attorneys.

Wearing business suits and carrying briefcases, some defendants are
visually indistinguishable from their lawyers before the trial begins. Sometimes I see jurors looking quizzically over at the defense table where two
well-dressed men are sitting behind a sign that says "Defendant," wondering who is who.[6]

Even when the defendant is identified by the judge, many people still
have a hard time regarding a handsome man in a suit and tie with dis-

gust, even when they know he is accused of a crime. In fact, they might even follow him across the street over the lunch break if he jaywalks—because research demonstrates that more people will break the law by following a jaywalker across the street who is wearing a suit and tie than one who is wearing denim.[7]

So what does a business suit tell you about the person wearing it? The first defendant I saw punch his lawyer in the face (yes I have seen this happen more than once) was wearing a business suit, as was a defendant I saw reach into his pants during a trial and throw excrement at the jury. Does that answer the question?

When Appearances Are Disarming

Sometimes appearances are not only deceiving, they are disarming—evoking an emotional response that causes us to misjudge what we see.

The first love letter I received from a criminal defendant was from a man who had killed and dismembered several victims. I did not suspect this caliber of criminal because his flowery letter read like Shakespearean poetry. The most brutal murder I ever prosecuted—committed by smashing the victim's head off with a rock, was perpetrated by a quiet man, slight of build, who never even peeked at the jury during the trial. So much for appearances.

One commonly evoked emotion that causes people to miscalculate character and criminal potential is sympathy. I have experienced this myself when I have had to arraign a criminal defendant who is lying in a hospital bed, bruised, swollen, and hooked up to an IV. The judge, defense attorney, court reporter and I are all there crowded around the bed because when an in-custody defendant is medically unable to travel to the courthouse—we bring the courthouse to him.

Looking down at the sympathetic figure lying in front of me, it is hard to believe he is capable of committing the violent acts for which I charged him. When I get to trial, however, I will show the jury photographs of what the defendant looked like the night before, when he committed the armed robbery (before running into rival gang members responsible for his current condition)—powerful images that evoke fear, not sympathy.

Appearances can also be disarming because they cause us to *underestimate* someone who doesn't look the part. This can be due to age, appearance, demeanor, or a host of other factors. I prefer to believe the following example was due to a youthful appearance.

Very early in my career as a prosecutor, I was on my way to domestic violence court pushing an enormous cart of files, reflecting the violent behavior that characterized Super Bowl weekend. As I approached, all of the defendants were lined up outside the courtroom. All men.

One by one, they began to comment about how "the little file clerk" was pushing a cart that was bigger than she was. "Oh, get the door for that cute little file clerk." "Hey little file clerk, can we push your cart? That's too big for you!" Comments that prompted much snickering and laughing from the rest of the group.

They weren't laughing for long. Because as soon as we got inside, they realized that I wasn't the file clerk; I was the district attorney prosecuting all their cases.

The Pretense of Public Persona

I am questioning an eyewitness to a racially motivated attempted murder at an investigative grand jury proceeding. She is employed in a respectable public position. When I have completed my questions, the grand jurors are passing me questions of their own. Now that they have heard what the witness *said*, and learned about the position she holds, they want to know who she *is*.

Political candidates can relate to this type of scrutiny. Running for office is like being exposed to a full body scan at the airport—and having all your luggage screened. Because transparency reveals truthfulness.

In contrast, when it comes to our personal lives, many people choose babysitters, employees, and potential romantic partners without knowing anything about them beyond that which is publicly observable. This can be a terrible mistake.

Some people hide behind a public façade of righteousness that requires strategic questioning to pierce the veil of virtue. The reality that a public persona is not always consistent with private behavior is illustrated through the process of jury selection.

One hundred potential jurors have just been seated. The defense attorney and I are both on sensory overload, scanning the sea of faces, trying to absorb as much information as we can in order to decide which individuals might be a good fit for our respective sides of the case.

The young woman on trial is sitting at the table, muttering profanities under her breath, drawing pictures of bunny rabbits, which she will proudly present to her attorney on a break. What did she do? She killed her mother. Stabbed her with a kitchen knife multiple times—chasing her down to finish the job. Then she called 911 and reported the crime. So . . . why are we here? She has pled not guilty by reason of insanity.

Because this case will consist in large part of a "battle of the experts," I want to select only those jurors who can process, interpret, and analyze full days of complicated psychological testimony. As I look around the room, however, at this point everyone looks the same. I am looking at a large group of nicely dressed, wholesome-looking citizens, sitting up straight and paying attention. They look like they are ready for a job interview. And in a sense, they are. That is why they are putting up a good front.

Merely observing these potential jurors sitting on display in the courtroom is not going to help me. They all look good. Sure, we will be asking them questions, but public presentation can be manipulated verbally as well. In front of a room full of strangers, these people not only want to look good, they want to sound good too. And as much experience as the defense attorney and I have, we still run the risk of believing every word they say.

This is because while some people fancy themselves good judges of character, most people take others at face value.[8] In reality, like a politician caught on a hot microphone, it is the things people say when they *don't* think everyone can hear them that are most revealing.

So if looks can be deceiving and talk is cheap, do actions speak louder than words? Not always. Outward manifestations of good behavior do not necessarily reflect motives. The juror who makes a big show of holding the door open for the rest of the panel may be acting out of the goodness of his heart, or in order to gain attention and respect.[9] The only way to tell for sure is to observe the person's willingness to engage in helping behavior when no one is watching.[10] But because we can't become stalkers and spies, we have to find other ways to accurately discern motives.

Seeing Behind the Façade:
FLAGs as Four Windows to the Soul

Some internal conditions are harder to read than others. The level of intoxication of a well-dressed, articulate driver of a Mercedes pulled over for a broken tail light will be harder to detect than the driver who is passed out behind the wheel of his pick up truck in the McDonald's drive thru.

Deciphering intention is much harder than detecting intoxication, especially with seemingly upstanding, attractive people.

Thankfully, even when someone presents a pleasing public image, there are still ways to perceive the person behind the persona. Once you have gleaned all the information you can from appearance, body language, verbal disclosures, and behavior, the FLAGs provide portals to look *inside* a person to detect motivation, character, and goals.

An analogy can be made to the home. A residence in an upscale neighborhood might have a stylish exterior, indicating good taste and material wealth. But you don't know anything about the character of the occupants until you view the inside.

As a prosecutor, I have accompanied law enforcement many times to interview witnesses in low-income areas of town. We have approached dilapidated, run-down apartment complexes only to enter an apartment that was meticulously clean and orderly, which provided a far more accurate assessment of the occupants in terms of their standards and values—and in our case their credibility—than the area of town in which they could afford to live.

With attractive people, the opposite is sometimes true. An impressive exterior does not necessarily ensure equally impressive values and morals. The FLAGs are designed to provide a view *behind* the veneer in order to learn critical information that is not immediately visible.

From a career's worth of experience, I have identified four areas that *consistently* yield information that can enhance your ability to separate good people from bad people who look good. Designed to stimulate observations that could otherwise fly under the radar, each area can help you identify manipulative and conniving people who do not wear their dangerous proclivities on their sleeves.

They are presented in the easy to remember acronym FLAG:

Focus
Lifestyle
Associations
Goals

These four areas are useful because of their ability to reveal subconscious information. Compared to aspects of impression management such as personal appearance that are easy to manipulate, the information expressed through these four areas is harder to fake. Let's examine each one separately to see exactly why this is true.

Focus:
Fixation Reveals Motivation

Think of how creepy it would be to be watching a tennis match where everyone's heads are snapping back and forth following the ball, when suddenly you spot a sinister-looking person on the opposite side of the court—staring intently at *you*. That might send a chill right up your spine.

Focus of attention reveals thoughts, feelings, intentions, and interests. It is rare to encounter someone who is completely zoned out on screensaver mode. Most people are paying attention to *something*. We can gain an enormous amount of insight about someone when we discover what captures his or her attention.

For example, a man may be physically present at brunch with his family on Saturday morning. But if a football game is on at the same time, he may be unable to follow the conversation because he is covertly watching as much of the game as he can on his smart phone under the table.

Think about your own selective focus. Have you ever noticed that when you are driving around looking for somewhere to eat because you are hungry, every sign you see looks like a restaurant marquee? Or have you noticed after the love of your life who drives a red Durango breaks up with you, you are amazed at how many red Durangos you see on the road? You think that model must have been the bestselling car of the year!

To use a more sinister example, in detecting pedophiles, one of the red flags I alert parents to watch for is an unnatural focus on a child. While most parents can spend no more than an hour sitting on the floor playing video games with a child, a pedophile can sit there *all day long* giving the child his undivided attention. Why? His focus is not in entertaining the child. His focus *is* the child.

Focus of conversation is another valuable piece of information. Whether it is sports, travel, ambition, or future plans, you can learn a great deal about someone through the topics he or she wants to discuss. And visually, consider whether the optics match the topics. Someone who smiles while relating a tragic event or displays mannerisms that contradict his or her message is likely to be viewed with suspicion and distrust.

Regarding social orientation, a person's use of "I," "we," and other pronouns can reveal inclusivity or exclusivity, indicating whether someone is focused on themselves or others.

Self-focus is also revealed through people whose primary conversation topic is themselves, or who respond to positive feedback with pride.[11] When presented with negative feedback, a self-absorbed individual is more likely to respond with "My bad" rather than "I'm sorry."

Selective Focus

Selective focus is often very revealing, especially when it is out of place under the circumstances. When we replay the video footage from the 2013 Boston Marathon bombing, we see thousands of fans focused on the race, watching and cheering on the runners. The bombing suspects, the Tsarnaev brothers, however, are not watching the race. They were there for another reason—to set off homemade bombs. Their focus is on carrying out their crime.

The 2014 protests in Ferguson, Missouri, following the officer involved in the shooting of Michael Brown, also demonstrated how different motives are revealed through selective focus. Lawful demonstrators exercising their First Amendment rights gravitated toward the news cameras, while criminal opportunists avoided the media to escape detection, traveling under the radar to exploit neighborhood businesses through vandalism and looting.

It is also suspicious when a person's behavior appears to be for show—when they are pretending to be engaged in some type of activity, but their focus is elsewhere. Surveillance footage reviewed after a burglary often shows a co-conspirator holding a telephone to his ear outside a liquor store about to be burglarized, yet his focus on the cars pulling in and out of the parking lot reveals that he is really functioning as a lookout.

Inadvertent Exposure

You can learn volumes about a person's interests the way I do with my potential jurors. By observing their behavior when they are *out* of the spotlight.

In the courtroom, jurors are in a fishbowl. They are literally the center of attention of everyone in the room, including each other, and are thereby motivated to showcase themselves in the best light possible. However, while they might be on their best behavior in the courtroom, in the hallway, their guard goes down.

Now I don't want you to think I sneak around and spy on them. But I make it a point to arrive at the courtroom early in order to see what prospective jurors are doing in the hallway as they wait for the courtroom to open. Here is the kind of thing I see when I arrive.

One of the men is blatantly defying social etiquette rules by pacing back and forth directly in front of the rest of the jurors, having a loud conversation on his cell phone.

A woman sitting directly in front of him is oblivious of his even being there. Wild-eyed, she is riveted to her iPad, totally engrossed in a fast-paced video game. The man next to her is equally distracted, but with a decidedly concerned look on his face as he stares at the morning paper. What section is he reading? The Horoscopes.

One demurely dressed woman is sitting by herself away from the rest of the jurors, with her nose buried in a book and a slight smile on her face. I intentionally walk by to see what book has so effectively captured her attention. *Fifty Shades of Grey.* Hmm, I have learned something about her, haven't I? Because as a sex crimes prosecutor many of my cases deal with unconventional sexual practices, this observation was very relevant.

FOCUS: FIXATION REVEALS MOTIVATION

- On a date: your body, your brain, or the ball game?

- In conversation: personal questions, puffery, or politics?

- At a social event: the host or the hosted bar?

- In general: pleasure, family, or career?

Lifestyle:
Personality Revealed

As the team leader in charge of prosecuting sexually violent predators, I deal with men who have *paraphillias*—the experience of intense sexual arousal to objects, individuals, or situations. From shoes, to children, to excrement (I don't make this stuff up), one of the ways we determine the existence and pursuit of these deviant proclivities is by examining their lifestyle.

Lifestyle transmits information about personality. Lifestyle includes preferences for activities, hobbies, and events, as well as pace and standard of living. Unusual activities are particular revealing. Learning that someone visited a nudist colony exposes (pun intended) much more than learning where he or she lives or works. We can learn about a person's lifestyle preferences in a variety of ways.

Lifestyle clues often leak out through a person's appearance. For instance, most people understand that a subpoena is a court order, not an invitation to a cocktail party. Yet when one of my witnesses shows up dressed like a waitress in a martini bar, I have been around long enough to understand that this might be the same outfit she would have selected if I had instructed her to dress as if she were going to church. She is not expressing disrespect for the court; she is revealing her comfort zone, personality, and lifestyle preferences.

I keep these same principles in mind when I am picking a jury. For example, I identify a woman whom I believe will be the perfect juror for my side of the case. Demurely dressed in a floral dress and pearls, gray hair in a bun, as a retired senior citizen, she volunteers her time with her neighborhood watch committee. So far so good.

At the next break, however, as she gets up to leave the room, I spot a marijuana leaf tattoo on her ankle. My mind races to rationalize the new (and inconsistent) information. *A relic left over from a wild youth?* No— the colors are too vivid (almost as if she recently hit the tattoo parlor). *A medical marijuana user due to illness?* Not a chance. She joked about being busier now than before she retired.

What I am left with is the likelihood that the marijuana tattoo reveals more about her lifestyle than does her conservative courtroom appearance. Due to the nature of the charges in my case, I politely excuse her from serving on the jury.

Lifestyle On and Off the Clock

Although most people don't have the luxury of choosing their dream job, in general, people are drawn to different types of work. Some people love to work outdoors, some prefer to work in groups, and some like to work from home. Some people thrive under pressure, while others feel stifled by structure and deadlines.

Some people choose to work when they don't need the money, which is an excellent way to gauge personality, passions, and goals. This type of selective employment is far more revealing of inner motivation than the occupation of the minimum wage laborer who considers himself lucky to be employed in any capacity. However, because many people work to live, not live to work, we learn more about their lifestyle by examining what they do once they are off the clock.

In the same fashion that I learn the most about the focused interests of my jurors by observing them after they leave the scrutiny of the courtroom, we can learn the most about someone's lifestyle when we follow them after they exit the fishbowl of public life. Not literally of course (remember, I also prosecute stalkers), but by taking advantage of opportunities to learn how they spend their free time.

At some companies whose employees work nine to five, if you stand outside the building at 5:00 PM you might think the fire alarm just went off, because it looks like you are watching a mass evacuation. What you are really witnessing is the fact that many people can't wait to get out of the workplace and on with their lives.

So, where do they go? If they head to the gym, you might infer a lifestyle of health and fitness—unless it is within the first two weeks of January, where it may reflect a short-term New Year's resolution.

If they head to the shopping mall video arcade, perhaps they enjoy unwinding with mindless activity (I of course am jaded and might suspect this person is a pedophile—but that would be stereotyping).

If they head to the local watering hole where they are on a first-name basis with the bartender, perhaps they are seeking to escape through self-medicating. On the other hand, maybe they only order ice tea, but enjoy spending time in an environment "where everyone knows your name," made famous by the television show *Cheers*.

Lunch hour activity is noteworthy as well. Someone who crams in a power cross-fit workout is more likely to embrace a lifestyle of fitness and discipline than someone who spends the time catching up on Facebook or watching TV in the break room.

And speaking of television, entertainment choices can be very telling. Recently, on a long flight from New York City, I sat next to a man who was wearing a business suit and an expensive Tag Heuer watch. I felt like I learned the most about him, however, through his video entertainment choices. Given his professional image, I expected him to prefer business or financial news, or the intellectual suspense of forensic crime drama. What did he watch? *South Park* episodes. *For the entire flight.*

Resisting the temptation to jump to conclusions, in order to fairly assess this man I wanted to know *why* he watched that show (which he brought with him), given the myriad of options on the flight. Mindless release? Rebellion against the stiff corporate culture of the workweek? I had to wait until the very end of the flight to find out because his focus never shifted; he was *riveted* to the screen from takeoff to landing.

The explanation was worth the wait. He was an animation technician, studying the show for a new series he was producing using similar animation techniques. He had the literature and business card to prove it. It was an explanation I would never have guessed.

THE LUNCH BREAK: LIFESTYLE SNAPSHOT

- Working out signals a lifestyle of health, fitness, and discipline.
- Catching up on Facebook indicates an emphasis on personal relationships.
- Heading home for lunch reflects family orientation.
- Running errands reveals a focus on productivity.

Professional Workspace: Personality Revealed or Concealed?

If you work at an office where you are permitted to personalize your workspace, I could tell a lot about you if I walked in and looked around.

I would notice the photographs on your desk, whether your walls were adorned with degrees, artwork, or your child's latest fingerpainting masterpiece, and what books you had on your shelves. I could most likely determine what you did for a living, what activities you enjoyed in your free time, and your relationship status. But my observations would only be as accurate as your transparency.

Many workplace settings are either sparsely personalized, due to office regulations, or strategically designed to convey a positive impression of success. For example, a married man with a family will often have photographs of his wife and children on his desk, not photographs of him and his buddies in Las Vegas. Those are on his smart phone. If he has a calendar on his wall, the theme might be historical, regional, or sports-related—although it will not be the *Sports Illustrated* swimsuit edition. That calendar is in his home office. Magazines in his waiting room will likely be *Time* and *Forbes*. At home he might have . . . well, you get the picture.

I don't want to pick on the guys. I have walked into the offices of successful women and felt like I should have paid admission because the spotless décor resembles a museum of fine art—when I have seen the slovenly state of their apartments—where they also showcase a selection of ill-advised photos from the most recent girls night out. Guess where they spend more time?

You can tell the most about a person by visiting their home, where you may find a person is every bit as tidy, classy, or family oriented as their office décor makes them appear. Or not.

Home Court Advantage: Natural Habitat

When we want to study animals, we study them in their natural habitat—in the wild. When we want to study people, we observe them in their natural habitat as well—in their home. This is where they feel the most comfortable, and the place that will yield the best information about their lifestyle.

I can still remember driving up with my case detectives to the gorgeous mansion of a wealthy businessman who had recently been arrested.

As we approached the immaculately landscaped mansion set back from the street by a sweeping driveway, I could already visualize the luxurious interior. Crystal chandeliers, artwork, marble floors. Wow, was I wrong.

We opened the front door and wondered whether a grenade had gone off inside. To describe the interior as unkempt doesn't do justice to the chaotic mess we found. Trash everywhere, sleeping bags strewn around the living room, filthy carpeting, and a stench that stunk up the police car for the rest of the day.

Can you guess the charges? If you only saw the exterior of the house, you might have guessed some type of white-collar crime like embezzlement or insider trading. If you saw the inside, you might have guessed correctly: drug dealing.

Unfortunately, within an indivualistic society, we work with people for years and never see the inside of their home. We might know the area of town in which they live, but that might only reveal their income bracket. Just as personal appearance can be a façade, so can the *outside* of a person's home or car. In order to perceive clues about a person's lifestyle, you have to see what's inside.

The difference between outward appearance and inward motivation is illustrated through the difference in expressing personality through *identity claims* and *behavioral residue*.[12] *Identity claims* convey how a person wants to be regarded—by oneself and others.[13] They include everything from the choice of photographs displayed to idealistic slogans or posters showcasing one's beliefs.[14]

Behavioral residue, in contrast, reveals unintentional traces of activity, such as sporting equipment or a disorganized file cabinet,[15] or the filthy mess we saw at the home of the wealthy businessman.

Sometimes we mistake identity claims for behavioral residue—such as when someone intentionally keeps sporting equipment lying around in order to look athletic.[16] I know plenty of young professionals who don't golf, but keep a golf ball and putter in their offices to convey an air of success to clients.

While some people will clean up their behavioral residue if they know you are coming (and you wouldn't drop by unannounced), you still have a greater opportunity to view someone's true colors on their own turf. Because even when a person has tidied up, their personality lingers.

For example, meticulous arrangement of the items in a person's home may reveal perfectionistic and controlling tendencies. We all remember Julia Roberts in *Sleeping with the Enemy*, playing the battered wife of a controlling husband who demanded perfection in everything from lining up cans in the cupboard to synchronizing the length of hanging towels.

Arrangement of household items can also represent familial priorities and emphasis on spending time together—such as a puzzle on a table surrounded by five chairs, as opposed to five separate computer terminals, each with its own set of remote controls and headphones.

To use an example I am familiar with through prosecuting stalking cases, items found in a person's personal space sometimes reveal jealousy or other destructive personality traits. A photo with an ex-partner whose face is scratched off like a Lottery ticket might reflect a level of obsessive anger. Most people would just throw the picture away.

Home Away from Home: Inside Your Ride

Our choice of wheels provides insight into our income bracket, personality, and character. A Bentley speaks volumes about its owner, as does a snappy Zip car. A flashy red sports car can convey self-confidence and financial security,[17] while a Hummer expresses an entirely different image.

In order to more accurately gauge lifestyle, however, just like with someone's residence, you have to see the inside of a person's vehicle, given the amount of time most people spend in them. In fact, a vehicle interior usually reveals far more information than the owner intends to share. Have you ever noticed that when someone ends up giving you an unplanned lift, they often apologize for the state of their car interior before you get in? Why? Because they haven't had the chance to clean up their behavioral residue.

A highly credentialed business executive whose car has a dashboard full of trash and candy wrappers looking like it was used by two detectives on a stakeout might reveal a lifestyle that is more chaotic than his professional image would otherwise lead you to conclude.

On the other hand, a spotless interior can be unnerving. Sliding into a sterilized, perfumed chamber without so much as a gum wrapper in sight, you may be afraid even to exhale lest you pollute the environment. You might feel more comfortable if you spotted a Big Gulp container in the backseat.

But a spotless car doesn't necesarily signal obsessive-compulsive tendencies or a lifestyle of perfectionism. It may reveal a desire to please a partner or spouse, or a boss with whom someone carpools to work. In other words, you have to know more in order to determine the significance of your observations.

Sometimes you learn things you never knew about the person once that car door is opened—where a mess of children's toys and car seats reveal a young family, or a blast of tobacco smoke suggests a habit you never suspected. Once they start the engine, unless they turn off the radio immediately, you might learn even more about them through their choice of pre-set music or talk radio stations.

Online Living

You receive a text message from your son during dinner: "D, p/p the butter. TIA" (translation: Dad, please pass the butter. Thanks in advance). He is sitting across the table from you. Welcome to the modern age of virtual living.

There is, however, a difference between the way people express themselves on and offline. Many people who are reserved in person express themselves in cyberspace with reckless abandon, liberated by the perceived unaccountability of disembodied existence. Differences in personality are even expressed through a person's preference for Facebook versus Twitter.[18] More gregarious and social people prefer Facebook, while people who are less sociable and more cognitive-oriented prefer Twitter.[19]

On Twitter, one of the loudest methods of virtually sounding off publicly in the modern world, a person's priorities and interests are revealed through the views they express about what is trending. Specifically, hone in on the hash tag—the ubiquitous symbol (#) used to signify the words and phrases with which a person indicates they want their tweets to be found.

Unlike Las Vegas, however, what happens in an online chat room often makes its way into a courtroom. Consider the defendant who appears in court for sentencing. With downcast eyes and head hung low, he is the epitome of remorse. What would I find if I looked online? While it is a safe bet that I am not one of his Facebook friends, in many cases, victims and witnesses are Facebook friends with the defendant, and give law enforcement access to their accounts. You would be amazed at what we find.

One college-aged defendant charged with drunk driving causing serious injury made an appearance two weeks later at a Halloween party in a black-and-white-striped "jail bird" costume. Posted on Facebook, these photos were used by the prosecutor to paint the young man as an unrepentant partier, an image that landed him two years in prison.[20] Regardless of how repentant he appeared in court, his lifestyle showcased a very different attitude toward the crime he committed and the injury he caused.

LIFESTYLE: PERSONALITY REVEALED

- Leisure time activities: healthy or hedonistic?

- Professional workspace: messy or meticulous?

- Scrapbooking or Facebooking: sentimental or social?

- Spending habits: splurging or penny-pinching?

Associations:
The Company We Keep

The well-dressed defendant has clothed himself, literally, with an air of respectability at the first court hearing. *He doesn't look that bad*, I think, peering over at the defense table. But the gig is up when I turn around and see the three "friends" he has brought with him to court.

Looking as if they have either been up all night or slept in their clothes (a lose-lose explanation), they are scratching themselves, fidgeting in their seats, and avoiding eye contact with either the bailiff or me. I begin to jump to conclusions. I wonder if there are warrants out for their arrest. They appear to be under the influence of methamphetamine, yet glassy-eyed too. In fact, is that alcohol I smell? Or merely power of suggestion?

When I look back at the defendant, he has lost the benefit of the doubt. Now he is guilty by association. My opinion has changed because I assume that his friends are revealing what *he* looks and acts like when he is not in court.

This dynamic opearates in a wide variety of cases. A man charged with speeding in a constuction zone will have his uber-conservative courtroom image undermined by his girlfriend in the audience, who in her bright orange pants suit looks like a walking traffic cone (we call this a fashion felony). The bottom line is that like it or not, we are often judged by the company we keep.

Accordingly, in law enforcement work, investigating a person of interest through his or her associations is an effective method of discerning a person's true colors. Because criminals don't congregate by flash mob, covert investigative techniques are often required to detect a network of confederates. A law abiding person's peer group is highly revealing as well—and usually much easier to observe.

However, judging a person through the company they keep can be deceiving for the same reason that appearances can be deceiving. One of my colleagues is occasionally horrified to turn around and see his pink-haired, tattooed teenage son sitting in the audience, having decided to surprise dad by coming to court and watching him in trial.

The running joke is that because courtroom seating is like a wedding, with each side's witnesses and supporters sitting behind their respective tables, when this man's son shows up, he tells him he is welcome to stay, but to please go and sit behind opposing counsel. I happen to know this colorful young man is a straight *A* student. However, that will probably *not* be the first assumption made by the jurors.

The point is that associations yield reliable information *once they are explored*. Actually *meeting* a person's friends will reveal the significance of those associations. The same principle applies online. Meeting a person's Facebook friends *offline* is much better than guessing what someone is like by looking at their social media avatar—which is often a photo of their dog or their favorite superhero.

In addition, beware of associations that are for show, as opposed to for pleasure. I have seen professional white-collar business people who lunch with community leaders at upscale restaurants in thousand-dollar suits, only to spend their time after work hanging out with drug dealers. Newsflash: it is the *after*-work associations that are most revealing. Usually the explanation is a drug problem.

Companion Choice

People reveal relational suitability through partner preference. Date rapists often have a history of first dates, as do individuals seeking impersonal sex. Other men only "date" prostitutes because they have no interest in a relationship.

Some of the sex offenders I have prosecuted admit that while they were married with children, it was only for appearances. They explain that sex offending is easier to pull off when you are seen as a family man.

Whether platonic or romantic, the depth of relational investment a person is willing to make speaks volumes about their emotional availability. Some people will dive into soul-bearing heart-to-hearts sharing deep topics, while other prefer to wade through superficial conversation at the shallow end of the pool. Some people still correspond with best friends from grade school, while others feel most comfortable among disembodied cyber friends they have never met in person.

Romantically, a man who is fifty years old and has never been married may view commitment differently than a man who has had five ex-wives and has just married wife number six. On the other hand, whoever marries the fifty-year-old holdout may be very lucky, because when he jumps in with both feet, it may be for life.

Here is where it gets creepy. Some adults prefer to hang around with children. One memorable red flag in a case where I charged a well-educated woman with having sex with a minor was the fact that although she was in her thirties, her best friend was *sixteen*. Adults who suffer from arrested development genuinely view children as peers and prefer their company over adults.

I have prosecuted sex offenders who have taken precautions to prevent creating future victims ranging from participating in years of sex offender treatment to having their testicles surgically removed and bringing them to court in a bag to prove it. We still want to know whether they are spending time with children. Because it doesn't take functional genatalia to touch a child.

Finally, some people are characterized by their *lack* of personal relationships. Some lone wolves are unable to form meaningful bonds with others, while others are merely introverts who are quite happy on their own. Therefore, it is helpful to learn *why* someone chooses to spend time alone.

Professional and Community Affiliations

In addition to personal relationships, associations also include professional affiliations and community involvement. The groups to which people belong often reveal interests, goals, and ambitions.

Some people are professional joiners. They have drawers full of lapel pins, representing all the different clubs and organizations to which they belong. Other people carefully select associations to join, and to advertise. With a Rotary pin, an American flag, or a Marine badge, people showcase what is important to them . . . or what they want other people to see. While a person's professional associations might accurately reflect interests and passions, they can also provide a pretense of respectability to hide insidious motives. I learned this first-hand.

One evening at a meeting of business leaders, I was introduced to a respectable-looking man, married with children, well credentialed, and active in local philanthropy. If you told me that evening that one year later, I would spend an entire month in trial prosecuting this man on multiple counts of child molestation, I wouldn't have believed it. But it happened. He is now in prison.

Respectable associations can provide the perfect façade to conceal clandestine motives and activity. We saw this principle in action with former assistant football coach and convicted child molester Jerry Sandusky, who founded a charity for at-risk children that was so well respected it was honored by President George H. W. Bush.[21] Unfortunately, Sandusky proceeded to molest the boys involved in the charity.[22]

So what we need to do is examine not the professional associations themselves, but how people *use* their involvement. Some people want to improve their community. Others want to improve their resume. And the people I prosecute for a living want to improve their chances of meeting potential victims. Whether seeking young children or wealthy widows, these guys are focused on the company rather than the charity.

ASSOCIATIONS: THE COMPANY WE KEEP

- Peer group: coworkers, childhood friends, or cyber friends?

- Quality time spent with; (real) family or fraternity brothers?

- Relationship history: one-night-stands or serial monogamist?

- Social orientation: isolationist or community builder?

- Home away from home: exclusive golf club, cigar club, or community service club?

Goals:
A Profile in Priorities

Think about it, if you knew what someone wished for when they saw a falling star or tossed a coin into a wishing well, you would gain insight into their character, values, ambitions, and motivations. You would also be better able to determine how you fit into the equation. While we can't read minds, we can read much more than meets the senses.

Knowing a person's goals help us to understand them and predict their behavior.[23] Goals are tied to personality profiles[24] as well as personality traits,[25] and include both tangible rewards as well as *implicit motives*—the subconscious pursuit of power, achievement, and affiliation.[26]

In many cases, a person's goals are evident through their demeanor, because aspirations predict psychological adjustment.[27] *Intrinsic* goals such as health, helpfulness, self-acceptance, and relatedness, goals related to personal growth, are more psychologically satisfying, and are linked with vitality, well-being, and positive affect.[28] *Extrinsic* goals such as money, fame, and image, which are dependent on the reactions of other people, produce the opposite effect. They are less satisfying and less likely to be linked with positive states.[29]

People who have life goals that revolve around maximizing their own happiness, contributing to society, or acquiring meaningful relationships (as opposed to status, approval from others, or money) are particularly likely to experience an increased sense of well-being.[30]

Goals can also reveal dark personality traits. Psychopaths and Machiavellians pursue tangible goals such as wealth, status, or sex.[31] Narcissists pursue admiration, respect, and status, rather than tangible resources.[32]

Goal-Directed Behavior

Goals are also expressed through goal-directed behavior. But before we jump to conclusions, we have to know the underlying motives.

Researchers use the example of an employee making a financial donation to a charity supported by his boss—knowing his boss would find out.[33] Coworkers are likely to attribute the donation to selfish ambition—a conclusion that may color perceptions about the donor in other areas.[34] If you didn't know the charity was a favorite of the boss, however, or knew the boss would never find out, you might view the donation as altruistic.

Sometimes perceiving goals through behavior is fairly straightforward—such as when someone runs several miles every night after work training for an upcoming marathon. But in order to really gain insight into a person's underlying motivation you want to know *why* someone chooses to pursue certain achievements.

For example, what inspires your colleague to keep running marathons? Is it the adrenaline rush of long-distance running, the challenge of beating her time from last year, or the desire to brag about having finished yet another race? The answers to these questions will be far more revealing of her true colors than the behavior alone.

Short-Term and Long-Term Goals

Different character traits are linked with short-term and long-term goals. Future-oriented people demonstrate stronger moral concerns than people who are present-oriented.[35] Future orientation encompasses personal values, low risk taking, and delayed gratification in pursuit of important long-term goals.[36]

The way goals are (or are not) pursued is also telling. Machiavellianism is characterized by ruthless pursuit of long-term goals,[37] while psychopaths are unlikely to formulate long-term goals[38] or realistic goals.

One of the men I prosecuted for economic fraud had an IQ higher than anyone in the courtroom. Having memorized all the facts of his prior police reports, he was virtually untouchable on cross-examination regarding the details of his financial crimes. And he had quite a few of them, because he was smart enough to evade detection for years.

So, with that level of intelligence, why didn't he pursue a PhD, become an accountant or financial advisor (given his pre-occupation with money), or otherwise put his brilliant intellect to positive use? Because he was a psychopath. Like many psychopaths, he lacked realistic life goals[39] and simply lived day to day, never formulating long-term goals or future plans.[40]

GOALS: A PROFILE IN PRIORITIES

- Selfish or selfless?

- Fame, fortune, or fun?

- Improve the world or conquer the world?

- Reach the peak of the highest mountain, or the top of the corporate ladder?

- Achieve the highest score on a test, or on the latest video game?

- Finish the race or win first place?

The Final Exam:
Consistency or Counter Intuition

Once you have thoroughly studied a person's FLAGs, you can compare your observations in each of the four areas to see if all of the clues point in the same direction. Consistency creates credibility, bolstering the confidence of your conclusions. Inconsistency evokes a sense of counter intuition, which breeds suspicion and distrust.

For example, focus, lifestyle, and associations often reveal goals. A man whose five-year goal is to become his company's CEO will lead a very different lifestyle from that of a man whose five-year goal is to find a partner and start a family. Focused on climbing the corporate ladder, the lifestyle of the CEO hopeful will reflect discipline and professional dedication. Focusing on his resume, not romance, he will associate to network, not to socialize.

A husband whose goal is to raise a healthy, happy family will be focused on setting a good example for his children. He will pursue a lifestyle of clean living, education, and morality. On Friday night, you are more likely to find him at home watching television with his family than on a pub crawl with his former college fraternity brothers.

Consistent FLAGs can also help you interpret ambiguous behavior. As a defense attorney I represented a woman accused of shoplifting. None of her FLAGs, however, signaled dishonesty. Focused on raising a family, working two jobs, and caring for aging parents, she explained that she simply forgot to pay for the merchandise. The jury believed her.

READING RED FLAGS: TRADING ROSE COLORED GLASSES FOR READING GLASSES

- Maximize first impressions: perceive as much as you can when you are most objective.

- Be wary of underexposure: secrets should signal suspicion.

---

continued

- Time lapse photography: observe behavior over time.

- Use a wide-angle lens: observe behavior in context, and in different settings.

- Solicit multiple exposures: introduce new partners to your family and friends.

- Vision enhancement: trust but verify. Seek corroboration on and offline.

No One Is Perfect

Despite scrupulous observation and attention to detail, there are still red flags that we might miss. Some shrewd individuals glide through life nondescript and unmemorable, leaving as light a trail as possible, yielding very little usable data.

I have seen thieves and burglars fly under the radar for years by blending into their environments like chameleons. These people are able to case businesses, infiltrate organizations, and maintain superficial relationships by quietly remaining in the background until they are ready to make their move.

Other people are hard to detect because they have spent their entire lives practicing techniques of manipulation and therefore have much more experience with the art of deception than law-abiding citizens who have focused their attention and energy on wholesome pursuits, healthy relationships, and honest living.

Nonetheless, proactive examination of people can help us to absorb as much information as we can. Now that you are familiar with the FLAGs, let us put them into practice.

1

The Optics of Illusion

The Power of Attraction

I step into an elevator at the courthouse. A well-dressed, handsome man gets into the elevator with me, smiles and says good morning. I assume he is a lawyer because like me, he is wearing a business suit and carrying a briefcase. I reciprocate his friendliness as we make small talk because I assume I am speaking to a colleague.

When I learn that we are going to the same department, I ask him which case he is on. He gives the name of one of the defendants I am prosecuting. Because I know the defense attorney on that case from past court appearances, I ask him if he is taking over the case from the lawyer who currently represents the defendant. Without missing a beat he explains that he *is* the defendant.

Well . . . this is awkward. Let me tell you, the man who got into the elevator looked *nothing* like his mug shot—or the way he looked in court in his bright orange jail-issued jumpsuit before he bailed out of custody.

Do you want to know the charges? Serial rapist. You see, although this guy had access to plenty of consensual sex partners, he was only aroused by nonconsensual sex. How did he make bail? He was successful in business for the same reasons he was successful in seducing women.

See if you can guess how he lured women into agreeing to spend the night with him. That's right. He used his charm, charisma, and handsome good looks—the same qualities that I found so engaging in the elevator. He used the same tactics to ingratiate himself with the women on the jury when he testified at his trial. Showing up looking like he just walked off an episode of *Miami Vice*, he sat through his trial making eyes at the women on the jury—some of whom I caught reciprocating the attention.

This is problematic, because a study that focused on the relative attractiveness of victims and defendants in rape cases found that attractive men who raped unattractive victims were less likely to be viewed as guilty.[1] Can you believe this?

In order to make sense of this phenomenon, let's approach the discussion of the disarming power of attraction by examining the psychology behind the seduction.

The Science Behind the Seduction:
Attraction Breeds Interaction

Attractiveness sparks relational contact.[2] Good-looking people draw others like a magnet, and generate positive feelings. Within romantic relationships, a person's perception of his or her partner as physically attractive boosts relational satisfaction and feelings of love.[3]

But we don't even need to know attractive people personally to have them make us feel good. Research shows that merely looking at photos of attractive individuals can be a source of erotic pleasure.[4]

On the other hand, physical attraction can overpower our will, cloud our judgment, and override our senses, causing us to see what we want to see—and ignore what we don't. And it doesn't take long. Because many of my rape cases begin as consensual encounters, consider the dynamics of attraction that are in play as early as the first date.

Annette meets Nathan at her fitness club where he is a new member. After about ten minutes of friendly treadmill conversation, he asks her out to dinner. Where? He tells her to choose the restaurant, explaining that he is new in town, instructing her: "Surprise me. Text me the name of the restaurant, and I'll meet you there at eight on Friday night."

Annette, infatuated with Nathan's good looks, agrees. Once she arrives at her venue of choice, however, Nathan is fifteen minutes late. But Annette forgets about that quickly as he makes up for his tardiness with effusive compliments, making her blush with the terminology he uses to describe his attraction to her when he first saw her in her leotard at the gym.

Nathan immediately orders tequila shots for both of them, to toast the beginning of their relationship. While Annette doesn't drink tequila, she does her best to ignore the fire in her throat as she tries to be a good sport. She is already feeling light-headed by the time he orders another round.

Although Nathan begins to make her uncomfortable with questions about her sexual preferences, he tempers her discomfort with generous flattery, telling her he could look into her beautiful eyes all night. After the third shot of tequila, however, when her eyes are probably more blood-shot than beautiful, Nathan wants to know how far she lives from the restaurant. Through a haze of straight shots and mixed feelings, Annette wonders where this is going.

Under the Influence in More Ways Than One:
Intoxication Through Infatuation

I can tell you where it went. Downhill fast. Nathan was the good-looking guy in the elevator that I mistook for a lawyer, and Annette was his latest date rape victim. Why did she agree to let him come home to her apartment after dinner? Because through the hazy mix of emotional and physical intoxication, Nathan looked really good.

So what should Annette have seen? Some women might have been put off by Nathan's suggestion that she pick the restaurant and meet him there. Setting up a first date is usually a man's job, as is picking up his date. Here, not only did Nathan reverse those roles, he didn't even arrive on time.

But it was a test. Annette agreed to it—something the Nathans of the world view as a sign of weakness and vulnerability. And some men are sexually attracted to women who exhibit signs of sexual exploitability.[5]

Single men like Nathan seeking casual sex are particularly likely to perceive this vulnerability.[6]

Looking back, Annette tells me that one of the reasons she thought Nathan was a safe guy was because he asked her lots of questions and appeared to be very interested in everything she had to say. The important question, however, is *why*. Was he interested in a romantic relationship or a one-night stand?

The focus of his questions—on sexual practices and how far away she lived—provide some clues. We gain more clues through examining other areas of Nathan's life that unfortunately Annette didn't know about because he made her do all the talking.

Nathan was new in town because he lives a nomadic lifestyle, switching jobs and partners frequently—which is both a sign of psychopathy[7] and indicative of general irresponsibility—also a psychopathic trait.[8] His shallow, superficial associations with romantic partners might be symptomatic of attachment difficulties, or psychopathic superficiality.[9]

But wait a minute, you might be thinking, lots of people have multiple sexual partners, move frequently, or change jobs. Some people are simply easily bored, happy-go-lucky, or not interested in a committed relationship.

That's all true. But in Nathan's case, his nomadic lifestyle and superficial associations facilitated his date rape behavior—which was always preceded by minimal contact beforehand, and very little self-disclosure, as Nathan always focused on his dates. Most women fell for his "reverse selfie" routine and were too flattered at his interest and attention to notice that he never revealed anything about himself. None of them saw his car, where he lived, or any forms of identification. This was no accident. Nathan wasn't even his real name.

More importantly, most women didn't report the rape because they were too ashamed to admit they drank as much as they did and invited a man they hardly knew to come home with them in the first place. That was all part of Nathan's plan. The alcohol also served the additional purpose of ensuring the women were fuzzy on the details after they left the restaurant, which would decrease the credibility of their allegations, if they were courageous enough to make any.

READING RED FLAGS ON A FIRST DATE

Focus: Does he ask about you, or tell you about himself? Does he emphasize financial status, relationship potential, or sexual prowess?

Lifestyle: Is he late and underdressed, or early and well groomed? Is he soft or muscular? Does his failure to make a reservation result in the two of you crammed like sardines onto stools eating at the bar, yelling to hear each other over the noise, or did he visit the restaurant the day before in order to select and reserve the best table?

Associations: Is his smart phone filled with photos from his best friend's bachelor party, or photos of his adorable niece and nephew? Does he live with his parents, alone, or in a fraternity house?

Goals: What type of impression does he try to make? Does he take you to a trendy hotspot, casual sports bar, or reserve a beachfront candlelit table for two? Does he express long-term ambitions, or a carefree, happy-go-lucky attitude toward life? Does he ask about your choice of career, or your preferred method of contraception?

Why Beautiful Looks Good:
The Halo Effect

Attractive people can deceive us due to our tendency to believe that "what is beautiful is good,"[10] even when it is not. The *halo effect* is well supported in research, and refers to our assumption that physically attractive people have positive qualities in other areas.[11]

Attractive people are consistently regarded in a more positive light than their less attractive counterparts.[12] We view good-looking individuals as honest, intelligent, talented, and kind.[13]

As powerful as it is, the halo effect is a perceptual bias.[14] Although people attribute positive qualities to good-looking people and negative qualities to people who are unattractive, these stereotypes are not accurate.[15]

The halo effect is dangerous because it can make bad look good. This is important because physical attractiveness is one of the most significant factors generating romantic attraction.[16] One particularly disturbing finding is that good-looking people are viewed as trustworthy when it comes to keeping secrets.[17] You can imagine the problems this causes when dealing with attractive manipulators.

Does the bloom ever leave the rose? In many cases, no. Attractive people are judged more positively even by people who know them.[18] Within friendship and dating relationships, this may cause the illusion of good to persevere, even despite evidence to the contrary.

The beautiful-is-good phenomenon operates in a variety of contexts. Good-looking political candidates gain more votes.[19] Attractive students are viewed more favorably by teachers.[20] And in the workforce, the halo effect is consistently blessing job candidates with perceived qualities they don't have.

Employers favor more attractive job applicants simply by viewing resumes—believing they will make better employees.[21] And in job interviews, physical appearance has more impact on job interviewer ratings than verbal behavior, nonverbal behavior, or impression-management techniques.[22] In fact, it has been suggested that managers consider structured phone interviews instead of in-person interviews in order to reduce the impact of physical attractiveness on rating potential employees. [23]

The beautiful-is-good phenomenon also operates online—debunking the notion that the Internet "levels the playing field" by allowing an attractive personality to compensate for a less attractive physical appearance.[24] Research shows that men with attractive photos in online dating profiles have the text of their profiles rated as more attractive as well.[25]

And on Internet dating sites, people select potential partners based primarily on their physical attractiveness as displayed in their profile photos.[26] They make judgments based on physical appearance, and proceed to filter subsequent information through those judgments—which are often inaccurate.[27]

When Bad Is Beautiful:
Seeing a Halo When You Should See Horns

I am in the courtroom getting ready to start trial. The defendant I am prosecuting is a wealthy young man who looks like a celebrity. The defense attorney is every bit as good-looking as his client. As I watch the prospective jurors file in, I notice that many of them smile at the two handsome men at the defense table. Some say good morning. With the psychological cards stacked against me, I realize that I am in for an uphill battle.

Most telling, however, is the jurors' reactions when they hear the judge read the charges. "Ladies and gentlemen, the defendant is charged with human trafficking." "Child molestation." "Being a sexually violent predator." "Forcible rape." My caseload consists of prosecuting the worst of the worst.

Instead of anger and disgust, I often see a look of confusion. *What? That guy? The handsome guy in the suit?* Yes. How do you think he was able to lure so many victims? A child molester doesn't drive to court in an ice cream truck with pockets full of candy and a bank robber doesn't walk into the courtroom with a stocking over his head. Yet the confusion on some of the jurors' faces suggests that these are the stereotypes they were expecting to see.

I face similar challenges with attractive female defendants. I have prosecuted beautiful women for crimes ranging from throwing their newborn baby in a dumpster to having sex with their pre-teen male students. Despite the seriousness of these charges, during some of these trials, I look over and see jurors staring at the pretty lady in the defendant's chair with a smile on their face, instead of paying attention to the testimony from the witness stand.

Sometimes the court of public opinion is already sounding off about the supposed guilt or innocence of an attractive criminal defendant before the newly arrested heartthrob ever sees a court of law. In a virtual age where retweeted images go viral overnight, criminal mug shots turned glamour shots have redefined the "most wanted" criminal—demonstrating how pretty faces are pre-judged.

The beautiful-criminal-gets-a-break phenomenon is supported by research both in field studies and in laboratory experiments.[28] Attractive defendants fare better in terms of both guilt and punishment. Research reveals that less attractive defendants were two and one half times more likely than attractive defendants to be found guilty by mock juries,[29] and attractive criminals receive more lenient sanctions.[30] One study found that handsome defendants were twice as likely to avoid custody as their less attractive counterparts.[31]

Not only do they receive better treatment from the criminal justice system, attractive criminals often do very well with the ladies. I prosecuted a white supremacist charged with a series of hate crimes who cut quite the handsome figure in the courtroom . . . until he turned around and you saw the large black swastika tattooed on the back of his shaved head. One of the most memorable things about his case, however, was his "better half."

A graduate student, she was demure, polite, and here comes the most interesting part: *Latina*. I couldn't resist. I asked her, given her heritage, how did she feel about being involved with a white supremacist? Did her parents like him? Was spending time together in public awkward with the swastika? She just shrugged. He is very good-looking, she explained. So there you have it.

The last I heard, they were still together. For her sake, I hope he grew out his hair.

As unbelievable as it sounds, becoming involved with criminals based on their good looks alone is well documented. Sheila Isenberg, in *Women Who Love Men Who Kill*, describes one woman who decided to replace her boyfriend with a convicted murderer serving a life sentence as soon as she saw his photo.[32] Isenberg explains her reaction—"He was gorgeous! I just sat there and looked at the picture. That is going to be my husband one day, I'm going to marry this man."[33]

Another woman describes her immediate attraction to a convicted criminal who had received a death sentence: "I was thunderstruck . . . There was something about him that was so compelling."[34] Explaining how her love for this murderer took priority over her career, this woman states, "I remember him as one of the most attractive people I had ever seen in my life. Nothing I have ever found out has altered that image or changed it in any way."[35] True to her words, after learning about his lifetime of criminality leading up to the murder, she left her husband for him.[36]

These shocking examples illustrate the extent to which, when presented with good-looking individuals, some people see a halo when they should be seeing horns.

When Red Flags Look Red Hot:
Discerning the Heart of the Heartthrob

Beauty blinds in a variety of settings. From the courtroom to the boardroom to the bedroom. What reveals the heart of the heartthrob, however, is the way beauty is used.

People with Dark Triad personality often engage in "effective adornment"—intentionally cultivating an attractive exterior as a "social lure."[37] They dress to impress in order to capitalize on the positive attention they receive, as well as to spark short-term romantic liaisons.[38]

Many attractive manipulators exhibit characteristics of narcissism. Just like the mythical Narcissus, who was mesmerized with his own reflection in a pool of water, narcissists are preoccupied with making themselves as attractive as possible.[39] Narcissists intentionally showcase themselves through wearing expensive, flashy clothing to enhance their appearance and perceived status.[40] Narcissistic women additionally enhance their appearance through cleavage and makeup.[41]

In addition to playing up their physical appearance, narcissists also exhibit attractive facial expressions, verbal humor, and confident body movements—all of which enhance their popularity.[42] They also seek to arouse potential mates through sexual language and exhibitionistic behavior.[43]

There are, however, lots of good people who are attractive, outgoing, and flirtatious, and who do not have dark personality traits. It is the underlying motivation and goals that separate the good from the just good-looking. In order to tell the difference, examine the FLAGs to see how people *use* their physical attractiveness.

Some people are self-focused, checking their appearance in every passing mirror, paying little attention to their dates. Others are focused on their partners, seeking to please by wearing their partners' favorite outfits of theirs when they go out together.

Some people lead a lifestyle geared toward using their physical assets to get ahead. Others believe that less is more. Some women with gorgeous figures avoid provocative clothing, choosing a more professional image instead. They prefer to showcase their intellectual side, knowing they look great in anything they wear. Some women with gorgeous hair maintain it with expensive salon treatments, while others routinely donate their locks to make wigs for cancer victims.

While many people use their physical beauty to achieve their goals, what separates the good from the bad is *how* they do it. There is a difference between using beauty to facilitate success, or to manipulate success by cutting corners.

Some people use their looks to pursue legitimate careers in modeling, film, or television. Others prefer a "casting couch" approach, using their looks to seduce people in power in order to circumvent the need to ascend legitimately through the ranks.

This distinction is similar to the operations of smart criminals. Sophisticated offenders cultivate elaborate schemes to perpetrate crime. With their intelligence, they could likely achieve the same results through legal means. The difference is that some people don't want to work for their goals; they want a shortcut. They would rather get what they want through manipulation than through legitimate effort.

Research reveals that people can recognize this difference. In a study aptly entitled "Beautiful but Dangerous," researchers found granting leniency to an attractive criminal to be related to whether or not the criminal *used* her attractiveness to facilitate the crime.[44] Subjects assigned more lenient sentences to the fictional defendant when she committed a crime unrelated to her attractiveness (burglary), but assigned harsher sentences when she was described as committing the attractiveness-related crime of swindling—which involved ingratiating herself with the victim.[45]

GAUGING WHEN BEAUTIFUL IS GOOD

Focus: How much attention does an attractive person pay to his or her appearance?

Lifestyle: Does a person get ahead through using beauty rather than brains?

Associations: Does an attractive person surround herself with fans, family or longtime friends?

Goals: Does someone use their physical attributes to benefit themselves or to help others?

The Multifaceted Lens of Attraction

Sometimes we can't put our finger on why we seem to be hopelessly attracted to another person. Actually, it can be a mix of factors. In *Erotic Capital*, Catherine Hakim describes the elements of erotic capital as a combination of both physical and social attractiveness that goes far beyond pure sex appeal.[46] She describes it as a combination of "beauty, sex appeal, liveliness, a talent for dressing well, charm and social skills, and sexual competence."[47]

In other cases, beauty may truly be in the eye of the beholder—particularly when it comes to judging facial attractiveness, where what is referred to as *private taste* may play a role.[48] In other cases, perceptions of attractiveness may stem from the "love-is-blind bias"—a positive illusion where people view their partners as more attractive than they really are.[49]

In some situations, we may find ourselves attracted to a certain look based on our current emotional state. In one study, men who were made to feel depressed expressed greater attraction for a "girl next door" who demonstrated warm expressiveness and low sexual maturity, over an inexpressive but sexually mature "ice princess."[50] Men who were made to feel elated, on the other hand, preferred the "ice princess."[51]

We are even attracted to people who are wearing certain colors. True to stereotype, research reveals that the color red causes men to view women as sexually desirable and attractive.[52] (Yes, I wear a lot of red suits.)

Researchers investigating whether or not the color red really is an aphrodisiac for men, due to what is referred to in the literature as the "red-sex" link, conducted a series of experiments showing men photos of women against backgrounds that were either red or a series of other colors, including white. The results? Men consistently perceived the women shown against red backgrounds to be more attractive and sexually desirable.[53]

What about the ladies? Sure enough, the color red also enhanced women's attraction and sexual desire for men that were shown in red clothing and against a red background.[54] Interestingly, in this study, the correlation was tied to the women's perception about the men's status, because higher status for males is linked to association with the color red.[55]

More Than Skin Deep

As the famous saying goes, there is more to attraction than physical appearance. How many of us have fallen head over heels for someone that made our best friends shake their heads in disbelief. *What does she see in him?* If you have ever had a crush on a less-than-physically-perfect suitor, you are not alone. There is much more to attraction than meets the eye.

While physical appearance is the most significant factor that we use to judge others,[56] attraction is also generated by nonphysical characteristics.[57] Physical attractiveness is enhanced through a wide variety of personality characteristics such as prosocial orientation[58] exhibition, and extraversion.[59] The perception of physical beauty is also enhanced by social status[60] as well as the perception of honesty.[61]

Psychologists have also recognized *dynamic attractiveness*—which includes nonphysical traits,[62] such as sense of humor, conversation skills, and nonverbal expression.[63] Perceived beauty can also be enhanced by a positive personality.[64] One study found that men who received positive personality information about women rated them to be more attractive across a broad range of body sizes, as compared to a control group.[65]

Within relationships, perceived physical attractiveness also stems from factors other than physical appearance.[66] *Social attractiveness* is generated through positive interaction within a relationship.[67] What kind of interaction makes people more socially attractive? It can be something as simple as being amusing, or having good communication skills.[68]

Sometimes, we find someone to be attractive because everyone else does. Researchers explain this as the *celebrity effect*—where peer esteem is a quality that is as desirable as wealth or physical attractiveness.[69] This has been demonstrated in studying *mate copying*, where mating interest is influenced by the opinion of others, and how much attention others pay to a person.[70] Receiving a high amount of attention from peers can compensate for low physical attractiveness, and can make another person appear more desirable, regardless of wealth.[71]

Attraction can also be generated through positive emotion, such as the warm feeling generated through likability.

Likability Covers a Multitude of Crimes

One Friday night when I was on a ride-along with the California Highway Patrol, we stopped a couple who were on their way to the airport to fly to Las Vegas to get married, and were wearing the clothes to prove it. They were speeding. They were also sober, sympathetic, and sincere. They got a warning—and hopefully made their flight.

While the cases I prosecute are far more serious than speeding, consider an example of how I struggle with the disarming power of likability in handling my own cases as well. As I take my seat along with the judge and probation officer in the judge's chambers for a pre-trial conference, the defense attorney breezes in wearing a bright orange suit with a bright smile to match. She greets everyone warmly and asks if we were able to take some time to enjoy the great weather over the weekend.

As we get down to business, she is in complete agreement with the heinous conduct of her client. "Vile and despicable behavior," she agrees, shaking her head in disgust. In light of the fact that I argue for a living (literally), her agreeableness is a breath of fresh air.

She assures us that she hasn't come to persuade us of her client's innocence or to attempt to sugarcoat the facts. Instead, she hands out packages of mitigating circumstances regarding what drove him to such horrific behavior.

She took the time to make a package for each of us, explaining that she wants to make sure that we are all literally on the same page so we can streamline our respective arguments at the next hearing. She is open, friendly, and respectful, emphasizing the fact that while we play different roles, our ultimate interests are the same—making sure that justice is done.

While ultimately I will make my decision on what to offer her client based on the evidence, I have to recognize and suppress my instinct to treat her client favorably not based on how I feel about his behavior, but because of the way I feel about *her*.

My feelings are explained by the *liking heuristic*, which states that we are more likely to give likable people what they ask for.[72] When we like someone, we will generally also trust and respect them.[73] This often leads to the desire to please them in order to gain their approval.[74] Other research suggests that we are innately predisposed to comply with the requests of people we like.[75]

In a professional context, likability can be enhanced further through personalization. For example, I might like the defense attorney even more had she breezed into the room and spilled her coffee, because clumsy blunders by people we perceive as competent often humanizes them, making them even more endearing.[76]

Why is likability so attractive in the first place? It is linked with happiness. Happy people are likable[77] and make others feel good because positive emotion is contagious.[78] Not surprisingly, happy people are viewed as more popular and attractive than their less cheerful peers,[79] which leads others to seek out their company.

In the workplace, for example, there is a tendency for both colleagues and superiors to extend greater accommodation to positive employees in order to increase interaction, which is consistent with research demonstrating that people in good moods intentionally seek to preserve their positive emotional state.[80]

While genuinely happy people attract others like magnets, some people project a false front of happiness in order to increase their perceived likability.[81] Consider the following example of cultivated likability that has fooled countless victims and witnesses throughout the course of my career.

"I Never Met a Child Molester I Didn't Like"

Did I get your attention? This quote is famously associated with victims, families of victims, employers, neighbors, friends, and law enforcement agents around the world, in describing their strong attraction to a person who later turned out to be a pedophile. The reason child predators are so successful is because they are so likable!

For child predators, likability is a lure. They ingratiate themselves with potential victims through constant smiling along with friendly conversation and remembering children's names.[82] One offender admits using his smile as his "entrée," describing himself "like a salesman, but I'm never off work." [83]

Yet there are ways to spot the phony. One predator notes that some smiles do not include the eyes—implicating one facet of psychopathy.[84] And while generally, smiling can prompt perceived sincerity,[85] authentic smiles produce a greater degree of emotional contagion and simulation than artificial grins.[86]

The Captivation of Charisma

While charisma is a concept that is hard to define, we "know it when we see it." Unfortunately, sometimes I see it in the courtroom—sitting on the wrong side of the table. Consider this case in point.

Portly, short, and losing his hair, one of the men I prosecuted had more girlfriends than you could count. Several of his girlfriends showed up to watch the trial. More of a harem, really. The ensuing drama of having these women in the same room together proved to be quite a distraction for the jury, effectively turning the courtroom seating area into an episode of the *Jerry Springer Show*.

With these histrionics already in full swing even before I called my first witness, I peered over at the defense table at the overweight, balding figure sitting in the defendant's chair. I was mystified. *What are these women looking at?*

Once the trial began, however, and I was in the courtroom with the defendant every day, I began to understand. This guy might not be much to look at, but his mannerisms, style, voice, and strong personality were *impressive.*

Sure, he was overweight. But he camouflaged problem areas with trendy clothing more effectively than a professional model on the runway. Yes, he was short. But he carried himself like John Travolta with a swagger to match.

When he testified, he had a voice like a radio disc jockey—cool, confident, and charismatic. Are you getting the picture? By the time he left the witness stand, I completely understood why this man did so well with the ladies. I began to worry about the women on the jury . . .

Positive Use of Positive Personality

You can imagine when we analyze the FLAGs of a guy who has managed to juggle multiple girlfriends while engaged in a life of crime we would find a lot of red. The jury did as well. Although even after he was convicted, I was told that the line of women waiting to visit him in jail was one of the longest they had ever seen.

Thankfully, it is not only criminals who attract others through their captivating personalities. Many good people use nonphysical tools of attraction in pursuit of benevolent goals. They use positive personality, charisma, and dynamic interaction skills to selflessly pour into the lives of others. They empower young people by serving as engaging role models, encouraging family members with their upbeat outlook on life, and using their social skills to enhance relationships both personal and professional.

They are open and outgoing. They are the ones at the party who always seem to be laughing and having a good time—but never at the expense of anyone else. They are focused on others. Their associations include family members and lifelong friends, as opposed to the type of superficial acquaintances that characterize the social circle of people who use others for ulterior motives. They make friends and keep them, not use them and discard them.

Their goals are to enhance the lives of others, and their other-focused mentality is demonstrated through their goal-driven behavior. They love to see others succeed, and it shows. These people are worth their weight in gold.

The bottom line with the power of attraction is that because appearances can be deceiving, it pays to take the time to evaluate everyone we meet in order to make sure that what looks good on the outside is also good on the inside.

2
Follow the Leader
The Attraction of Power

have known him all my life and can tell you that he is as honest as the day is long," declares the navy-blue–suited corporate executive the defendant has called as a character witness. "Are you aware that he has a felony conviction for grave robbing?" I ask her. She is unfazed. "Yes."

You would think this woman's refusal to change her opinion based on the defendant's prior theft conviction would sway the jury. But did I tell you she was the president and CEO of a major financial firm?

You should have seen the jurors by the time she was done reciting her impressive credentials. Some of them were leaning so far forward in order to catch every word she spoke I was worried they were going to fall out of their chairs. I was expecting some of them to hang around afterward to ask for an autograph. This powerful woman, who knew nothing about the defendant's current charges, was the best piece of "evidence" in his case.

Power is attractive. Whether a person is a business executive, politician, or community leader, we are impressed by members of the upper echelon. And even if we logically understand that power often stems from the possession of resources—whether it is money, job title, or elected office, power is nonetheless seductively attractive.

Powerful people are often viewed as physically attractive, extroverted, dominant, and charismatic.[1] Members of powerful groups are evaluated more positively, and believed to have more positive traits than members of groups with less power.[2] This might be driven by the desire to validate social hierarchy, or due to the halo effect, which, as in physical attractiveness research, causes us to attribute positive traits to people who belong to groups that are powerful and successful.[3]

We also enjoy the way powerful people make us feel about ourselves. We place more significance on the endorsement of people we respect, and greater weight on the opinions of those in positions of power.[4] The more power they have, the more confidence we place in their promises or assurances.

When it comes to gravitas, we think we know it when we see it. Nonetheless, power is most appealing when it is actually possessed as well as perceived.[5] A person whose power stems from a position of status, strength, or affluence may nonetheless lack influence if that power is not perceived by others.[6] A person must be a leader and be seen as a leader in order to be an aphrodisiac.[7]

The perception of power is not difficult to portray. Even vertical position can indicate perceived power. Researchers testing the theory that men with status and resources are viewed as desirable found that perceived physical attractiveness can be manipulated merely by where a photo is placed on a computer screen.[8] They found that men were perceived to be more attractive when their images were shown near the top of a computer screen, while women were judged as more attractive when their photos were shown at the bottom.[9]

Power Is Sexy

For many women, there is nothing more alluring than becoming involved with a powerful man.[10] Whether by virtue of position, wealth, or social status, powerful men are like magnets. In some cases, power can even make up for the lack of physical attractiveness.

Abundant research demonstrates the attractiveness and desirability of men who have attributes associated with power, such as status and resources.[11] In "Is Power Sexy?" John Levi Martin conducted a study demonstrating that men who exercise interpersonal power are sexy to both men and women.[12]

He notes that past research found that women desire men of high social status.[13] Recognizing that social position is linked to resource control, he explains that women find men with resources to be sexually desirable.[14] Martin's study, however, demonstrated that men's social status was not viewed as attractive in itself, but rather as something that can compensate for the *lack* of attractiveness.[15]

The Allure of the Alpha Male

One of the men I represented as a public defender was the stereotypical king of the jungle. Head of a large family, he was used to being regarded as a dominant figure, and expected to be treated with no less reverence from the criminal justice system. Even his charges fit his image. Cockfighting.

As he pranced around the courtroom like a peacock, it was amazing to see how, sure enough, he garnered respect just through his dominant actions and behaviors. Everyone treated him with deference. The explanation? Very simple. Dominance is desirable.

Dominant men are attractive to women.[16] Women perceive physical dominance to be linked not only with attractiveness, but social dominance as well.[17] Ogi Ogas and Sai Gaddam in *A Billion Wicked Thoughts: What the World's Largest Experiment Reveals About Human Desire* have a chapter entitled "Ladies Prefer Alphas." In this chapter, they note that male dominance is erotically appealing, demonstrated through the preference for dominant male voices, scent, facial features, and movements.[18] Dominance is also expressed through behavior, such as direct eye contact for example, and increases the sexual attractiveness of men, although not their likability.[19] In fact, dominance is consistently portrayed through angry expressions—including lower eyebrows.[20]

Some women who are attracted to men who dominate them are aroused by the power inequality.[21] In *Money, Sex, and Power*, Nancy C. M. Hartsock notes that within the realm of social science and power literature, domination is linked to virility.[22] She cites Henry Kissinger's observation that "Power is the ultimate aphrodisiac" as an example of Western culture's association of manliness, power, domination, and virility.[23]

Hartsock also notes, however, that there is societal consensus regarding the centrality of domination and hostility, rather than physical pleasure and intimacy, in producing sexual excitement.[24] While perhaps counterintuitive, she quotes a number of scholars discussing the link between sexual excitement and hostility.[25]

Chasing the Alpha Female

Powerful women are attractive as well. Men find high status women to be sexy,[26] and are satisfied with women who are self-empowered. Men with feminist partners have reported more sexual satisfaction and relationship stability, debunking the stereotype that feminism is incompatible with romance.[27] Research does not support the stereotype of feminists as unattractive, single, or members of the lesbian community.[28]

While it's true that some men "marry up," powerful women are not always a good match for men who are seeking to assert dominance in all aspects of a relationship. A man who is looking for a woman to stay home and take care of the household should not be eyeing the pretty faces at the top of the corporate ladder. Most of these women are not going to climb down. And if they did, they might not be perceived as attractive because in many cases, their powerful position is part of their allure.

Some people are better matched with women who would rather spend their time in their living room than in the corporate boardroom. Many relationships are more successful when partners have goals that are compatible rather than similar.[29] A relationship where one partner seeks financial success while the other wants to stay home and raise the children may be more successful than a relationship in which both partners are pursuing professional advancement.[30]

Yet some people are aroused by the challenge of pursuing someone powerful and out of their league—and even more exciting to catch them. But the pursuer can become frustrated when they realize that they caught exactly what they chased. And the tiger isn't changing her stripes.

The first time a man succeeds in diverting the attention of a powerful woman from her smart phone—which everyone knows doubles as a "do not disturb" sign—he may feel ten feet tall. Although if she is intimidating enough, he might at the same time be so nervous about what to say next he feels like he is about to melt into a puddle.

Why pursue a woman who creates such anxiety? For the thrill of landing an impressive partner. Some powerful women have several pursuers—often resulting in competitive love triangles that sometimes lead to brawling suitors (literally), which, depending on the injuries, might shoot the case in my direction.

The Invincible Nature of Power:
Boardroom Eyes

It has been famously observed that "power tends to corrupt,"[31] Some powerful corporate figures embody this maxim, boldly pursuing female subordinates while most of their troops turn a blind eye to their misbehavior.

As a result, many workplace harassment cases are hard to prove when the offender is in a position of power. As soon as a complaint is made, many witnesses don't seem to remember much of anything, leaving the victim's allegations uncorroborated.

Some powerful men use language in the boardroom that belongs in the locker room, including terms we would never expect to hear in mixed company. They use the same language with female cocktail servers during company happy hours, showcasing a lifestyle of devaluing women.

And then there is the staring—conduct that goes largely unnoticed by most of the board members, who are glued to their computers and smart phones. As one board secretary explained, there is nothing quite like the challenge of trying to take the minutes at a board meeting with the boss leering at you—discomfort that often causes her to make typographical errors, which adversely affects her perceived competence.

One of the most troubling aspects of these cases is that some of these men are honestly not aware of the inappropriateness of their conduct. Comments after allegations break include, "Don't women like to know they are attractive?" and "What woman isn't interested in dating the boss?"

Why would a man have this perspective? One possible reason is because he only associates with subordinates in order to sustain a perpetual power trip. Within a carefully selected crowd of admirers, his behavior is never challenged.

In addition, some people in power direct sexual behavior toward subordinates because they overperceive their receptivity.[32] This overperception is one way in which power can lead to sexual harassment.[33] Under these conditions, the victim's discomfort might not be as obvious to the perpetrator as it would be to an outside observer.

In addition, power may prompt goal-driven behavior in the power holder, who is aware of the influence they have by virtue of their control over valuable resources.[34] This behavior is enabled by the fact that many offenders have avoided consequences for sexually harassing behavior in the past. Too often, power and punishment operate as an inverse proportion, with higher power linked to a decreased likelihood of punishment.[35]

Power You Should Not Follow:
The Dark Side of Leadership

While outstanding leadership is linked with character strengths,[36] less desirable individuals also possess traits that serve them well in leadership positions. This is important to recognize, because charismatic leaders have the ability to influence people to behave in ways that contradict their moral values.[37]

Power in the form of leadership potential is linked with all three Dark Triad personality traits: narcissism, psychopathy, and Machiavellianism.

Narcissists have characteristics that under certain circumstances make them desirable as leaders—even when people are aware of their narcissistic features.[38] This is because in situations of uncertainty, the narcissist's confidence, dominance, strength, and toughness can generate psychological comfort and a sense of security.[39]

Psychopaths can make good leaders as well. Because many noncriminal psychopaths lack anti-social behavior,[40] other psychopathic traits such as heightened physical and social fearlessness can predispose them to effective leadership in areas such as the military or in politics.[41] In the corporate world, some businesspeople with high psychopathy scores hold positions of senior management.[42]

One study specifically found that fearless dominance, which embodies the boldness characteristic of psychopathy, was linked with more highly rated presidential performance, crisis management, persuasiveness, leadership, and congressional relations.[43] Fearless dominance was also linked with other indicators of presidential performance such as project initiation and being seen as a world leader.[44]

Another characteristic of psychopathy that can bolster leadership potential is the absence of morality. Famous politicians and ruthless world leaders such as Hitler and Stalin are recognized as examples of psychopaths whose rise to power would not have been possible were it not for their lack of conscience.[45]

This research does not prove that psychopaths make good presidents or world leaders any more than it proves that they make good corporate executives. It only means that some of the traits linked with psychopathy are also linked with power and leadership.

Machiavellianists can be good leaders as well. They are power-oriented, which decreases their social desirability, yet they are judged positively and desired as leaders.[46] With their talent for strategic, long-range planning and expertise in impression management,[47] they are often well suited for leadership roles and administrative positions.

Yet while people high in Machiavellianism often show stronger leadership and ability to form alliances than those with less of the trait, they are also prone to exploitation, and their concern for others is limited to their own self-interest.[48]

Perceiving Power Imbalance

A significant number of the crimes I prosecute are facilitated by the imbalance of power. From domestic violence to child molestation to embezzlement, many people fail to recognize the signs of exploitation by someone they view as a romantic partner, caretaker, mentor, or role model.

Some pedophiles automatically have power over their victims by virtue of age and position of authority.[49] They deliberately exploit status disparity, and sometimes feel justified in doing so.[50] Other times, however, power imbalance masquerades as a relationship of equality.

Some pedophiles lead a child to believe they share a friendship, which involves relational equality and the absence of power imbalance.[51] In reality, however, the relationship between a pedophile and a child is asymmetrical, making the sexual seduction a "perverse seductive game" where a child's acquiescence cannot be considered reciprocity.[52]

Predators gain power over parents of victims as well, often through fulfilling unmet emotional needs.[53] Some offenders specifically target parents with special needs children,[54] or single mothers seeking physical, emotional, or financial support.[55]

Other types of illicit bonds are also controlled through power imbalance—such as relationships between pimps and girls who sell their bodies for sex for them.[56] Some of these relationships start with a pimp helping a woman to kick a drug habit and promising financial assistance[57]— behavior which can lead the woman to believe he truly cares for her. But as time goes on, many pimps seduce women into a life of vice through cultivating dependence.[58]

These men feign false romantic interest and jealousy to prompt women to prove their love and devotion, often through severing ties to others in order to give the offender their full attention.[59] Pimps strategically isolate their victims from other people, increasing reliance on the pimp for both material and emotional needs.[60] While many of these women continue to refer to their pimps as "boyfriends," the relationship is now characterized by an abuse of power.

One of the most common ways of creating power imbalance is paradoxically clothed with the perception of altruism: helping behavior.

Too Good to be True:
Spotting Ulterior Motives

The mother of a young molest victim is emotional on the witness stand as she recounts all the wonderful things the defendant did for her. Grocery runs. Painting. Mowing the lawn. And . . . picking up her son from school—where conveniently, he was alone with the child.

Reaching for another Kleenex, she explains that she considered the defendant to be her knight in shining armor, coming to the rescue when she was struggling to raise a family on her own and couldn't afford hired help. As she learned the hard way, it is wise to be skeptical of things that are "free."

Sexual predators strategically use helpfulness to ingratiate themselves with victims and their families.[61] They offer to fix things, help with errands, or babysit, free of charge.[62] Their assistance often leads beneficiaries to describe them as "too good to be true." [63] They are.

Helping behavior allows predators to infiltrate families through several means. It enhances interpersonal warmth because helping is believed to demonstrate kindness.[64] Helping also generates perceived competence through demonstrating valuable skills or information that others need, resulting in elevated status attributed to the helper.[65]

Unfortunately, however, as important as the assistance might be to the beneficiaries, helpfulness can lead to the blurring of boundaries, affording the predator increased access to the family through creating a sense of indebtedness.[66] One mother describes (reluctantly) allowing a neighbor who had been working on her car for several years to simply walk into her house and pour himself a cup of coffee.[67] In fact, the first time it happened, not only did she refrain from objecting because he had spent time working on her car, she even offered to make him a sandwich.[68]

Helping behavior can generate power imbalance. Masquerading as prosocial altruism, helpfulness can be designed to cultivate social dominance.[69] Some argue that helping relationships are inherently unequal, because helpfulness generally stems from power and the possession of valuable commodities such as abilities, resources, and information—which give the helper higher status than the beneficiary.[70] Helping behavior also generates power because providing necessary services or essential benefits cultivates dependence.[71]

Both professionals and predators themselves warn that seemingly one-sided altruism is a huge red flag.[72] Child molesters are not behaving charitably to make new friends, nor do they expect legitimate compensation.[73] The repayment they want is sex with the children.[74]

Overcoming the Truthfulness Bias:
The Ambition Behind the Altruism

When someone offers to assist you in ways that will include interaction with your child when the basis of their relationship is supposedly with *you*, the FLAGs can help you to determine the ambition behind the altruism.

When evaluating the sincerity of helping behavior, consider the impact of the *truthfulness bias*—which explains that most people cannot distinguish between behavior that is honest and behavior that is deceptive, thus making the easier judgment that others are truthful.[75] To make things even more difficult, when we view others positively, we tend to believe they are telling the truth—even when they are lying.[76]

One way to overcome the truthfulness bias when examining a person's seemingly altruistic behavior is by becoming suspicious of his or her motives.[77] Researchers give the example of a man who rescues a colleague who is having car trouble. If those are the only facts you have, he is viewed as helpful and nice.[78] If you learned the colleague was attractive, the man was single, and he is not helpful in other situations, you might perceive the ulterior motive of romantic interest.[79]

Parents with young children who receive offers to "rescue" them through providing helpful assistance should similarly gain as much information as they can about these helpful individuals in order to more accurately perceive their motives. Beware of people offering assistance that focuses on interaction with the *children* as opposed to the adults, such as babysitting, or driving kids to and from school or sports practice. Be particularly wary of activities that afford secluded access to the child such as camping trips, sleepovers, or even dark movie theatres.

Beware of helpful neighbors or coworkers who have a lifestyle that involves unsupervised access with *other* people's children. Legitimate organizations usually involve group activities or on-site events, not overnights with a child or driving a child home. You would think this goes without saying, but I continue to see these reports every day.

Researching the Rise to Power

Before you clothe someone in a position of power with positive attributes they do not deserve, consider how they achieved their post. Researchers Joey T. Cheng and coauthors (2013) explained that two distinct ways to achieve influence and social rank is through using strategies of dominance and prestige.[80]

Acquiring social rank through *dominance* involves creating fear through coercion and intimidation, while using *prestige* refers to acquiring recognition and respect through expertise, knowledge, or success.[81]

Their research revealed that power is not merely a popularity contest, finding that people who achieved influence through prestige were likable, while those using dominance were not.[82] It also shed some light on why we tend to notice powerful people, finding that we pay more visual attention to individuals high in dominance and prestige.[83]

Regarding practical examples, relationships of dominance include both an employer-employee situation, as well as a bully-victim dynamic.[84] Prestige, on the other hand, creates a desire to emulate the knowledgeable individual—which can lead to following their instructions even in light of disagreement, as a means of seeking favor.[85]

Cheng and coauthors note that the difference between dominance and prestige is consistent with the recognized difference between power and status—two concepts that, while linked, have distinct methods of producing influence.[86] Dominance operates in a broader range of contexts than power—which produces inequality within hierarchical groups where individuals have control of resources.[87] Prestige is consistent with the concept of social status as it is defined in social psychology—to include receiving respect or admiration from others.[88]

But there is a more important distinction. Within relationships, people using a dominance strategy are more likely to be narcissistic, Machiavellian; and aggressive, whereas those using prestige are more likely to be agreeable, socially accepted, and high in self-esteem.[89] Prestigious people also tend to possess valuable skills such as altruism, academic achievement, and other intellectual and social abilities.[90]

Examining the Use of Power:
Malevolent or Benevolent

"Punish me, judge! Punish me!" the schizophrenic defendant shouts at the judge. The veteran jurist is unfazed. With the wisdom of many years on the bench, he continues to articulate the reasons for his decision based on the law, the facts, and the equities—not on the defendant's outbursts. He uses his power to achieve justice, regardless of how the defendant behaves in court.

In the wisdom of Plato—*the measure of a man is what he does with power.* As an extension of a person's motives, power can be used selfishly or altruistically.[91] While civic-minded individuals make benevolent leaders who seek to benefit others, psychopaths seek positions of corporate leadership to attain power and personal rewards.[92] They engage in unfair supervision practices and are workplace bullies.[93] Corporate psychopaths engage in bullying behavior to humiliate subordinates, perhaps because they like hurting others.[94]

On the other hand, many people use power to help others succeed. Power in the form of legitimate authority can empower group members to succeed in meeting objectives.[95] In close relationships, positive use of power may involve partners each using their influence to benefit the relationship.[96] And within mentoring relationships, power imbalance is used to benefit the protégé.[97]

A person's FLAGs can reveal how they use power. Some powerful people empower subordinates instead of dominate them.[98] This type of relationship, although unequal, can benefit the weaker partner.[99] *Transformative* power is described as a method of empowering a weaker relational partner that not only benefits the subordinate, but also serves to equalize the power imbalance through teaching skills to the weaker partner.[100]

The link between power imbalance and influence through expertise is illustrated through the example of a master-apprentice relationship—where the master teaches the apprentice through sharing his or her knowledge and abilities.[101] Within such relationships, the more powerful partners use their power to benefit the subordinates, who submit to the power imbalance willingly in order to enjoy the benefits of the association.[102]

POWER: POSITIVE USE OR ABUSE

Focus: Self-service or serving others?

Lifestyle: Ruler or role model?

Associations: Peers or protégés?

Goals: Empowerment or exploitation?

Spending Power:
Where the Heart Is, the Wallet Will Follow

In the words of Tony Montana in the movie *Scarface*: "In this country, first you get the money, then you get the power, then you get the women."[103] How true that is in many cases.

This phenomenon is certainly not limited to any particular country. It is a universal truth. Ogas and Gaddam observe the premium placed on material wealth as demonstrated through the fact that Amazon's romance titles include 286 billionaires, 415 millionaires, and 263 sheiks.[104] Research even demonstrates that women walking along the street are more likely to give their phone number to a stranger who asks them out on a date when he appears to be of higher financial status.[105]

There are both good and bad people with money. How can you tell the difference? Read the FLAGs. Consider the biblical wisdom that your heart will be where your treasure is. [106] Consider whether money is the focus of a person's existence, or merely a way to facilitate other pursuits and goals.

For example, when someone can afford to live a lifestyle of enjoying the very best—do they? Some people dress to impress, teetering around black-tie galas in $500 shoes, light-headed from the tight confines of the latest designer fashions, while others relax in comfortable clothing, choosing function over flash. Some people showcase their wealth through arriving in style, alighting from expensive, flashy cars, while others prefer the ease of public transportation over sitting in traffic in a Bentley.

Some rich folks prefer to associate within their income bracket by rubbing elbows with similarly situated wealthy people at high-end social clubs, while others strike up conversations with homeless people every day during their morning walk. Community associations are revealing as well. While there is nothing wrong with belonging to an expensive golf and tennis club, some wealthy people also belong to service clubs such as Rotary, Kiwanis, and other orgnaizations dedicated to philanthropic pursuits.

Regarding goals, some people place a high premium on money and resources, using them to "buy" friends and lovers, making a public showing of picking up the tab at group dinners. On the other hand, some wealthy people live a modest lifestyle and donate generously to charity.

As with the other areas of examination, it is the inner motivation of how people use what they have that is most revealing of their true ambitions and character.

3

Perceiving is Believing

The Comfort of Credibility

I am cross-examining a middle school teacher, called as a character witness for the defendant, who is accused of child molestation. "I can't believe that about our principal," she declares with indignation. "He has two master's degrees, has been here for fifteen years, and is married with children. He would *never* hurt a child. How dare you bring these charges!"

"Do you even know what the charges are?" I counter. She does not. This is common. If I had a dime for every defensive and often downright hostile reaction I have heard after shameful allegations have surfaced against someone in a position of respect, I would be able to retire.

I have prosecuted scores of educated, credentialed members of society who deceived, defrauded, manipulated, and exploited friends, family members, and employers for financial gain—using their status as a shield to deflect suspicion of wrongdoing. I have also prosecuted intrafamilial crimes such as incest and spousal rape—crimes that are already hard to prove due to the lack of independent witnesses—that are made even more challenging when the perpetrator holds a position of prestige in the community.

The common denominator is that respectable, educated, impressive people receive the benefit of the doubt through the comfort and security created by the perception of credibility.

Above Suspicion:
Honorable Mention

My jaw dropped the first time the mother of a child molestation victim told me she agreed to allow the perpetrator to take a shower with her son in order to teach him how to wash himself properly. Sadly, I quickly became accustomed to hearing this sort of thing. Why would a parent allow this? Because the perpetrator was a school administrator. Or a minister. Or a public official. Someone with an honorable title that conveyed credibility.

Newsflash: Not all pedophiles work as clowns for children's parties. Many of them hold lucrative, high-status jobs. No one wants to believe that a person in an esteemed position of respect would sexually abuse a child. This intentional disbelief allows well-credentialed predators to continue their deviant activity virtually unchecked, sometimes for years. Consider the vast number of victims a credible child molester can rack up in a school setting.

An established athletic director at an elementary school has flawless credentials, a stellar reputation, and the trust of the children's parents.[1] Despite having been accused of inappropriate sexual behavior with children over the years, his employment continues, with parents of the children who have complained explaining that they knew he loved children and that there "must be some mistake."[2]

Finally caught and incarcerated at age thirty, he explains that in fact there was "no mistake at all."[3] How many victims did he have in the seventeen years he admitted sexually abusing children? Approximately one thousand two hundred and fifty.[4] I wrote out this number so you wouldn't think there was a typo.

How did he get away with it? The same way many others do. People are easy to fool if you have the right credentials, qualifications, or position in society. Welcome to the comfort of credibility.

Credibility Is Comforting

In a world filled with uncertainty, credible people are welcome sources of security. We feel comfortable taking their advice, relying on their guidance, and believing what they say. Unfortunately, this mindset can create emotional blinders that cause people to miss, misinterpret, or discount red flags, enabling deceptive individuals to exploit misplaced trust.

Like other sources of attraction, credibility is not a trait of a speaker, but a *perception* of expertise and trustworthiness created in an audience.[5] Similar to the halo effect in attraction research, credible communicators are believed to possess a wide range of attractive traits including reliability[6] as well as trustworthiness, goodwill, expertise, dynamism, sociability, extroversion, and composure.[7] Other characteristics attributed to credible communicators include in-group membership, similarity, physical attractiveness, likability, high social status, and being viewed as an authority.[8]

Credibility includes both *expertise* and *trustworthiness*.[9] Expertise is persuasive even without supporting information.[10] *Expert power* is a process through which an audience is influenced by an expert source, without necessarily comprehending the reasoning behind the expert's message.[11]

Determinations of trustworthiness are based on a variety of different factors, including academic credentials, profession, gender, age, and ethnic group.[12] These areas generate perceived competence and motives for trustworthiness.[13] Stereotypes often dictate the significance of culturally respected characteristics, leading to trustworthiness through perceived competence based on certain characteristics alone.[14]

A third dimension of credibility is *goodwill*—expressed through caring.[15] Goodwill is recognized as a speaker's "honorable intentions" toward the listener,[16] and generates inspiration and trust.[17]

The Deceptive Security of Status

The public is repeatedly shocked at the scandalous behavior of credentialed professionals. Particularly when the behavior involves misconduct by high-ranking corporate or government officials. Why? Because some people equate high status with high morals.

Most of us have seen enough high-profile scandals to know better. From extramarital affairs, to insider trading, to sending scantily clad selfies on Twitter, there are a wide range of examples of people in high places behaving badly. The astonishing thing about high-profile misbehavior, however, is that despite the (eventual) admissions of many offenders, we still clothe people in high places with a veneer of credibility that even they recognize they do not deserve.

This is often true even if you know nothing about a person except for his or her title. For example, you wouldn't be afraid of passing a stranger in a dark alley if you knew the person was the CEO of your company. On the other hand, upon encountering an unknown, shadowy figure, you might turn around and walk the other way.

If the president of your company told you that she intended to promote you within the next several months, you would likely feel much more secure about this actually happening than if you were assured of such advancement by a mid-level supervisor. This is because status carries credibility. Why? Let's have a closer look at the concept.

Status is the admiration, respect, or regard a person receives from others.[18] Status involves a publicly recognized hierarchical ranking that comes with certain privileges.[19] Low-status individuals defer to those with high-status through social coordination,[20] and we are more likely to comply with the requests of high-status people than those with low status.[21]

How does this work? From research on prestige comes an *altercasting* theory where credibility is generated through relational dynamics.[22] Examples include authority-agent relationships—where authority entitles a person to exert power over others—which can stimulate obedience, and high-status admiration—where famous or popular people elicit preferential treatment—which can generate influence.[23] This follows from the fact that many people admire, want to identify with, or seek approval from high-status individuals.[24]

The influence of status is also demonstrated through *social modeling*—where a person's behavior prompts similar behavior from others, providing "social proof" of appropriate behavior in different contexts.[25] People frequently imitate social models who have a high degree of status, power, and prestige, as well as people who are capable and attractive.[26]

HIGH STATUS DOESN'T ENSURE HIGH STANDARDS

Focus: Financial shareholders or community stakeholders?

Lifestyle: Lavish perks or corporate phalanthropy?

Associations: Elitist segregation or engaged cooperation?

Goals: World peace or political re-election?

Unfortunately, both good and manipulative individuals hold positions of status. Some predators use community status to ingratiate themselves with adults in order to obtain access to children, and then to deflect suspicion when allegations surface, because many people refuse to consider incriminating evidence against a person with an unblemished reputation.[27]

Status yields other benefits as well. Some perpetrators, by virtue of their positions, may be viewed as safe and nonthreatening.[28] Offenders can also use their position of high status to give victims a taste of enjoying a higher standard of living than they have with their own family.[29] In addition, an offender's position of authority may facilitate victim seduction[30] and discourage resistance to the abuse.[31] And in many cases, high status can guarantee victim silence.[32]

Note, however, that as with credibility in general, status is sometimes just a perception. One that can be created through a cultivated image, as well as through nonverbal behavior.

One example involves arrogant people. Do you know any of those? Displays of pride lead some people to believe that a person with a high self-view also has high status.[33] This is true when the person displays pride as compared with other emotions such as happiness, shame, and anger, and when a person reacts to a positive event with pride instead of gratitude—causing people to believe the person is more likely a company boss than an employee.[34]

Credibility Through Authority:
Blind Obedience

Many people instinctively obey authority. When you see flashing red and blue lights in your rear view mirror, you pull over. You don't call 911 to make sure the car behind you is really a police car, although you know that some women have been sexually assaulted after being pulled over by someone pretending to be a cop.

When the officer asks for your license and registration, you open the glove box and begin rooting around for the paperwork. You don't demand to see the officer's credentials, although you have probably read about the rare but highly publicized cases where police officers have threatened drivers with citation or arrest unless they pay sums of money or perform sexual favors.

But beware of authority without accountability. The famous 1963 Milgram experiment demonstrated destructive obedience in revealing that people will obey orders to shock protesting victims in a laboratory condition, indicating the power of perceived authority.[35] Under the guise of a "learning experiment," subjects obeyed orders to shock a victim (actually a confederate), over half of them complying with directions to increase voltage up to the highest degree of the shock generator.[36]

The extent of obedience demonstrated in this experiment highlights the need to ensure that perceived authority is legitimate, because both good and bad people can play the part.

When Credibility Is a Costume:
Beware of the Staged Appearance

Credibility can be conveyed through appearance. One common example that I have experienced in settings ranging from watching an autopsy as a prosecutor to participating in laboratory experiments as a psychology major at UCLA, is the "white coat" phenomenon. We often trust doctors and lab experimenters merely because they officially look the part. In addition to doctors, other occupations that convey authority through uniforms include police officers, military employees, firefighters, and professional athletes.[37]

In contrast to people who wear uniforms or distinctive clothing in the course of legitimate professions, manipulators strategically dress to impress by selecting attire that conveys credibility. Don't automatically assume the guy you see walking through your parking garage at night in scrubs is a doctor. That is a powerful disguise when used by a criminally minded individual because of the strong air of credibility. Yet all it demonstrates is the power of a credible *appearance*.

One popular courtroom "disguise" is the use of non-prescription eyeglasses. Designed to convey an air of righteousness and virtue, some defendants walk into court looking like Clark Kent, ready to find a phone booth to make the transformation from criminal to crime fighter.

Speaking of phone booths, more people will admit finding change in a phone booth when asked by a well-dressed experimenter than by one who is poorly dressed.[38] Similarly, people are more likely to make change for[39] or lend money to well-dressed requesters.[40]

Some people gear their appearance toward their target audience. Some cults,[41] for example, desire to attract newcomers who are intelligent, successful, and talented.[42] So instead of dressing like hippies and handing out flowers on street corners, modern cult recruiters might wear pin-striped business suits, reflecting the evolution of cult appeal.[43]

Business suits in general are one common type of "costume" that men have used to pull off a multitude of crimes, including raping women at knifepoint who willingly invite a well-dressed stranger into their homes, believing his story about responding to advertisements they posted in the classified section of the newspaper.[44]

Consider, however, how despite a clean-cut image on the job, a man's after-hours behavior can reveal the character beneath the corporate image.

Beneath the Business Suit:
FLAGs After Five

I prosecuted a man who avoided suspicion for years by hiding behind the credibility of a professional image and behavior to match. He was the perfect gentleman in the office from nine to five. Unfortunately, he moonlighted as a sexual harasser.

This pattern of extracurricular activity was revealed in part through his focus on keeping Friday nights free to participate in a very different lifestyle than he leads during the week. On Friday nights, this man hit the town solo, a custom he had been enjoying for years. One Friday night was his birthday. Instead of celebrating with friends or coworkers, he engaged in his usual Friday night routine, venturing out to kick up his heels by himself. This time, his luck ran out.

While other patrons might only have seen him buying drinks and tearing it up on the dance floor (alone) at several different clubs, video surveillance footage revealed that his celebration included more than club-hopping. Amid the crush of people, Friday nights being the busiest night of the week, he blatantly groped several women at each nightclub. While the victims couldn't identify the culprit in the thick crowd, security cameras could. Oops.

After the fact, several other women came forward and reported having been groped at the same nightclubs—on Friday nights. We now understand why this man kept Friday nights free.

This example illustrates the reality that even with seemingly credible business professionals, a person's focus and lifestyle off the clock can be much more revealing of his or her true colors than the polished appearance and tempered behavior exhibited on the job.

Regarding social preferences, while we can't conclude that everyone who chooses to party alone has malevolent motives, that preference means *something*. For this man, who lived alone and had few friends, his lack of associations (and consequent unaccountability) facilitated his after-hours lifestyle and goals.

Penetrating the Camouflage of Credentials

Smiling, with dreamy expressions on their faces, the jurors are mesmerized with the smooth, articulate recitation of facts coming from the witness stand. As a highly credentialed professional, the witness exudes expertise and proficiency in his field, which has captivated the jurors. They are leaning forward, paying attention, and nodding with approval when he makes a point.

Because most of my cases involve a battle of the experts, I am routinely either pleased or horrified to watch this phenomenon . . . depending on whether or not the witness is on my side. Anyone who marvels at a jury verdict that is contrary to the evidence presented should spend some time in the courtroom to experience the often beguiling magic of expert testimony.

Here is the formula behind the illusion: credentials create credibility, and credibility generates believability. Professional witnesses come in with a resume longer than the defendant's rap sheet and dazzle the jury with their knowledge and expertise. Once these witnesses have completed reciting their qualifications, credentials, training, and experience, some jurors are ready to buy a beachfront condominium in Arizona from them based on their background alone.

As many people find out the hard way, however, credentials do not always equal credibility. Professional accomplishments on a curriculum vitae demonstrate academic achievement, experience, and expertise. Period. They tell you nothing about the person's honesty and integrity. Consider the valuable information received through exploring the character behind the credentials.

I am picking a jury and come across a nurse. I know that nurses consistently top Gallup poll surveys rating the most honest and ethical professionals.[45] But instead of stereotyping, I have some questions.

"Juror Number 5, as a nurse in a large hospital, what is the most challenging thing about your job?" What if I had received the following response: "Having to deal with annoying patients all day long! I swear as soon as I leave one room, the guy is ringing his call button again, and then the patient in the next room starts ringing hers; it starts to sound like a bunch of dogs barking when a firetruck goes by!"

Can you imagine if I just stereotyped instead of following up? *Oh, a nurse! She must be nurturing, patient, kind, and empathetic. She will surely sympathize with my high-maintenance, attention seeking victim.* I would have been terribly mistaken.

Or in response to that same question, imagine that the juror shares that she loathes her job as a nurse, resentful that after slaving away for years to put her husband through medical school, he ran off with his assistant, leaving her with insufficient funds to further her own medical career. That juror defies the stereotype as well, and would be a terrible choice for a case where the victim was a man who had been unfaithful to his wife.

These examples demonstrate why we cannot simply make assumptions about what someone is like based solely on a credible occupation.

Reading Behind the Resume

There is a tendency to attribute heightened trustworthiness to people who look good on paper. This tendency is so strong that some employers will hire employees based on their impressive qualifications, even if they discover that their resume contains dishonest embellishment.

Kristine M. Kuhn and coauthors (2013) conducted a study of the desirability of job applicants who embellished their resumes.[46] They found that misstating employment dates of a previous job to cover a period of unemployment had little effect on the way favored applicants were evaluated in terms of ability, trustworthiness, and likability, but negatively impacted the view of less-favored applicants.[47]

The researchers suggested that these results provide evidence of motivated reasoning, manifested in the tendency to dismiss or attempt to justify deception, if possible, having already formed a positive impression of another person.[48]

One factor to consider in deciding whether a highly credentialed person is someone you want to hire, consult with, or associate with is to read beyond the resume by examining how their FLAGs indicate they *use* their talents, expertise, and position.

For some lawyers, the primary goal is success, not justice. Their focus is on obtaining outrageous fees, targeting big-name clients, and holding press conferences on the courthouse steps to boost their visibility and drum up business. Their focus and lifestyle reflect their goals, as they flaunt their wealth to boost their perception of prestige and success in order to attract potential clients.

For other lawyers, the focus is on fairness, not finances. They limit their practice to the pursuit of causes about which they are truly passionate, and even handle cases pro bono for the disenfranchised in order to promote access to justice. These lawyers showcase a lifestyle of modesty and transparency as they pull into the courthouse parking lot in an inexpensive car with a standard license plate, amid a sea of flashy sports cars with vanity plates spelling witty legal acronyms. With these civic-minded advocates, what you see is what you get.

There are numerous examples of these distinctions in many other professions. In the medical field, some doctors pursue lucrative niche practices in upscale communities where they perform expensive cosmetic surgical procedures, while others travel regularly to third world countries in order to treat underprivileged children for free. Business leaders from all walks of corporate life routinely volunteer their time at career fairs to help young people craft the perfect resume.

Another factor that can reveal the true colors of accomplished professionals is the extent to which they share their expertise through donating their time to educate others. Whether they offer free seminars, guest lecture at universities, or provide complimentary consultations, many people demonstrate authenticity through the desire to share their knowledge and expertise without expecting anything in return.

So the next time someone hands you a business card with their name followed by a string of degrees, consider these educational achievements to be merely a starting point for your analysis.

Credibility Crashers:
Dishonesty and Hypocrisy

I am dashing to court in the middle of trial when my paralegal catches up to me and hands me a rap sheet, stating: "You are going to want to read this right away." My first thought is that because the defendant bailed out of custody, he probably picked up a new case over the weekend. *Some people just can't stay out of trouble* I think to myself as I begin to read what I have been handed.

I literally stop in my tracks when I realize the rap sheet doesn't belong to the defendant. It belongs to my expert witness who is about to take the stand.

Why didn't I know? Because my expert has an illustrious resume. I never imagined she was a convicted felon. Even worse, the prior conviction involved a crime of dishonesty, which of course is always relevant to witness credibility.

Sometimes I come across evidence about highly credentialed people that doesn't directly relate to dishonesty, but impacts authenticity through hypocrisy.

Earlier in my career I worked in our office's issuing department, where my job was to read police reports all day and file the appropriate charges for the crimes committed. Every now and then, I was shocked at what I read. A police report would come in, describing a person pulled over for weaving all over the road, who was obnoxious, combative, blew an alcohol reading three times the legal limit, and then threw up in the back of the police car.

It wasn't the conduct that shocked me; I read about this type of intemperance every day. It was the identity of the perpetrator. When I arrived at the page with the name and photograph of the offender, sometimes I discovered that it was one of my well-known professional acquaintances. A university professor. A famous expert witness, renown in his field. A local public official. Sometimes it was someone I knew so well that I had to hand off the case to another prosecutor to issue because I would have a conflict of interest charging the case.

Of course, impressive people are human and make mistakes just like the rest of us. It is a huge blow to credibility, however, when someone's lifestyle contradicts his or her professional claims. After all, we expect people to practice what they preach.

If the drunk driver described in the police report had been a toxicologist who routinely testifies about the negative effects of alcohol and the dangers of drinking and driving, the facts of his arrest would undermine his credibility and the weight that should be given to his testimony. It wouldn't matter if he was honest about his overindulgence. The jury would still view him as a hypocrite.

CREDENTIALS DO NOT GUARANTEE CREDIBILITY

Focus: Does a person use credentials to enjoy special privileges, or to help the underprivileged?

Lifestyle: Do experts practice what they preach? Does your doctor smoke? Does your financial advisor gamble?

Associations: Does a person belong to professional associations within their field of expertise, or prefer to socialize with fans and followers? Do they prefer to work alone or as part of a team?

Goals: Does a person capitalize on their expertise by charging expensive fees for their services, or do they donate their time? Are they motivated by greed or generosity?

The Smoke Screen of Success:
Spotting the Corporate Psychopath

Is there anything worse than an outwardly credible person who is a liar or a hypocrite? Yes. The corporate psychopath—who is both.

Psychopaths are alive and well in the corporate world.[49] These "snakes in suits"[50] glide through posh corporate hallways, slithering their way into boardrooms around the globe using cleverly devised tactics of manipulation.

Using smoke and mirrors, they charm their way into organizations, modeling behaviors that are misinterpreted as leadership traits, get to know as many coworkers as possible, and then selectively form "psychopathic bonds" with individuals in order to exploit their weaknesses and areas of vulnerability.[51] In fact, some psychopaths intentionally target coworkers, knowing these people are unlikely to report them because they will be ashamed that they fell for the scam.[52]

In *Corporate Psychopaths* (2011), Clive Boddy describes psychopaths as "smooth, charming, polished extroverts who are in control of themselves and their environment," presenting the illusion of success.[53] Exploring the link between psychopathy and criminality, in *The Wisdom of Psychopaths: What Saints, Spies, and Serial Killers Can Teach Us About Success,* Kevin Dutton notes that some attributes of psychopathy are more common in business leaders than in criminals.[54] These attributes include superficial charm, persuasiveness, independence, focus, and egocentricity.[55]

The success of corporate psychopaths as productive members of society stems from the fact that their ruthlessness and manipulation are their least discernable traits.[56] This allows them to win the confidence of others and climb the corporate ladder.[57] Some psychopaths are on the management track,[58] described by those in power as intelligent, charming and likable.[59]

The term *successful psychopathy* recognizes that psychopathy is manifest within a range of severity, as opposed to being an all-or-nothing condition.[60] People on the low end, often referred to as *noncriminal* psychopaths, do not exhibit anti-social behaviors but have other psychopathic personality traits such as fearlessness and superficial charm, which can be beneficial in some professions.[61] These professions include politics, law, law enforcement, corporate business, and high-contact sports.[62] Other psychopaths hold respectable professions ranging from doctors and lawyers to academics and entertainers,[63] and even judges.[64]

But it gets even more interesting. Some psychopaths are *heroes.* Researchers exploring the link between psychopathy and heroism note several cases where people with psychopathic traits performed volunteer work and stunning acts of heroism that saved other people.[65] The explanation? Heroism is believed to be linked with a psychopath's fearless dominance.[66]

Right about now, some of you may be alarmed, wondering: *Holy cow, am I a psychopath?* Not to fear. Many people have positive traits that are associated with psychopathy, while lacking the negative ones. In order to pick out the bad apples, we have to look beneath the surface.

FLAGs Reveal the Venom Beneath the Veneer

Most people don't quit jobs, they quit bosses. Therefore, we want to spot corporate psychopaths sooner rather than later. Fortunately, as crafty as they are, "snakes in suits" often reveal their venom. A psychopath's coworkers often see through the façade and expose their true nature as manipulative, deceitful, and abusive.[67] How? Psychopaths have distinctive FLAGs.

They are self-focused, not team players who work toward common goals.[68] Instead of fostering an atmosphere of cooperation, corporate psychopaths frequently use other people and even take credit for their work[69] due to their parasitic lifestyle.[70]

You may, however, not notice this dynamic right away because coworkers often willingly pitch in to help the psychopath, whom they describe as a close friend and whom they are "fixated on pleasing."[71] Even after manipulation comes to light, some of these people miss the "special relationship" they had with the psychopath, and blame themselves for the relational failure.[72]

Despite their successful careers,[73] psychopaths also expose their true colors through a lifestyle of dishonesty. As Paul Babiak and Robert D. Hare explain in *Snakes in Suits: When Psychopaths Go to Work*, "In the great card game of life, psychopaths know what cards you hold, and they cheat."[74] In fact, be on the listen for admissions that some of them find dishonesty to be enjoyable. One psychopath, when asked about spending more than his expense budget, admitted to his boss that he felt "like a kid in a candy store!"[75]

And when talking with these slippery characters around the water cooler, beware of form over substance. Individuals in the workplace with high psychopathy scores often have good communication skills—which likely made them attractive job candidates, and now make them successful employees.[76] Their oral communication skills, however, can be illusory.[77] They often impress others with presentation over content—making use of clichés, jargon, and clever phraseology to make up for a lack of substance.[78]

Psychopaths are also distinguished by the types of goals they pursue. You may remember *Wall Street's* "greed is good" mantra, delivered eloquently by Michael Douglas playing the role of Gordon Gekko, a psychopathic businessman who sacrificed morality for financial gain.[79] Some people who share his goal also share his traits, as psychopaths pursue tangible goals such as wealth and status.[80]

A good rule in the corporate world is to keep your guard up at the office. Even with enhanced efforts at screening for psychopathic and other problematic traits, it is predicted that "sour cream will continue to rise to the top."[81]

The Illusion of Competence:
When Experience Is Misleading

Competence is attractive. Ogas and Gaddam point out that the fictional romantic hero is always competent.[82] He is not a couch potato or a mid-level manager; he is usually the best in the business—whatever his field.[83]

Competence is also comforting—instilling confidence. We believe that someone with the appropriate credentials, training, and expertise is competent to deliver the services we need. When we go to a doctor and leave with a prescription, we take the medicine. When we hire a reputable chef for an event, we do not expect our guests to end up with food poisoning.

Sometimes competence is both attractive and comforting, as in the handsome tennis instructor who is tanned, talented, and at the top of his game.

However, competence, like other attractive traits, is a *perception*.[84] A perception that can be misleading—particularly when it is based heavily on expertise through experience that you have not personally observed. Because while you can watch your tennis instructor consistently demonstrate his athletic prowess on the court, you cannot stand in an operating room and watch the surgeon you are thinking of hiring while he is operating on other patients.

As a result, some people place undue emphasis on prior experience. I have asked many victims of criminal negligence the same question: "Why didn't you change your mind after you saw *that*?" The answers are often some version of the same sentiment: "Because he has been doing this for twenty years," or "because everyone else uses him."

Blinded by the impressive background and successful history of a respected service provider, many people ignore FLAGs that fly in the face of qualifications and credentials. Past experience does not necessarily guarantee present competence. For example, perhaps you should think twice about hiring a world-class surgeon whose focus is shifting from the operating room to the golf course as he is in the middle of a lifestyle change, transitioning into retirement. You want to hire someone who not only has the right skills, but also has his head in the right game.

Pay attention to an office bookshelf filled with a disorganized mess of files, which might constitute *behavioral residue*,[85] reflecting lack of focus on a current job. Notice whether a professional's lifestyle is consistent with success in his or her profession. You wouldn't hire a day care provider with an after-hours lifestyle of impulsive risk taking and recklessness, or a security guard who is addicted to Facebook and spends all of his waking hours glued to his smart phone.

Take note of professional associations, including leadership positions, which indicate interest and involvement in one's chosen field. Also notice whether a person has allowed professional memberships to lapse, which might indicate pending retirement or contemplation of a career change.

Regardless of past experience, these types of observations can corroborate or contradict credentials and experience that can assist you in gauging competence.

4

Suddenly Smitten

The Pleasure of Positive Attention

A woman meets a handsome man who treats her like a queen. Their relationship leads to the altar. A prestigious company CEO, husband, and father of three has an affair with his intern. The scandal lands on the front page of the newspaper. A thirty-five-year-old schoolteacher, married with children of her own, begins a sexual relationship with a twelve-year-old boy in her class. Her case lands on my desk.

What do all three of these cases have in common? Each relationship was fueled by the seductive power of positive attention.

We are attracted to others who give us attention.[1] We are particularly drawn to people who make us feel desirable, important, and sexy. We can understand the woman enjoying the royal treatment in the first example. But what about the other two?

The CEO's affair with his intern was fueled by her enthusiastic affirmation of his sexual prowess in a way that his wife had never expressed. The schoolteacher's infatuation with her pre-teen male student stemmed from his hormone-fueled adoration of her in a way that her age-appropriate husband did not express.[2] In other words, all three relationships were motivated by the pleasure of positive attention.

Thankfully, many people who make you the center of their world really adore you. They are the real deal, and are as good as they look. Authentic attention produces longstanding friendships, solid family ties, and wonderful marriages. Other people focus on you for other reasons. The key is to be able to tell the difference.

The Muted Lens of Loving Attention:
A Lighter Shade of Red

When I ask people who have been victimized to explain how they became involved with the offender, their faces often light up as they describe how the defendant made them feel. Whether they were made to feel like they were the most beautiful, sexy, intelligent, or caring people, these victims ate up the offender's compliments, captivated by his professed assessment of them as "special." Here is the fascinating thing: many of these people also saw red flags, which they chose to downplay or ignore in order to continue to enjoy the warm glow of attention.

"Didn't you know he had a criminal record?" I ask during an interview with one of these victims, attempting to break through the dreamy reminiscence. Certainly she did. Who told her? *The defendant*. She explains that his honesty only added to his credibility. "Besides," she explains, "everyone makes mistakes." She should know—she fell for the scam.

Within families, I have prosecuted cases where defendants have fathered children with their own biological daughters (confirmed through DNA)—resulting in confused youngsters who don't know whether to call the defendant "dad" or "grandpa." Believe it or not, the horrendous nature of the conduct usually doesn't change the fondness the victims have for the offender.

Having spent years watching forensic interviews of toddlers through a one-way mirror, I am continually amazed at how a young child can smile as she is asked to describe the perpetrator—often a close relative she loves. With older children, when I am questioning them in court, some admit on the witness stand that the offender was the only person in their lives who paid them any attention—a factor that outweighed having to endure the sexual abuse. "Do you still love him today?" I ask. Almost always, the answer is a tearful "Yes."

The mothers of the victims sometimes still love the defendant too, because as they explain to me, despite his flaws, he was an attentive, caring husband. Even when they know that he molested their own children? Yes.

Do these women change their minds after the men are convicted and sentenced to prison? Not always. Many spouses promise to visit the pedophiles regularly—with the hopes of reuniting if they are ever released. "Did you hear the judge? He just got a fifty-year sentence." I explain to one of these women at the sentencing hearing. She will wait as long as it takes, she explains. In her words, her husband's loving attention is a drug and she will be "hooked" till the end.

Bestowing attention to facilitate abuse does not just occur within families. It happens within all types of relationships. Predatory educators target vulnerable students for sexual abuse,[3] often honing in on those whom they believe will be particularly responsive to positive attention.[4] Family friends, "Big Brothers," and a variety of other adults who play different roles in a child's life do the same thing.

Attention is used to camouflage sinister motives when manipulating adults as well. Consider the abusive husband who continues to give his wife beautiful gifts, even after he has become violent. As time goes on, however, some of the gifts begin to carry veiled warnings—threats really—in the form of instructions.

For their first wedding anniversary, a man gives his wife a beautiful diamond watch. I ask the victim to read the instructions to the jury: "My darling, I hope this gift will help you have dinner ready on time." A few of the jurors start to laugh, until they realize that it wasn't a joke. Wait until they hear why this was the most terrifying gift the victim had ever received.

Her husband, you see, was a psychopath. Here are some of the things she wished she knew before she said "I do."

I Only Have Eyes for You:
The Seduction of Selectivity

I prosecuted a man who seduced a juror . . . during the trial . . . in the courtroom. How much personal contact does it take? Would you believe, none at all? Unless you count eye contact, that is.

While being tried for attempted murder, the intelligent, charismatic defendant spent most of the trial staring at the jury. Most of the jurors were visibly uncomfortable with this attention. But not everyone was offended. Apparently, he had been focusing his gaze on one woman in particular—who refused to convict him. When asked about it afterward, she explained that she felt like she knew the defendant, because of the way he had been looking at her throughout the trial. They had bonded, although of course they never spoke. Not with words, anyway.

The defendant was clever, and his technique was simple. He found a receptive female in his audience, and focused his attention—*selectively*. With a courtroom full of people, he only had eyes for *her*. Too bad she didn't think about *why*. Could it have been because she was deciding his fate? Believe it or not, that was something she did not consider.

Our receptivity to focused attention is demonstrated in a variety of practical contexts from the way we treat e-mail to the way we respond to romantic attention. For example, while we routinely disregard mass distribution e-mails where everyone appears to have been blind copied, we usually respond when someone sends an e-mail only to us—sometimes even if we do not personally know the sender. In a dating context, you are more likely to be attracted to people who appear to be uniquely captivated by *you*, as opposed to being equally interested in everyone they meet.

The allure of selective attention has been documented through studies on speed dating. One study revealed that partners who exhibited a unique desire toward his or her partner were more likely to have the feeling reciprocated.[5] This suggests that the study participants who appeared to be equally impressed by every one of their speed-dates were viewed as undesirable due to their unselectivity, whereas those participants who transmitted a unique desire for a particular partner evoked a feeling of unique chemistry.[6]

Another interesting aspect of speed dating research is that the results seem to indicate that the need to feel special operates *immediately* within romantic contact[7]—demonstrating how quickly we subconsciously respond positively to people who show us special attention.

The attraction to selective suitors is consistent with research exploring the success of "playing hard to get." Contrary to popular wisdom, hard-to-get dates are not always viewed as more valuable.[8] Instead, researchers found that a woman was viewed as most attractive when she was easy for the subject to get, but hard for *other* men to get.[9]

Catering to Our Favorite Subject

Having selected well over one hundred jury panels in my career, I am familiar with the reality that people embrace the opportunity to talk about their favorite subject—themselves. For prospective jurors, even in front of a room full of strangers (including the defendant), being able to talk about oneself, without interruption, in a venue where you are the center of attention, is empowering. A moment in the sun. Many prospective jurors will raise their hands repeatedly in order to continue to provide information, as if they have been deprived of human contact for a significant period of time. With all eyes and ears on them, they just can't get enough airtime.

This phenomenon reflects the reality that people enjoy talking about themselves, and are more likely to initiate conversation about themselves than about other people.[10] People are also eager to show off their family. Just think about a friend's response when you ask about her daughter's recent birthday party. Her face lights up as she whisks out the smart phone. Why tell you when she can show you? For the next fifteen minutes you are dizzy watching the camera roll of photos from the party, accompanied by a running narrative that she barely interrupts to take a breath.

Why all the excitement? People love to share their lives. When you express interest in someone, you have become more attractive to that person than you can imagine. The next time you leave a social event thinking about how much you enjoyed spending time with someone, consider who did most of the talking. Perhaps it was you.

For people who want to share their lives with as many people as possible from the comfort of their own homes, such self-disclosure is now literally at their fingertips.

Welcome Attention:
Friends, Fans, and Followers

A sixteen-year-old girl glances at her computer to see the new message in her in-box: "The Prince of Shadows is now following you on Twitter." Her reaction? Fear? Anxiety? Does she call the police? Nope. She breaks into a smile. The whole reason she has a Twitter page is to gain followers. And this guy sounds interesting.

Two months later this sixteen-year-old is sitting in my office. "Did that name concern you?" I ask, once charges had been filed in her case. "Nope," she says. "He sounded like a video game superhero." Unfortunately, The Prince of Shadows turned out to be a stalker. And he was no prince. Although we did catch him lurking in the shadows underneath her bedroom window.

Having been through this experience, has my victim terminated her online profile? No way. Welcome to the age of online promotion.

Social media users are able to share volumes of personal information with the world with a click of a button. But the attention they receive in response is not always the type of positive attention we want to see. While some people love the limelight and consider attention of *any* type to be a goal in itself, people like me worry about the predators lurking in cyberspace, looking for provocative screen names and exhibitionistic selfies, searching for victims to target.

Unfortunately, predators have a wide range of candidates to choose from because in contemporary society, becoming an Internet sensation is part of the new definition of success. Let's face it, people don't tweet and blog to read their own posts. The goal is to attract attention—the more the better. When success is measured by the number of Facebook likes, Twitter followers, and hits to a YouTube page, repeat customers are welcome. This can be dangerous, because online, we don't call them cyber stalkers. We call them friends, fans, and followers.

Social media sites exploit this quest for attention by teasing their customers, informing them that "Three people viewed your profile in the last week—upgrade your membership to find out who." Although framed in terms of a sales pitch, this is good advice, because not everyone looking at you online harbors good intentions.

If you decide to research who has been viewing your information, what will you find? Sometimes, not much. Many people create online identities for the sole purpose of interacting anonymously. Learning that "John Doe" has viewed your profile fifty times in the last several days might creep you out—but it won't tell you whether this person is on the other side of the world or in the cubicle next to you in the office. It also won't tell you about his or her intentions.

When frequent contact is made with someone the user actually knows offline, there is a greater sense of security. When we receive online accolades from coworkers, neighbors, or other acquaintances, we tend to overlook the significance of their online admiration. We should not dismiss such focused attention too quickly.

Someone who knows too much about us can become suspicious on that basis alone. It depends on the nature of the relationship. A job interviewer, for example, might expect interviewees to Google him or her before the interview. In a world where online research is so easy, such preparation is often expected. We would not, however, expect the same level of research from a coworker who was just assigned the cubicle next to us.

Many attention seekers, however, are not frightened but flattered by the high level of interest expressed by cyber fans. Yet when a cyber stalker sets his sights on a high-visibility, attention-seeking target, suddenly, being an Internet sensation doesn't seem so cool. And because you can't read the FLAGs of anonymous admirers, it can be virtually impossible, pun intended, to determine when Internet fans are dangerously fanatical.

"Last Call":
When Desperation Masks Deception

Believe it or not, some people still meet potential suitors the old-fashioned way: in person. Such meetings often take place in designated public gathering spots that are notorious for facilitating sexual encounters: bars.

While people indulging at a bar usually appear progressively less attractive as the evening wears on, singles hoping to partner up often have the opposite perception. For unattached singles, romantic prospects in a bar become *better* looking the closer it gets to closing time, demonstrating a situationally induced lack of selectivity.[11]

The perception that a person is running out of time to find a partner can cause attentive suitors to look very good—a perception that stems from desperation rather than desirability. Clever con artists looking for women with resources to exploit are able to spot this desperation faster than a drug-sniffing dog can find cocaine.

Some of these guys never steal anything tangible, they just take advantage of a woman and deplete her resources. Even when there is nothing for me to "charge" these guys with except being pathetic freeloaders, we can nonetheless learn about potential warning signs by examining their routine. Consider the following example.

A handsome scam artist named Phillip targets Shelly, a woman of humble appearance, but quite wealthy. Shelly also had the unenviable distinction (in her mind) of being the only one in her circle of girlfriends who was still single. For Shelly, the only sound worse than the chatter of her friends gushing about the joys of couplehood was the deafening tick of her biological clock.

Phillip spotted Shelly in the imported fruit section of a gourmet market in her upscale neighborhood. Guessing by her appearance that she wasn't accustomed to receiving male attention and aware that receptivity to attention is often more pronounced in people with low self-esteem,[12] Phillip did not waste any time.

Rolling up with his cart, which contains a number of expensive grocery items carefully selected for show, he tells Shelly that she is beautiful, asking if she is a native, or an exotic import, like the fruit she is buying. I can see you rolling your eyes. *Give me a break*, huh? Except that Shelly, who has never been called beautiful in her life, bought it hook, line, and sinker. When Phillip asks whether she lives in the neighborhood, Shelly, still reeling from the unexpected compliment, stammers that she does.

Fast-forward to the weekend—where we find the pair cooking a gourmet dinner together—at Shelly's place. Fast-forward two more weeks and Phillip is cooking dinner with Shelly several nights a week, pairing entrées with expensive wine from her wine cellar, swimming laps in her pool, and running through the neighborhood on the jogging track in her posh gated community.

Shelly is delighted with Phillip's desire to "spend time with her." In fact, as far as she can tell, he does not appear to spend time with anyone else. She does want to know one thing though. Considering the amount of time he spends at her home, why hasn't Phillip made any moves on her physically? What a great question.

When Shelly finally asks Phillip about the status of their relationship, he doesn't respond, and stops coming over. He does not return her calls, and as much as she searches for him at the grocery store where they first met, she never sees him again.

Where is Phillip? At an upscale grocery store in a different affluent neighborhood, pushing another cart full of props. This time he is loitering amid the fine wines . . .

When Red Looks Green:
The Readiness Effect

Shelly fell for Phillip because of his flattering attention and expressed romantic interest. She also fell in love with him because as the last single woman standing among her friends, *she wanted to*.[13] Demonstrating what is known as the *readiness effect*, Shelly was driven by a strong desire to find love.[14] People like Shelly might inadvertently advertise their vulnerability by making admissions of "wanting it badly," "needing someone to love," and other statements indicating a strong desire to find love.[15]

Shelly's mindset caused her to miss a number of red flags. One of the biggest red flags was the fact that Phillip's focus was never on Shelly, but on her resources. Sure enough, it was Phillip's *lack* of interest in Shelly physically that prompted her to ask him about the status of their relationship.

Phillip was not a paramour, he was a parasite. The first question he asked Shelly was very telling: whether she lived in the neighborhood. Men like Phillip aren't looking for romance, they are looking for a roommate. Actually, because they don't pay rent and often overstay their welcome, they really are squatters.

Lacking other meaningful relationships, how did Phillip spend his time when he wasn't in the pool or on the jogging track? Had Shelly looked, she would have seen Phillip's lifestyle documented on his computer—where a virtual deck of solitaire cards reflected the intensity of his day. She also would have seen pornography, because Phillip wasn't the slightest bit attracted to Shelly.

Phillip did, however, have one consistent goal: to find a woman who would support him. With Shelly no longer available, Phillip was off in search of his next host.

Focus of Attention:
Relationship or Resource

When examining focus of attention, you want to know whether someone's attention is focused on you, or something that you possess. As a prosecutor, by the time I meet the Shellys of the world their whirlwind suitors have stolen more than just their hearts. Many of these women are manipulated because they have access to desirable commodities, such as money or resources.

One thing these women often notice in retrospect is the shift in focus. These guys come on strong, and then after they make the transition from handsome stranger to houseguest, the women no longer feel like the focus of attention. There are no more candlelight dinners or quiet times together, if there ever was.

Focus of attention also reveals a person's mating preferences, style, and goals. Research has gone beyond merely demonstrating that some people enjoy looking at others who are attractive, and has investigated literal focus in terms of visual fixation, termed *attentional adhesion*—referring to the inability to pull one's attention away from an attractive target.[16]

People with an unrestricted sociosexual orientation (seeking sex without emotional commitment)[17] in search of strangers to have sex with focus their attention on physically attractive members of the opposite sex.[18] People worried about competition, on the other hand, focus on attractive same-sex rivals.[19]

Assessing the Authenticity of Affection

We have all seen couples in public who are all over each other. "Get a room!" we joke. However, such effusive displays of attention are often an integral part of relationships, because one common form of attention is affection.

Affection is one of the most basic human needs.[20] The expression of affection enhances relationships ranging from the casual to the intimate,[21] and generates positive emotions.[22] People enjoy more love, closeness, and satisfaction within affectionate relationships, and affectionate communication is linked with health, happiness, and contentment.[23]

Most people, however, require both show and tell. They need both *affection* and *affectionate behavior*—concepts that do not always overlap.[24] In other words, we desire both the emotion and the expression of affection.[25] Many people are not satisfied with emotion without physical affection, as in a long-distance relationship, or affection without emotion, as in anonymous sex.[26] Unfortunately, affection may be expressed disingenuously for purposes of manipulation.[27]

When the Powerful Become the Prey:
Spotting the Ego Predator

Some of the cases I handle involve nontraditional victims—successful, wealthy, prominent citizens who selected paramours who viewed them not as partners, but as prey. While not all of these strategic pairings result in criminal conduct, the manipulation within the honeymoon phase often follows a similar pattern. Here is how it happens.

Milton, a wealthy philanthropist, meets Helen at a charity gala. Fresh from the salon and dressed to the nines in faux designer wear, Helen is alone and on the prowl, seeking to meet someone of Milton's financial status. After being introduced by a mutual acquaintance, Helen quickly makes Milton the focus of her attention for the rest of the party—and the focus of her *affection* for the rest of the night.

Although she is thirty years younger, Helen makes Milton the center of her world. Why? Is she in love with him? No, nothing like that. With little education and no marketable skills, she views Milton as an opportunity to improve her standard of living.

Milton needs Helen's affection for several reasons. Sure he enjoys showing off an adoring young date at black-tie functions and dinner parties. But his needs run deeper. He is not a handsome man, and his fragile ego requires the attention of a woman like Helen around the clock.

Her affection is an ego booster. A confidence-enhancing elixir. She makes him feel young, sexy, and attractive, even when the mirror insists otherwise. What Milton doesn't recognize, or is not willing to admit, is Helen's true motivation.

Milton sure looks like a sugar daddy, doesn't he? Milton doesn't see it that way. He is accustomed to doing well with the ladies and resists facing the reality that his wealth might have something (everything?) to do with it.

Ironically, although power and wealth can sometimes make bad people look good by masking red flags signaling danger or deception, here the tables are turned. Powerful, influential, wealthy people are potential *victims* in the eyes of someone like Helen, who seeks to exploit their resources for personal gain.

Helen's biggest red flag is her price tag, because her affection doesn't come for free. Milton gives her a luxurious place to live, a weekly allowance with which she now purchases *real* designer clothing and bags, and a lifestyle that allows her to continue her goal of upward mobility. Capitalizing on her role as an arm charm as her ticket to mingle with the upper echelon of society, Helen's eyes are wide open.

Slow Down and See the FLAGs:
The Speed of Psychopathic Seduction

Just as it takes a spike strip on the freeway to halt a speeder on a police chase, sometimes only brutal revelations about a paramour will put the brakes on a runaway relationship—hopefully sooner rather than later. Because while only a small percentage of attentive people are psychopaths, those who are manage to cause an enormous amount of damage—quickly.

Sandra L. Brown in *Women Who Love Psychopaths* notes that psychopaths often instigate emotionally intense whirlwind courtships designed to sweep women off their feet and prevent them from seeing red flags signaling danger.[28] She explains that these women often find themselves "unable to slow down the race to the altar, to their beds, or into their homes."[29] Such men may propose marriage within months, or sometimes even days, claiming to have "never felt this way before."[30]

Some women fall right into the trap, because charismatic psychopaths often portray themselves as the perfect relational partners.[31] They shower women with attention, flowers, and expressions of public affection that leave other women longing to find such a perfect mate.[32] Their attention may include both gifts and compliments designed to make women feel wanted and special.[33]

In *Dangerous Liaisons: How to Recognize and Escape from Psychopathic Seduction*, Claudia Moscovici describes the progression of psychopathic seduction as illustrated in the movie *9 ½ Weeks*, starring Mickey Rourke and Kim Basinger, where romantic attention and gifts that make the woman feel special and desirable lure her into a relationship of domination and control.[34]

Once relationships begin, psychopaths often end up taking a woman on the ride of her life—emotionally as well as financially. Some psychopaths even have families with their victims in order to exploit their financial resources.[35] Consequently, the string of discarded individuals psychopaths leave in their wake often include both ex-spouses and unsupported children.[36]

Looking at the FLAGs, watch for a focus on environmental control, including both situations and people. Or a focus that shifts from romance to resources in order to fuel a parasitic lifestyle.

Look for superficial associations, because regardless of how strong psychopaths come on, they don't bond. In fact, even the speed with which they move in forming relationships is a red flag indicating shallowness as opposed to true love.[37] And their goals are not to please others, but themselves—often at the *expense* of others.

When Associations Are Accessories:
The Arm Charmer

Have you ever dated someone who showered you with attention and loved to take you out on the town and to parties . . . but never made any effort to get to know you or spend time with you alone? You probably began to wonder what the person was after. Beware of the signs that a doting suitor views you not as a paramour, but a party favor. Consider the difference in how that might look from the perspective of the attention recipient, compared to that of her coworkers.

Morgan meets Shane, a famous screenwriter often featured in the Hollywood society columns, at a black-tie charity event. Shane makes a beeline to introduce himself shortly after she arrives. He tells her that with her black hair and piercing green eyes she is the most striking woman in the room, making her feel very attractive and special.

A few days later, he invites her to be his date at an annual screenwriting gala, an invitation she eagerly accepts. She interprets his desire to introduce her to his colleagues in the industry as a sign of his budding commitment.

At the party, however, Shane introduces her to very few of his colleagues. He does not use the word "girlfriend," nor does he even hold her hand. Morgan is disappointed, but tries not to take it personally, telling herself he likely has to maintain a certain public image. Ironically, she will soon find out how true that is.

Shane and Morgan begin seeing each other weekly. Their time together is spent at A-list parties, galas, and other public events, where Shane always ensures they are photographed together. He explains that he loves to "show her off." Morgan is flattered by his compliments, which boost her ego and motivate her to make sure she always looks her best.

Morgan's coworkers notice the change. She is wearing more makeup, getting her hair and nails done each week, and sporting a stylish new wardrobe with an attitude to match. As they watch her striding confidently down the office hallway like she is on a catwalk during Paris fashion week, they are amazed at the transformation.

There is, however, one very suspicious twist. Shane has not once suggested they spend time alone together. No walks on the beach, no movies, not even a single dinner date or quiet evening at home. Nothing but galas, banquets, and charity balls. Morgan's coworkers are crying foul. What is this guy really after?

After a few months, Shane abruptly stops calling. When Morgan calls him to find out what happened, Shane calmly explains that he met another woman who is more beautiful than she is. His cold, ruthless, explanation is like a punch in the stomach. Morgan's enchantment with the relationship is shattered—along with her ego. Needless to say, the fashion show at the office is over as well.

As Morgan thinks back months later after the fog of disillusionment lifts, she realizes that the red flags indicating Shane's superficiality were there all along. The entire experience is a difficult lesson that she never forgets.

Recognizing the Real Actor:
Red Flags on the Red Carpet

Shane looked good to Morgan because of the way he made her feel. Having captured the attention of a successful man who wanted to be seen with *her* made her feel attractive, desirable, and self-confident. Shane's social status also increased Morgan's sense of significance, as her photograph now appeared in the social columns as well, alongside her handsome date.

These positive feelings masked the reality that for Shane, Morgan was nothing but an arm charm. Shane paid as much attention to Morgan as he did to his cuff links. After all, she served the same purpose—as an accessory. Overwhelmed by his flattery, she deluded herself into believing he was interested in her, instead of the way she enhanced his image.

Shane's goal was to see and be seen—with a string of different women. It would have been a waste of time for Shane to introduce Morgan to his colleagues because she was going to be replaced. It was only a matter of time.

The Narcissist and His Trophies

Shane's FLAGs suggest that he is a narcissist. Narcissistic traits such as self-focus[38] and self-centeredness[39] explain Shane's lack of affection for Morgan.[40] He led a lifestyle of superficiality, gala-hopping his way through a very public existence of rubbing elbows with fellow socialites and wealthy philanthropists. Unlike people who spend time with friends and family whom they genuinely care about, narcissists use associations to fuel their self-esteem.[41] They date supermodels, hang out with high-status friends, or affiliate with popular groups in order to fuel their sense of importance.[42]

Narcissists like to show off and impress other people.[43] They use relationship partners as trophies in order to make themselves look good.[44] Shane liked to show off Morgan, and told her as much. With her exotic looks, she was the perfect accessory because narcissists prefer exclusive, custom-designed products that positively distinguish them as unique.[45]

They appreciate the symbolic value of possessions to convey uniqueness and superior class,[46] and seek to customize personal style.[47]

The trophy date/arm charm phenomenon is not confined to men. There are plenty of women who attend social events with attractive young men who are ten or more years their junior. Whether male or female, on the dating scene, narcissists are attracted to others based on how the person can enhance their self-image, not because they care about them.[48]

Continually seeking admiration,[49] narcissists prefer romantic partners who admire them rather than partners who offer intimacy and caring, because admiration increases the narcissist's self-esteem.[50] They are also less committed due to the perception of and attention paid to relational alternatives.[51] As you might expect, narcissists have high levels of infidelity and find it easy to embark on new relationships.[52]

While narcissists often enter relationships infatuated with an idealized view of their significant other, the bloom may be quickly off the rose as soon as they find someone better,[53] as Shane did. He had no problem ending things with Morgan because to a narcissist, relationships are fungible and easily replaced.[54] Just like material possessions.[55] Out with the old, in with the new.

However, becoming disentangled from a narcissist might be for the best. Because as relationships progress, narcissists play games, run hot and cold, are deceptive and dishonest, and engage in other methods of relationship sabotage.[56]

FLAGs Reveal the Intention Behind the Attention

Given that most people enjoy basking in the glow of positive regard, how do you perceive the intention behind the attention? Here are some suggestions.

As a starting point, consider *when* a person began to make you the focus of their attention. Celebrities and politicians often express skepticism about how many more friends they suddenly have after their rise to power. Usually these friends have accompanying requests. Lawyers who become judges often remark that their jokes have apparently become so hilarious overnight that they feel ready for open microphone night at the comedy store.

People with ample resources are particularly likely to view attention with cynicism. Those who are in a position of responsibility and control over money or assets might consider ulterior motives. We are all aware of this phenomenon on some level. "What do you want?" we sometimes joke when someone gives us a big compliment. Actually, that is a very good question.

Are you really the focus of someone's attention, or are they more focused on what you can do for them? Authentic people consider quality time with you to be driving through the countryside or walking your dogs together, not having you pull strings for them at work, take them somewhere they cannot afford to go on their own, or introduce them to people who can help them further their careers.

The same dynamics operate in the romance department. One study showed that for men, the most effective method of initiating sexual encounters with women was investing attention and time, as well as expressing love and commitment.[57] But because that initial "I love you" might be designed to get you into bed,[58] you have to look further. How do you know whether your love interest is showering you with attention because they want to spend the rest of their life with you, or spend the night with you? Here are some clues.

People who are interested in a casual relationship are more likely to use flash, charm, and emotional warmth to attract attention.[59] A person interested in a short-term encounter may set the mood on the first date by creating a sensual but superficial mood through candles, soft music, and by slipping into "something more comfortable," demonstrating a "player" mentality.[60] Providing liquor while showing off an expensive car is more likely to indicate a predatory mating style, seeking easy sex with no strings attached.[61]

People interested in forming long-term relationships are more likely to attempt to win your affection by providing support—such as helping you accomplish something, and through honest praise.[62] Such other-orientation distinguishes them from manipulative players whose focus is on themselves and getting what they want.[63] A person who is interested in a long-term relationship is also more likely to engage in supportive behaviors demonstrating genuine care and concern, to avoid bragging, and to offer sincere compliments.[64]

Perceiving the focus of a potential romantic partner is also important because people are drawn to different attributes depending on what type of relationship they are seeking.[65] Someone seeking a casual fling may place more emphasis on sex appeal and physical attributes, while someone looking for a long-term relationship will be more interested in qualities such as dependability, commitment, and love.[66]

READING THE INTENTION BEHIND THE ATTENTION

Focus: Are you the focus of his or her attention in private as well as in public?

Lifestyle: Does the person network frequently, or selectively spend time with you?

Associations: Does the person have a history of intense, but short-lived relationships?

Goals: Do you have something the person needs to achieve his or her goals?

Too Much of a Good Thing:
When Attention Becomes Obsession

As much as people love attention, there is such a thing as too much of a good thing. Sometimes, welcome attention becomes unwelcome obsession—both on- and offline. These crimes of *unwanted* attention range from obscenity, to threatening messages, to full-blown stalking.

I have prosecuted stalkers who targeted a wide range of victims—from local news anchors and community leaders to Bible-study prayer partners. What some of these cases have in common is that at the beginning of these relationships the victims enjoyed the stalker's attention. But sometimes, positive attention becomes pathological obsession as the warm glow of pleasure is transformed into the icy grip of fear. Here is how it happens.

Gina and Bob meet at the bookstore. He approaches her as she is browsing the self-defense aisle and remarks that a pretty young lady like her can never take too many precautions to stay safe in a dangerous world. After some polite conversation, he asks for her e-mail address, joking that a pretty woman should never give her phone number to a stranger who may turn out to be a stalker. How true that comment turns out to be.

A week later Gina agrees to meet Bob for coffee. He brings her a present. A self-defense kit, complete with mace, a prepaid cell phone, and a "screamer" alarm system. She accepts the gift, believing that this man she has just met is genuinely concerned about her safety.

As they begin to date, Bob is very protective of Gina. He offers to accompany her when she runs errands at night and comes over to inspect the locks on her front door and windows.

One sleepless night Gina peers out her window and sees Bob sitting in his car across the street. A chill runs up her spine as she begins to realize that Bob's behavior may not be entirely for her benefit. When she refuses to see him again, she will find out that she was correct.

FLAGs of Fixation

I meet women like Gina when Bob doesn't take kindly to her rejection and continues his (now unwelcome) pursuit—which ironically makes her glad that she allowed him to install all her home safety features. Although she should probably change her locks, because someone like Bob is likely to have made himself a key. In retrospect, Gina asks herself, how did she permit the relationship to progress to this point?

Like many stalking victims, Gina missed warning signs signaling jealousy and possessiveness because she was flattered by Bob's attention and apparent concern for her safety. She failed to place enough significance on the fact that she was the sole focus of his attention. He didn't seem to have much of a life otherwise, lacking steady employment or close friends.

Also, while she originally believed Bob was motivated by concern for her well-being, Gina finally realized that Bob's pursuit of overexposure to her personal life was to determine who she was spending time with, to gain access to her home to establish his territory, and to invade her privacy more quickly than she was willing to grant access. Unlike manipulators who infiltrate a person's life to gain access to their *possessions*, for a stalker, his victim *is* the coveted possession.

As the case progresses, one of Bob's ex-girlfriends comes forward. Where do you suppose he met her? In the self-defense aisle of a different bookstore.

5

The Not-So-Secret Admirer

The Allure of Affirmation

Wow, Ms. Patrick, you really destroyed that witness. You are such a great advocate. I sure hope you go easy on me." Who do you suppose that compliment came from? Would you believe, the defendant? I have prosecuted defendants who spent the entire trial complimenting me on my quick thinking and trial advocacy skills, despite their attorney's repeated admonitions not to talk to me.

Their objective? Obtaining a reduction or dismissal of charges of course—a request they include with the compliments.

Here is the part that is hard to believe. Although their ulterior motives are crystal clear, much to my dismay, the compliments strike a chord. *Even though I know they are insincere.* Welcome to the alluring world of affirmation.

Affirmation Is Appealing

Both good and bad people affirm us through compliments, recognition, validation, and other methods of making us feel understood, important, and special. Affirmation not only makes us feel good, it makes the person providing the positive reinforcement appear attractive—even in the face of insincerity.

How does this work? Abraham Maslow in *Motivation and Personality* explains that we all share common desires,[1] as well as a hierarchy of human needs.[2] The satisfaction of lower level needs (such as hunger) causes higher needs to emerge.[3] This brings us to what Maslow describes as *esteem needs*—which reflect the reality that everyone wants to have a positive self-view based on the respect they receive from others.[4] This includes the desire to feel a sense of confidence, achievement, prestige, appreciation, and attention.[5]

Sexual predators use affirmation to attract children through techniques of acceptance and attention.[6] They portray themselves as the one person in the child's life who believes in the child and accepts him or her just the way they are. They affirm their victims through expressing agreement with their views and understanding their feelings,[7] because by acknowledging and validating the feelings of others, confirming messages build close relationships.[8]

Predators use affirmation online as well, portraying themselves as confidants to provide support to troubled teens.[9] However, their true colors are evident when we examine their goals—to connect offline. Their intention is not merely to offer emotional support; it is to facilitate sexual abuse. They take the time to listen to and talk with their victims not because they care about the well-being of the children, but because of their strong selfish interest in the children themselves.[10]

People also seek affirmation through validation—defined as the recognition, understanding, and reasonableness of one's feelings.[11] They pursue validation through relationships in order to boost self-concept.[12] Good people *satisfy* this need, while psychopaths *exploit* this need by learning what traits another person values in themselves, and reinforcing those traits, making the other person feel validated and special.[13]

Regarding the most common forms of affirmation, one of the most familiar methods of making someone feel good is flattery.

Flattery Gets You Everywhere

Flattery feels good. And not only is it pleasurable, it causes us to like the flatterer.[14] This can be true even when the flatterer has a clear ulterior motive, such as in the world of marketing.[15] In fact, even when the flatterer is known to have a manipulative intent, people generally like them anyway.[16]

Some flattery research yields mixed results. While some studies conclude that flattery recipients tend to believe in the sincerity of the flatterer,[17] others demonstrate that ingratiation attempts through flattery or bestowing favors are consistently ineffective due to the blatant transparency of motive.[18] Still others conclude that while positive attention builds positive emotions and self-esteem, excessive flattery arouses suspicion.[19]

How do we really know that flattery works? Through the results. Everyone can relate to how compliments make us feel. Especially compliments designed especially for us.

The Pleasure of Targeted Praise

The type of flattery we like the most depends on our individual areas of vulnerability. In the context of an initial meeting, some people are more comfortable with compliments about accomplishments and attire rather than physical attributes.[20] On the other hand, many people love to hear how great they look. Some people have spent years dieting or weight training, or have opted for plastic surgery (or all three) and welcome positive recognition of their effort and expense.

When it comes to physical compliments, however, beware of short-timers. People with an unrestricted sociosexual orientation (those who have sex outside committed relationships) emphasize physical attractiveness when pursuing relational partners, even to the exclusion of other positive attributes.[21] As wonderful as they may make you feel with their attentiveness, if this is their orientation, you will not have their attention for long because they prefer short-term relationships, and are unfaithful.[22]

Flattery can be strategically designed to boost self-esteem in an area of physical insecurity. In the course of my work I meet young boys who are teased in school because they are small and possess characteristics seen as feminine. The reason I meet them is sometimes because they have a teacher who makes them feel strong and masculine—within the context of a sexual relationship.

Most of these relationships only come to light when the pair is caught in the act (having sex in the teacher's car in the parking lot for example), as opposed to the victim spilling the beans. Why? Female pedophiles can seduce an underdeveloped boy into sexual activity through appealing to his developing ego, assuring him that he is "sexy and desirable and manly."[23] For many victims, that type of affirmation outweighs the abuse.

Other people suffer from cognitive insecurity, and are affirmed through confirmation of their thoughts and feelings. Confirming messages not only recognize and acknowledge thoughts and emotions, they endorse a person's ideas or importance—which is the strongest type of confirming message, conveying the highest level of value.[24]

Detecting False Flattery

As good as it feels, it is common knowledge that flattery is not always genuine. Some people even pride themselves on their ability to detect insincerity. But can you? Even if you suspect ulterior motives, can you prevent yourself from responding to the flattery?

In *Without Conscience*, Dr. Hare recalls one of his female interviewers describing how one of the men she interviewed in prison made her feel unusually pretty by the end of the interview, through complimenting her on her appearance.[25] Describing herself as usually able to "spot a phony," she commented afterward that she couldn't believe she had fallen for the prisoner's lines.[26]

He describes another psychologist, with a great professional reputation but no social life, who ran off with one of her psychopathic patients.[27] Within two weeks, this man had stolen all her money and discarded her like trash.[28] In retrospect, in explaining her horrendous lapse in judgment, she admitted that she simply surrendered to his promises and sweet talk.[29]

It is not only psychopaths who are adept at fooling others with flattery. Machiavellians use flattery in a way that is both calculated and manipulative.[30] Speaking of manipulation, there are plenty of otherwise "normal" people who resort to flattery in pursuit of sex, advice, training, financial prosperity, or career advancement. How do you know when flattery is genuine? One preliminary factor to consider is whether the flatterer intends for you to hear the compliment.

"If you really want to learn the ropes, watch the master at work," declares one of your coworkers loudly, motioning toward you. That puts a smile on your face. But it could be even better. That same compliment made out of earshot and shared with you by someone who overheard it is clothed with authenticity because it is now more likely that the speaker's goal was not merely to flatter you. In other words, it is evidence that the person really believed what they said. This type of compliment is much more satisfying, and perhaps even one you might share with your family.

In addition, consider who is delivering the compliment. We often value praise from strangers more than praise from friends.[31] Yet it is often friends and associates who successfully manipulate us through inauthentic affirmation. Consider the following scenario.

Frenemies with Benefits:
Spotting the User

A new employee at a department store constantly compliments her manager on her mastery of store procedures, remarking at how lucky she is to be "learning from the best." As time goes on, however, this employee continues to ask her boss about the location of even easy-to-find items, and for help in minor tasks. Her boss continues to indulge her, enjoying the regular dose of positive reinforcement.

It isn't until a coworker brings to the manager's attention that the new employee is spending more time on Facebook than helping customers, that the manager realizes her role as an enabler. Why would the new employee need to learn anything when she can just ask her boss for help? The time the manager has been spending indulging her complimentary new employee is time that could have been spent managing the store.

Can we relate to this? Who needs an employee-recognition plaque to hang on your wall when you can be inundated with positive reinforcement all day long? How rewarding is that? Often rewarding enough to ignore the signs of inauthenticity.

While some employees are just lazy, flattery in the workplace can be motivated by darker personality traits. Psychopaths size others up as a potential source of money, power, influence, or sex,[32] and use flattery as goal-directed behavior to get what they want.

And you do not need to be at the top of the food chain to be targeted. Using other people to fulfill their goals, psychopaths not only manipulate those in powerful positions, but they also use people with *informal* power, which includes connections and assets the psychopath considers to be useful.[33]

This could mean buttering up the boss's scheduler or secretary, or having someone in the mailroom pull strings to ensure a package is sent out earlier than scheduled.[34] More often than not, the people enjoying the affirmation have no idea they are being used.

So how do you separate friends from frenemies? Examine the focus of the friendship. Consider whether some "friends" are only complimentary and affirming when they have something to gain. Whether they need a favor, a party date, a ride, or an introduction to someone you know, be wary of individuals who view you as an instrument or an intermediary instead of a friend.

On the other hand, you may have friends and family members for whom you are the main event. Their focus is on *you*, not on what you can do for them. As far as they are concerned, spending time with you is a goal in itself. Not surprisingly, with friends like this, friendship itself is a valuable source of affirmation.

Linked with well-being and happiness,[35] genuine friendships fulfill fundamental human needs.[36] Friendship is even affirming on a basic level, because the simple act of spending time with someone conveys an appreciation of value.[37]

Friendship also involves affirmation through social support—which plays a fundamental role in cultivating and maintaining intimate relationships.[38] Social support expresses affection through providing assistance,[39] elicits feelings of comfort and warmth, and creates intimacy.[40] Emotional support in particular leads to fulfilling personal relationships.[41]

A Loyal Following

Some famous trial lawyers have scores of young attorneys who idolize them. Everyone knows when they are in trial, the TV vans are stationed in front of the courthouse, and the courtroom is packed with observers. The young lawyers in the audience don't want to deceive or manipulate their rainmaking role models, they want to *learn* from them. When there is time for brief conversation with these trial stars, their fans don't express cheap flattery, but authentic admiration.

Similarly, in the workplace, many people want to learn from the best, sincerely admire the boss, and are not afraid to say so. They are not afraid to risk a trip down the hallway to the boss's office to request clarification when an assignment is unclear.

Many people in senior management are pleased with this type of proactivity. It demonstrates initiative, a desire to succeed, and helps to ensure a quality work product. However, here is what you won't often hear them admit. Many of these managers also enjoy the company, because true to cliché, it can be lonely at the top.

Believe it or not, even successful people like to be reassured of their value and worth. No one wants a secret admirer. People want to be publicly recognized for their accomplishments and complimented on a job well done. No one displays a brag wall full of awards without hoping someone will see them. Instead of assuming that people at the top of their game are ultra-confident and self-assured, we always score points by verbalizing authentic respect and admiration.

Legitimate admirers in the workplace are distinguished by their positive FLAGs. They are focused on learning and success. Their lifestyle and social activities reflect their professional goals, because networking and participation in professional associations add credibility to their ambition. They discuss their career goals with their superiors because they value their advice. The result? When promotion time rolls around, these authentically affirming employees find themselves on a short list of qualified candidates.

The Reward of Recognition

In the *Seinfeld* episode "The Calzone," George tosses some money in the tip jar, but then realizes his generosity wasn't noticed by the restaurant. Determined to get credit for his actions, he attempts to fish the money back out of the tip jar and is accused of stealing.

As funny as this is, can we relate? Sure, some people donate anonymously out of selfless benevolence. Most people, however, are like George. They enjoy receiving credit for their generosity.

Think about this the next time you are at the coffee cart. With a busy barista or lots of background noise, people tip with coins because they are loud. They want their tip to sound like a jackpot payout at a casino. If the barista is not able to see or hear the coins, people often narrate their actions, "here is the rest of my change," to draw attention to the tip.

This phenomenon is not limited to the coffee cart. People are more likely to give to charity in front of other people than on their own.[42] Why? Enhancing one's reputation within a group is a factor motivating charitable behavior.[43]

People are also motivated by social worth in terms of feeling valued by others.[44] Social worth evokes feelings of being needed and useful to the lives of other people, which results in feelings of belongingness.[45] Consider how this motivation can be satisfied by bestowing recognition through appreciation.

Juror Number 29 finishes his answer: ". . . and for my occupation, I drive a garbage truck during the week and paint houses on the weekends." The judge asks how many children he has. "Two at home, three in college—which is why I have to work seven days a week." He explains that he is widowed and raising his family on his own. By this point I have promised myself I will never again complain about having a tough day.

Selecting as many juries as I have, I am always humbled by the hardworking and devoted people who juggle all their other obligations to answer their jury summons. Not only do they honor their civic duty and dutifully report to the courthouse, many of them show up in their Sunday best, to demonstrate respect for the judicial process. Why do they report for jury duty instead of attempting to get out of it? One of the reasons is the genuine affirmation they receive from the judges and lawyers.

Like the rest of us, these jurors desire respect and appreciation.[46] In addition to making us feel good, appreciation and acknowledgment build self-esteem and self-confidence.[47] One of the things judges and lawyers do during jury selection that often makes all the difference in the world to these citizens is take the time to recognize the sacrifice of their valuable time.

Just as employers who recognize and reward hard work cultivate the most loyal employees, judges and lawyers who recognize and appreciate the often complicated arrangements many jurors make to put their lives on hold in order to serve on our cases end up with the most dedicated jury panels.

For those jurors "lucky" enough to be selected, once the trial begins, the jurors witness a different form of affirmation: professional respect.

Professional Respect:
The Ultimate Attitude Adjuster

"Ms. Patrick, you may cross-examine," the judge announces. The defense expert visibly stiffens in the witness box and nervously reaches for his bottle of water as I approach the podium.

He has just testified that one of the reasons the defendant stuffed her newborn baby in a plastic bag and threw him in a dumpster is because she suffered from postpartum psychosis—a theory he knows I am going to tear apart.

"Good afternoon, Doctor," I greet the witness with a smile. "Thank you for coming in to testify. It sounds like you have quite a bit of experience dealing with psychotic patients."

Right out of the chute, the witness's expression reveals that he is confused by my approach. I am not going for the jugular; I am beginning the examination by affirming his expertise. Why? Depending on the facts of the case, with a practiced and polished expert, I will often get much farther with honey than with vinegar. By conceding expertise, which is often warranted, I can spend my time instead eliciting information that bolsters my side of the case.

After all, I am not going to change the opinion of the opposing side's expert witness. Professional witnesses do not charge the expensive fees they do to suddenly change their mind on the witness stand. In addition, if I am overly confrontational, I will get less valuable testimony, will risk having an argumentative objection sustained, and might alienate the jury.

Instead, I use a tactic that will allow me to establish rapport through genuine admiration of hard-earned education and experience in order to easily procure the information I need, rather than engaging in a futile attempt to elicit testimony that I would never get anyway. My paralegal watching from the audience has joked that some of my expert witness cross-examinations were so congenial that she wondered if the witness and I were going to have dinner together after court.

What I am appealing to, although we "agree to disagree" on the substance of the issues, is the expert's desire for professional respect. This is one element of Maslow's *esteem needs,* where people receive an ego boost as a result of the respect they receive from other people.[48] Expert witnesses have worked hard for their credentials, and people desire respect and admiration for the attributes they possess.[49] Giving them the respect they deserve while eliciting the testimony I need is a phenomenon you rarely see in a courtroom: a win-win situation.

The Search for Significance

You might remember Steve Martin's thrilling exclamations in *The Jerk*: "The new phone book's here! The new phone book's here!" Ecstatic to see his name in print, he predicted things would begin to happen to him now that he had achieved a measure of importance. Sure enough, another form of interpersonal affirmation targets our desire for significance.

Everyone wants to feel important. Some manipulators cater to this need quite effectively—especially when focusing on someone who lacks emotional fulfillment from other people in her life. As one victim explains, her (pedophile) teacher made her feel special and "worth spending time with."[50] While her parents and other teachers treated her like a child, the offender treated her as an equal and seemed genuinely interested in what she had to say.[51]

People satisfy the need to feel important in many ways. They surround themselves with friends and acquaintances who treat them with respect, and select partners who make them feel valuable and worthwhile. Not surprisingly, the premium we place on the need to feel important is highlighted through the negative emotions we experience when we feel unimportant. This occurs when we are made to feel anonymous, insignificant, or forgettable.

The Insult of Anonymity

While the jury selection process makes jurors feel important, recognized, and appreciated, it often has the opposite effect on the lawyers trying the case. Which is probably a good thing because it keeps us humble.

One of the first questions the judge asks a panel of prospective jurors is whether or not they recognize any of the attorneys. Some lawyers who have practiced in their community for years are sometimes a bit disappointed to look out into the crowd and see that not a single hand is raised.

Then they are introduced by name. Again, no hands. *Never heard of him.* The sting of obscurity is even more painful in small towns where some of the local courtroom talent who fancy themselves resident celebrities are brought down a peg or two when their apparent anonymity within their own community indicates otherwise.

A related example is the perception of insignificance you feel after the way you are treated when making an important phone call. After you confidently announce your name to the receptionist, asking to be transferred to your close friend, the company president, the humiliating questions begin. "Who?" she asks. You state your name again. "The president is very busy. Will she know what this is about?"

Ouch. Our sense of importance quickly deflated, we plunge back down to earth. Most of us, however, would rather not make that hard landing.

Yet it gets worse. You are placed on hold for more than five minutes while the receptionist proceeds to answer other calls. Now you are both humiliated and insulted. The message is loud and clear: not only are you unknown, you are unimportant.

Consider how differently you would feel if when you called, the receptionist had said "Oh, John, of course! The president is waiting for your call. I'll put you right through."

Now that feels good. Because aside from the disembodied personalities in the blogging world and the secret admirers who send letters to my stalking victims, most of us do not want to be anonymous. We want to be recognized. When we are, we become immediately fond of the person who has acknowledged us. As we will see, however, sometimes that fondness causes us to miss red flags.

The Pleasure of Being Memorable

For some people, even worse than being unknown or insignificant, is being forgotten. Have you ever read the minutes from a board meeting you attended and noticed your name was omitted from the record of attendance? Some people are offended by this type of oversight.

Adding insult to injury, sometimes by the time you see the error, other board members have confirmed the minutes as accurate. Clearly, you made quite an impression at the meeting. Why are we upset with this type of oversight? Because no one wants to be forgotten.

It should therefore come as no surprise that being *remembered* in today's world of multitasking and distraction is a big compliment. Research demonstrates that even remembering a person's name prompts compliance with a request.[52] Does it matter who remembers you? Perhaps not. Consider the following example.

In a case of an assault with a firearm, I had a defendant who memorized everything the jurors revealed about themselves during the jury selection process. He then incorporated their information into his testimony, making eye contact with each juror as he restated something each juror had shared, whether city of residence, occupation, or other information. Most of the jurors felt extremely uncomfortable and sent notes to the judge expressing concern over the fact that the defendant had apparently memorized all their personal information.

One juror, however, was not uncomfortable. He was flattered. An admitted introvert who was unaccustomed to anyone remembering anything about him, he told me afterward that he was impressed that the defendant apparently found him interesting enough to remember the details he had shared. He felt validated and important. Perhaps that is why he voted not guilty, deciding that the defendant's gun discharged by accident.

Being remembered is particularly flattering when a period of time has passed. Have you ever been introduced to someone who exclaims, "I remember you! How could I forget? I met you at the company picnic last year." Last *year*? That makes you feel pretty good. And when someone remembers you after an extended period of time, they might just become your new best friend.

Consider how you would feel if you were approached on the street by a woman who introduces herself as a high school classmate, who confesses that while you probably don't remember her, she always looked up to you in school and thought you were one of the most brilliant students on campus. You might think that whatever happens after this, your day is complete. You are flying high.

Well, not to rain on your parade, but if her comments made you feel that good, it means you took them at face value. But should you? I participated in the investigation of a woman who used this ploy to research the current assets of people she had known in her youth, using the ruse of false idolization to lower their defenses and increase their willingness to answer personal questions. Here is the part that is hard to believe: not a single one of the people targeted doubted the sincerity of the woman's gushing sentiments of admiration.

Having examined a variety of different types of affirming behavior, let us turn our attention to an example of how to detect inauthenticity.

Retired but Worth Remembering

Retirement from a distinguished profession is bittersweet, and often leads to depression as some people begin to perceive a loss of identity and significance. This depression can be enhanced when a person lives alone without a family, because isolation can compound negative emotion. Some older people even become suicidal, due to several factors, one of which is feeling invisible and disconnected from other people.[53] Sometimes this vulnerability is exploited.

I have prosecuted elder abuse cases where young people have befriended older adults, manipulating their need for significance and connection in order to create a relationship they could profit from financially. In many of these cases, the victims are heartbroken when they discover the truth. Consider a fact pattern that illustrates one of the many ways in which this can happen.

Harold, an aging, decorated military veteran, meets Brittany at the local senior center, where she volunteers once a week serving lunch. As the two become acquainted over time, Harold shares some details about his military career.

One day, Harold admits to Brittany that he spends time at the senior center because he doesn't have any children and lives alone in a large house. For the first time, Brittany expresses interest in learning more about his military career, explaining that her father served his country as well. She explains that she doesn't know many details, because he passed away when she was very young.

While Brittany is impatient with most of the senior center clients, she begins to treat Harold like a king. Her newfound interest in his military service makes Harold feel a renewed sense of significance, after many years spent feeling invisible. He relishes the opportunity to reminisce about the career he considers to have been the high point of his life.

Harold is aware that Brittany routinely skips out early on her shift, slipping out through the back door. One day she suggests to Harold that they both leave early so she can visit his house to see his collection of medals and military photos, explaining that she was never able to celebrate her father's pride of service. Harold happily invites Brittany to his upscale home and proudly shows her his collection of medals.

Not long afterward, Brittany offers to assist Harold at his home by running errands for him—a gesture for which he is very grateful—and which requires him to give her a key to his house. You can probably guess where this is going.

Harold's house is burglarized one day while both he and Brittany are at the senior center. Brittany expresses shock and condolences when they discover the break-in. But it doesn't take long for police to tie the burglary to Brittany's boyfriend and several of his companions. It turns out that Brittany gave them her house key, and kept Harold busy while they burglarized his home.

When he is subpoenaed to testify, it will be with tears in his eyes that Harold will take the witness stand, looking over at Brittany, the woman who brought him back to life—and whom he had grown to love as a daughter, now charged as a co-conspirator.

FLAG-ing the Agenda Behind the Affirmation

If Harold had observed Brittany's FLAGs, what might he have seen? In this scenario, timing was everything. When did Brittany become interested in Harold? It wasn't when they first met; nor when she learned about his military background. It was the day she learned that he lived alone in a large house.

Unfortunately, Harold didn't know anything about Brittany's lifestyle and associations. Had he met her circle of friends, he would have discovered that she hung out with thieves and burglars, often sharing in the loot. *Birds of a feather.*

Regarding Brittany's goals, we are faced with inconsistent information until we examine everything in context. Brittany's choice to volunteer at the senior center appears to demonstrate an interest in working with an aging population. But *why*? Does she genuinely care about helping these people—or is there a more sinister motivation? What about her interest in Harold? Was it altruistic or opportunistic?

The process of becoming suspicious involves acquiring more information to resolve ambiguity.[54] This is illustrated through an experiment where participants were presented with a story about a man who courted a wealthy widow—presenting the possibilities that he was in love with her, or was after her money.[55] The ambiguity was resolved when they learned what the man did when a grocery clerk gave him too much change.[56]

When they learned that he returned the extra change, they believed the man was truly in love with the widow, but when they learned that he kept the change, they concluded that he was motivated by greed and was after her money.[57]

It was learning about behavior related to honesty and greed that helped the participants evaluate the man's motives in the experiment.[58] Learning that the man offered a seat to a pregnant woman on a bus, for example, would only demonstrate that he was friendly.[59] In other words, it is information about the specific characteristics in question that helps us confirm or deny suspicions.[60]

Applying the same rationale in deciphering the motivation behind Brittany's "courting" behavior, Harold could have attached more significance to her cheating the senior center by consistently fudging her hours. It turned out that her dishonesty was not confined to one area of her life.

In fact, it turned out that Brittany lied about everything. Brittany's father was not deceased; nor was he serving his country. He was serving a prison term in another state for armed robbery.

Affirmation Through Affair:
Mr. Wrong to the Rescue

In relationships, why do people cheat? Just ask them. In a study of marital infidelity, some people described extramarital affairs as providing validation and affirmation of their personal worth.[61] Women in particular described the most important thing about the affair as being treated as "special."[62] They loved being viewed as sexually attractive, interesting, valued, and desired—particularly when those elements were missing from their lives.[63]

While there are many variations of this theme, here is an example of how Mr. Wrong disguises himself as Mr. Right Now.

A woman whose husband spends all his time at the office is home alone, feeling rejected and neglected. Deciding to take golf lessons at the local club to fill her time, she meets a handsome golf instructor, who lays on the charm.

While her husband has not complimented her on anything in years, her golf instructor raves about her skills on the golf course and her positive attitude. One day, when in the process of guiding her swing he is close enough that she can smell his cologne, he tells her that she has a beautiful body—a compliment that actually makes her blush.

While this man is twenty years her junior, melting under the heat of his attention, she begins an affair that ends up costing her the trust of her husband and children, as well as her reputation at the golf club. Once the affair is exposed, she never hears from her golf instructor again. Although it isn't long before she hears through the grapevine that he is dating another of his clients.

Red Flags on the Green

I see these cases after the woman's husband comes home, catches them in the act, and levels the imposter, sometimes with one punch. At trial, these smooth operators make very unsympathetic victims.

Men like this are focused on having fun. They live a lifestyle where these types of affairs are, pardon the cliché: par for the course. Many of these characters have quite the reputation around the golf club, tennis club, or wherever they work, for targeting wealthy older women, with the goal of enjoying short-term pleasure and variety. They often brag about how easy it is to seduce these women for gratuitous sex, no strings attached.

In other words, many of these guys are displaying warning FLAGs that women can see from the far end of the fairway—if they are looking.

The Value of Human Life:
Acknowledging Priceless Goods

Sometimes instead of flattery, confirmation, or recognition, affirmation comes in the form of selfless value of human life and dignity. I experienced one of the most vivid demonstrations of this type of affirmation on a Friday night in Pohang, South Korea. It was on a dark street lit only by fluorescent lights emanating from the storefronts. The merchandise was different in every store, showcased with flashing lights and music.

Customers didn't show up until after midnight . . . due to the nature of what was for sale. The merchandise, you see, was *women*. Welcome to the Red Light district of Pohang, South Korea.

What was I doing there? In connection with teaching a course on human trafficking at Handong International Law School, I accompanied a group of Christian students to minister to the sex workers. While our trip was cut short by "enforcers" in ominous dark vehicles patrolling the scene, our interaction with the sex workers was an unforgettable experience in the power of affirmation.

Unlike customers who view the women as merchandise or tourists who scoff at the indecency of the life these young ladies have "chosen," we warmly greeted the sex workers, bearing gifts—cans of iced coffee.

As we spoke with the girls, we watched their initial expressions of skepticism turn to some of the biggest smiles I have ever seen. Not because we gave them a can of iced coffee. But because through our words and actions, asking for nothing in return, we gave them perhaps the first dose of respect and self-worth they had experienced in years.

The expressions I saw on the faces of those girls was familiar. It is the same expression I see on the face of a sexual assault victim after I fly across the country just to speak with her in person about her case. It is the same expression I see on the face of a convicted felon who has been sexually assaulted in prison when I tell him that I plan to relentlessly pursue justice on his behalf by prosecuting the perpetrator to the full extent of the law.

Authentic affirmation doesn't come with a price tag. It's a gift without expecting anything in return. It is congratulating a child on the quality of a school project, a compliment from a passing stranger, or a man praised for his intellectual acumen by an anonymous blogger who reads his post. Sometimes the best rewards really are free.

SPOTTING THE AGENDA BEHIND THE AFFIRMATION

The Focus Behind the Flattery: Some people dole out superficial compliments en masse. Others are uniquely focused on you. The less they need from you, the more likely their affirmation is authentic.

Empowering Lifestyle: A selfless lifestyle of encouraging others lends credibility to a person's affirmation of you.

Assessing Authenticity through Associations: A compliment from a colleague who spends all of his time networking will be less credible than one from your company president, who spends her free time with her family.

Gauging Goals: Consider whether a person validates your ideas because they sincerely believe in you, or see you as a means to an end. Reflect upon whether their affirmation ensures their success, or yours.

6

Born to Bond

The Seduction of Similarity

C rouched down in the front seat of an undercover police car, I peer over the dash at the entrance to a convenience store where a young girl has just gone inside. While neither I nor the members of the vice team I am with can see or hear what is happening inside, from past experience, we might discover it is some version of the following scenario.

Chelsea stops at the corner market on her way home from school to buy a soda. Belle, who has been loitering outside, spots her and follows her in. She watches what type of soda Chelsea selects and immediately chooses the same brand. Meeting her at the counter, Belle jokes about great minds thinking alike and offers to pay for both.

In the friendly conversation that follows, Chelsea learns that they are both fifteen, both from similar family backgrounds, and that they share the same taste in music, movies, and boys. Having begun the bonding process, Belle wastes no time. She invites Chelsea to meet her at the market the following day after school to "hang out." Chelsea happily agrees. Just wait until she finds out why Belle was so eager to meet with her again.

For Belle, time is money. She is not just a fifteen-year-old girl; she is a human trafficking recruiter. In many cases, young girls are more likely to be lured into the sex trafficking business when approached by a same-aged peer instead of the trafficker—who is often a much older (and much scarier looking) man.

Belle will slowly introduce Chelsea into a lifestyle of deviance. First modeling, then dancing, then introducing her to her pimp, selling sex for money. I wish I could say that this was an unusual case, but unfortunately, it's not. It happens every day.

Young girls are lured into the sex trade by other young women under the guise of friendship.[1] This type of recruitment effort is one that pimps are using more and more often.[2]

The Soothing Lens of Likeness

The insidious strategy used by the Belles of the world is successful because it exploits the seduction of similarity.

Similarity attracts. In fact, the *similarity effect* is described as "one of the most robust phenomena" in attraction research.[3] When we perceive others as similar, we like them more [4] and spend more time with them,[5] hence the observation that "birds of a feather flock together."[6]

Regarding types of similarity, we are attracted to people with whom we share similar backgrounds, personality features, hobbies,[7] values,[8] attitudes,[9] and social or personal traits.[10] Similarity in the form of shared values or viewpoints is also *affirming* because it validates our own beliefs,[11] which is one of the ways similarity generates attraction.[12]

Similarity increases the perception of beauty,[13] and can increase attraction through the expectation that people who are similar to us will like us, which motivates us to pursue those relationships.[14] And similarity not only enhances attraction, it also increases relational quality.[15] In this respect, similarity both "breeds connection"[16] and facilitates bonding.[17]

Similarity can even increase the perception of trustworthiness.[18] Perceived trustworthiness can stem from simple facial similarity.[19] In one study, perceived trustworthiness was increased by combining photos so that the person in the photo looked similar to the observer.[20]

So having heard all this, how powerful is the bond of similarity? Let's just say that it forges some very unlikely alliances. Consider the following examples.

Birds of a Feather:
Similarity Breeds Connection

In a case of driving under the influence, the defendant is an admitted alcoholic. One of the jurors refuses to convict him, despite the evidence. He even cancels a family vacation in order to stay on the jury to make sure the defendant is not convicted.

Why? Because his wife is a recovering alcoholic, so he has incredible sympathy for the defendant, and the challenges he no doubt struggles with as a result of his addiction. (It would have been nice if he had revealed this information during jury selection when the judge specifically asked about it.) By identifying with the defendant through common (vicarious) experience, the juror prevented the conviction (that time).

To share a counterintuitive example, early in my career I prosecuted a woman for joyriding who shared many of my physical attributes and mannerisms, ethnic heritage, and sense of fashion. One day we both showed up wearing blue suits with white blouses, with matching strands of pearls. What were the odds?

When we were in court, this defendant repeatedly attempted to engage me in casual conversation against the advice of her attorney. She said she couldn't help it. She wanted to talk to me because she felt like we shared common ground.

It was true, as different as we were, there were superficial similarities. Although she was convicted, I have remembered her case, hoping she cleaned up her act.

Resemblance Generates Relationships

Should I have been horrified to have a jury file into the courtroom with the defendant and I looking like twins? Not according to research. Studies show that we are not only attracted to others who dress like us, but we are even more likely to assist them and trust them without question.

Experimenters in the 1970s discovered that on a college campus, when they asked for money for a phone call while dressed in a fashion similar to the students—either "straight" or "hippie"—students were more likely to give them the money.[21]

Another study found that anti-war demonstrators who were approached by others dressed in similar attire were more likely to sign a petition without even reading it.[22] Imitation creates influence through generating positive feelings toward the imitator.[23]

Accessories have the same effect. If you walked into a room full of people you didn't know and had to find an empty seat, would you choose a seat next to someone whom you noticed was wearing the same watch as you? Chances are, even without knowing anything else about her, you would.

Really? A watch? Yes. One study found that even when a researcher *told* a stranger at a crosswalk that they had the same kind of wristwatch, it resulted in the stranger spending more time close to the researcher, illustrating how similarity generates the desire to build relationships and prompts behavior to further that objective.[24]

In the episode "The Invitations," Jerry Seinfeld meets and falls in love with Jeannie Steinman, a woman who is incredibly similar. Both Jerry and Jeannie read Superman and Supergirl comic books, love cereal, and also share the same initials.

OK, we can understand the comic books and the cereal, but would sharing the same initials really generate attraction? Research says yes. In fact, some research demonstrates that people are more likely to *marry* others who have similar names.[25]

Incidental similarity promotes emotional attachment,[26] and trivial similarity wields social influence.[27] Even sharing the same first name or birthday increases compliance with requests.[28]

How about language? One of the more distasteful parts of my job is having to recite the "F word," the "N word," and even the dreaded "C word" in front of a jury in order to accurately quote witnesses in furtherance of proving my case. When cameras have been permitted in the courtroom to film some of these cases, the footage is completely unusable, sounding like Morse code with the number of words bleeped out.

Such language is always preceded (and often followed) with apologies to the jury, explaining these are the defendant's words, not mine. Yet after one trial involving particularly colorful language, one of the jurors approached me and said that he felt a real connection to *me* because the language reminded him of the community where he grew up. This connection was perceived despite the fact that I was quoting someone else.

There is, however, an important caveat to all this. Our attraction to similar others is not based on actual similarity, but on *perceived* similarity.[29] And sadly, similarity can be faked.

Synthetic Similarity as Targeted Appeal

One of the ways in which bad people make themselves look good is through false similarity. This occurs in many different situations.

Sexual predators take extensive steps to make themselves similar to victims they want to attract. They familiarize themselves with the hottest Internet sites, video games, and television programs that appeal to youth, in order to help them identify with victims.[30] Using age-appropriate terminology, they often speak a child's "language" better than the child's own parents.[31] Through establishing similarity, offenders create peer-like relationships with their victims where they are viewed more as a friend than as an adult figure.[32]

Intelligent, educated offenders often start by seeking out adults with whom they share areas of similarity, and establishing relationships with them first before pursuing sexual activity with their children.[33]

Psychopaths bond through similarity as well. However, unlike real bonding, which takes time to develop, psychopaths can bond with you within a few hours on an airplane.[34] How? Through cultivating a simulated persona—a mask specifically designed to make them appear similar.[35]

This is effective because in a world of diversity, it is refreshing to meet someone who shares our beliefs, worldviews, and life experiences.[36] We feel understood, accepted, and safe.[37] This can even lead us to disclose private information, believing the person will keep our secrets.[38]

Psychopaths also use false similarity in weaving elaborate personal stories to perpetrate "affinity" fraud—inducing people to make false business deals through expressing shared personal values and beliefs.[39]

The attraction to similar others is even exploited within the prison system, where inmates use similarity to manipulate correctional staff in order to seek privileges and favors.[40] Their techniques include identifying with staff through ethnic, demographic, or other circumstances.[41]

Detecting the Cyberspace Chameleon

Of all the methods of portraying false similarity, the Internet is one of the easiest places for manipulators to misrepresent themselves in order to get what they want. This is because one of the most valued features of the Internet is the ability to connect with others who are similar.[42] But tread carefully, because a social media footprint can be a misleading representation of its creator. Consider one of the more outrageous cases of Internet dating gone wrong.

A young woman named Anna thought she had met the man of her dreams. Living with her dog, engaged in an isolating profession as a poet, she ventured out into cyberspace to meet men. Harboring a healthy skepticism about online dating, she chose a site for dog lovers, believing that a man who shares her passion for canines would be a safe bet. Anna was wrong. Here is how she explains what happened.

Browsing through screens of various men posing with their dogs, she notices Tyler's profile right away. Occupation: veterinarian. *Impressive.*

Although she is admittedly distracted by the photos on his profile page. Taken at the beach, they showcase much more than his dog. Tyler is in superb physical shape.

Tyler's page is also filled with links to songs and YouTube videos. However, Anna never looks at any of that until later, because the handsome photos and respectable profession were enough for her. And because his profile indicates that he has been a member of the dog lover's site for three years, Anna feels comfortable making contact.

Tyler wastes no time in cultivating the illusion of similarity. He launches right into a series of questions, asking Anna about her preferences in dog food, dog grooming, and favorite walks. Once Ann submits her answers, Tyler expresses similar preferences on every topic. Anna is comfortable immediately.

Common ground established, Tyler gets down to business. He begins to ask Anna personal questions about past relationships. Her guard lowered, she answers these questions as well.

The next step? Photographs. Claiming that his favorite place to walk his dog is at the shoreline, Tyler asks Anna to send photos of herself with her dog at the beach—in her swimsuit. Wisely tempering a request that might otherwise have tipped his hand too soon, he assures her that the part of her he is looking forward to seeing the most is her gorgeous smile.

Oh, brother, you might be thinking, *what a line*. But Anna, who doesn't get out enough, eats it up. So much so that when Tyler skips over the typical "safe" first offline date in a public place and instead suggests a "house call" so he can make dinner for both she and her dog, she enthusiastically accepts. She gets off work early and spends the afternoon getting ready, looking forward to meeting Tyler in person.

Tyler arrives with flowers and groceries—including dog food, and immediately asks to meet her dog. So far so good. But the evening is about to be over as quickly as it began.

When Anna turns to invite Tyler into the dining room where she has prepared a beautiful, candlelit table setting for two, Tyler reaches out and grabs her buttocks. When Anna gasps in surprise, Tyler laughs dryly and remarks that he just wanted to "check out the merchandise" before he conducted a full physical exam.

The mood totally destroyed, instead of suffering through a horribly awkward evening, Anna politely asks Tyler to leave. Appearing surprised but without apology, Tyler heads for the door. He leaves his bag of groceries—which Anna discovers also contains a packet of condoms.

The unpleasant physical contact was not the worst part of the case; it was what Tyler did with the racy photographs he talked Anna into sending. Anna sat down at her computer one morning and felt all the blood drain from her head when she looked at her screen. Her in-box was filled with messages from men responding to crude offers made on a phony profile on the dog lover's site, created using her real name and the photos she sent Tyler.

Cyber Optics:
Reading the Person Behind the Profile

Internet savvy predators like Tyler can cause both emotional and reputational damage through virtual exploitation ranging from revenge porn—sexually explicit content posted to embarrass or shame the subject, to sextortion—posting sexually explicit photos and then extorting money from the subject to take them down.

With online dating, it is cases like Anna's that emphasize the necessity of exploring the authenticity behind the avatar. You can't simply believe what you see.

Personal Web sites present an ideal venue for showcasing identity claims without behavioral residue, because people can deliberately create a specific online identity without the interference of inadvertent traces of behavior.[43] And as demonstrated in Tyler's case, the background information provided on Internet dating sites is strategically presented, in order to compete with other users who are using the same strategy.[44]

With regard to red flags, Tyler showcased more of his true colors in terms of lifestyle, personality, and relational goals on his profile page than

Anna perceived. Deliberately presenting himself based on the type of relationship he was seeking, as many people do,[45] Tyler's page contained YouTube videos and song lyrics full of double entendres that glamorized a lifestyle of casual sex. Anna didn't see any of this because her attention was diverted by his attractive photographs.

And speaking of photographs, Tyler's request to see Anna in as much skin as the dating site would permit was another clue about his relational goals. He never once asked to read any of her poetry.

Had Anna researched other dating Web sites, she would have seen Tyler's profile on quite a few of them. Although he always used his own picture and the same suggestive songs and videos, he tailored the rest of his information to maximize his desirability to potential sex partners on each site.

On a sports and fitness dating site he presented himself as a ski instructor. On an adventure-seeking dating site he was a mountain climber. As a (genuine) dog lover herself, one of the things that would have shocked Anna the most is that on all the rest of Tyler's online profiles, his answer to the question about pets was: "None."

Misery Loves Company:
Missing Red When Feeling Blue

Some of the most heartbreaking cases of emotional exploitation involve people who are lonely or have lost a loved one, who believe they have met a like-minded partner who understands what they are going through, only to discover the person they thought was a kindred spirit was a conniver. Here is an example.

An elderly man named Frank lost his high school sweetheart and spouse of fifty years. Devastated and desperate for company, he joins a grief share group for widows and meets June—who is attractive, friendly, and age appropriate.

June does not share information or emotion in the group setting; her focus is as a supportive listener. Frank really bonds with her one day when, after telling her how big his house seems now that his spouse is gone, she immediately expresses having the exact same feelings about living alone without her late husband. When she suggests they go for coffee to continue the discussion, Frank heartily agrees, delighted to have found someone who understands what he is going through.

Once she and Frank begin to see each other regularly, June suggests that they alleviate their respective loneliness by living together . . . under Frank's roof. Anxious for companionship and enjoying his time with June, Frank agrees.

Shortly after moving in with Frank, June drops out of the grief share group. It has served its purpose. Honestly, she thinks to herself, she can't believe she endured the sob stories and psychobabble as long as she did. The mourning period apparently over, she now spends most of her time on her own—shopping and driving around in Frank's Cadillac.

When Frank receives notice from the bank that they are foreclosing on his house, June only asks one question: when do they have to move out? The day before they are set to move into a small apartment Frank can afford, he wakes up and finds that June is gone.

Where did she go? June, now "Jane," hopped a bus to another state. One week later, she is sitting in a new grief share group for widows. Once again the supportive listener, she focuses carefully on the stories of each of these new men, deciding who can now best care for her needs.

She doesn't contribute anything to this new group either. How could she? She doesn't have the slightest idea what it would be like to lose a spouse—because she has never been married.

Becoming Colorblind:
The Isolating Lens of Loneliness

Frank missed the red flags because he was lonely and looking for someone to fill the void. June was right there ready to step in—but for all the wrong reasons. Believing he had found someone who truly understood him, he downplayed other clues that could have revealed June's true motivation—a comfortable, rent-free roof over her head.

Yet the warning FLAGs were there. Sure, June focused on Frank, playing the role of a supportive listener. You bet she was listening, but not to offer support. Like a shark tasting blood in the water, she honed right in on Frank's disclosure of his resources and areas of vulnerability, and made her move.

What did Frank know about June? Not much. Believing they shared common ground emotionally, Frank overlooked the fact that June never discussed any details about her personal life. This was a huge red flag because authenticity involves interacting in ways that exude transparency,[46] which enhances relationships.[47] And people are more authentic within emotionally important relationships than in more casual relationships.[48]

June's carefree lifestyle once she moved in with Frank was also a red flag—to the extent that it is arguably inconsistent with having been recently widowed. Frank also never met anyone who corroborated her story, since she never mentioned any friends or family.

The only association they had in common was the grief share group—which itself generated a sense of connection. *Social identity theory* holds that we maintain our concept of self by affiliating with particular social groups[49] and trust other group members,[50] even when they are strangers.[51] This is what the Junes of the world are counting on.

Affinity groups, whether mobilized around politics, religion, or other shared beliefs, also appeal to psychopaths because of the shared trust among group members—which facilitates the ability to perpetrate fraud.[52] Religious affinity groups are particularly vulnerable to the wiles of psychopathic fraudsters due to their acceptance of members from all walks of life and their belief in forgiveness.[53]

I meet men like Frank when a woman like June steals more than just their heart. Regarding the extent of the deception, in one of the cases I handled, the female defendant not only misrepresented her intentions but also her age—*by several decades*. As the elderly victim and I sat looking at her in the courtroom, we were scratching our heads as we compared her appearance with her date of birth recorded on the police report. In a sweater, thick glasses, and with her gray hair in a bun, she looked like a kindhearted grandmother. All that was missing was the rocking chair.

How old was she? Fifty. She intentionally made herself appear decades older in order to bond with men of the victim's generation, to avoid being exposed as the gold digger she was.

Similarity Through Shared Experience

It is disappointing, to say the least, when my star witness shows up in court high as a kite. Or being able to smell the alcohol blasting from a victim's breath while she is on the witness stand (when I am sitting much farther away than the poor jurors).

Yet the often counterintuitive bonding power of similarity is illustrated in grand fashion through witnesses just like these. Due to the significantly different lifestyles between many of my witnesses and my jurors, bonding has to occur through similar experiences. Here are some examples of how it happens.

When my rape victim is a prostitute, she deserves to be treated with the same dignity and respect with which we would treat a victim who was a nun. In the eyes of the jurors, however, she is not clothed with the same degree of credibility, neither literally nor figuratively. This makes the case more difficult.

Cultivating jury appeal for victims like this can be challenging, because many jurors are not sympathetic toward women who are in the business of selling sex. It doesn't help when these women come to court looking like they just got off work.

Jury selection in these cases often degrades into a chaotic mess. "You are going to hear that the rape victim is a prostitute," I explain during the jury selection process. A murmur reverberates through the courtroom as the jurors look at each other in bewilderment. A few of them begin to verbalize their confusion. "What?" asks a juror loudly in the front row.

Soon, the courtroom is buzzing with comments, gaining volume. Some jurors are laughing. Very demoralizing. This situation often deteriorates into a scene that in the movies would lead to the judge banging his gavel on the desk barking "order in the court." I get no such help.

Nonetheless, I press on. The challenge in cases like this is to have the victim bond with the jury. How? Through shared experience. Not job experience—emotional experience.

Fast-forward to the testimony of the victim in one of these trials who tearfully relates how a man posing as a "customer" lured her into his car, raped her, then dared her to report him, laughing about how no one would believe her—or care.

I am watching the jury. They are riveted. Some of them are nodding as she speaks. I see a few of them glance over at the defendant, eyes flashing with anger. Because while they cannot relate to her specific predicament, *all* of them can relate to having been made to feel worthless. To being taken advantage of because someone knew they could. The result? The jury found her to be credible and believed her testimony.

Crimes that occur in correctional facilities present similar challenges. They include everything from sexual assault, to drug smuggling, to throwing urine at correctional officers.

Because remember, who witnesses crimes that occur in prison? Not nuns, military captains, or high school valedictorians. *Convicted felons.* When I call one of these witnesses to the stand, as with a prostitute victim in a rape case, the testimony will carry a lot more weight if I can establish a connection between the witness and the jurors.

This is not as difficult as you might think. Despite their own misadventures (usually an understatement), some of the criminals I call as witnesses are outraged by fellow inmates who prey on smaller, weaker men in custody, some of whom are mentally challenged. While no choirboys themselves, their condemnation of what they observe and often physically break up strikes a chord with jurors who share their disdain of bullies.

In other cases, however, much to my dismay, the witness who bonds the most with the jury is the defendant. He begins crying during his testimony as he describes his difficult childhood. I am expecting the jury to recognize his performance as crocodile tears—until I hear sniffling from the jury box, and look over to see several of the jurors crying with him.

As a public defender, I represented clients where identification with the defendant won the case. And I am not just talking about cases of illegal possession of a shopping cart or having a dog off a leash. With more serious charges as well, similarity facilitates bonding, even between people who are drastically different in other ways.

Connecting Through Common Ground

Some defense attorneys deliver very effective closing arguments by establishing common ground with the jury through identifying areas of similarity. Not similarity with their clients, but with themselves.

I knew one lawyer who within ten minutes could have the whole jury box mesmerized, looking like a stage full of hypnosis subjects. How? By shifting the focus from defending his client to bonding with the jury.

He begins by telling the jury about the slow pace of life in the town where he grew up. I can see some of the jurors clearly relating to the lifestyle he is describing, because they are smiling and nodding. The corner drugstore where the kids went after school to get ice cream sodas. *Yes, we had one of those.* Playing in the sprinklers during the hot summers. They are still nodding and smiling. *Did that too.*

It is only after the jurors have been lulled into a nostalgic haze of pleasant memories that the defense attorney finally turns to the facts of the case. By that time the jurors are feeling good, and are in a receptive frame of mind to consider his defense.

I don't criticize this technique. Everyone uses it. Particularly when the facts of a case are gruesome, disturbing, or otherwise unappealing, the jury needs to be softened up to be receptive to the fact that they have to decide the case based only on the evidence that was presented in the courtroom.

The point is that whether the connection is made through a passion for chocolate, a love of warm weather, or frustration with the long lines at the DMV, emphasizing areas of similarity is an incredibly effective way to overcome differences.

THE SEDUCTION OF SIMILARITY

Focus: Similar interests are more reliable indicators of common ground than similar appearance.

Lifestyle: Similar lifestyles predict relational success more than similarity in areas such as profession or income level.

Associations: Even when someone is physically similar to you or has the same job, examining the types of people a person chooses to spend time with is more likely to reveal their true colors.

Goals: Merely because someone shares your ethnicity, gender, or background doesn't mean they share your ambitions.

Spotting the Phony:
FLAGs of False Similarity

As a Christian minister, I have the privilege of performing marriages. One of the weddings I performed included a big reception at a downtown venue where the festivities attracted several wedding crashers. Well-dressed, outgoing, and friendly, these guys wandered in off the street and helped themselves to over an hour's worth of free drinks from the hosted bar before they were identified as the freeloaders they were.

These imposters would never have been detected, however, had they kept their mouths shut; because they looked like everyone else. It was their insistence in initiating conversation (the more they drank) that gave them away. Because almost every conversation at a wedding reception contains some type of "bride or groom" inquiry, too many wrong answers will sound an alarm.

Not all manipulators, however, give themselves away so easily. In order to detect the ones who appear to blend in, you can often spot the phony by looking below the surface. If despite superficial traits in common, a person's FLAGs reveal *dissimilarities,* you are left with yet another example of how appearances can be deceiving.

Consistency is important because inauthentic similarity involves adopting different personalities with different people. An equal opportunity rapist who assaulted both adults and children at knifepoint described his chameleon-like existence as one where he "changed colors with the wind," personalizing his language and behavior to match his social group, whether they were foul-mouthed drug users or mild-mannered Christians.[54]

We can catch this type of insincerity if we are paying attention. When salespeople dress differently depending on which client they are meeting with, or to close a sale, we may perceive them as disingenuous.[55] Their clothing does not reflect consistency, but strategy.

The FLAGs are designed to expose this type of manufactured similarity by shifting the focus to inward motivation and dispositions. Someone who really is similar to you is more likely to share more significant areas of common ground than buying the same brand of milk. They will share interests, ambitions, and lifestyle choices, and associate with the same types of people.

You might also catch false similarity through noticing reciprocal behavior, because studies show that while unconscious synchrony increases positive feelings toward another person, false synchrony does not.[56]

One way to detect false synchrony comes from studies in mimicry. Mimicry studies demonstrate the *chameleon effect*—unconscious imitation of a partner's mannerisms, behaviors, and expressions.[57] Mimicry increases liking, and facilitates interpersonal interaction.[58]

Individuals low in empathy do not display mimicry.[59] Because Dark Triad individuals are characterized by low levels of affective empathy, which relates to emotional contagion, [60] lack of mimicry can serve as one indicator of potentially aversive personality traits.

In addition, Dark Triad individuals might be exposed through their inappropriate emotion. Emotions help us perceive authenticity, and enduring emotional states reveal a person's genuine identity.[61] This is important because emotions may be expressed disingenuously,[62] in pursuit of strategic self-presentation or ingratiation.[63]

People are sensitive to the link between emotion and underlying circumstances, disliking people who display inconsistency. A study measuring brain activity of subjects watching actors describe a tragic event found that when the actor smiled while recounting the tragedy, the subjects' brains registered the detection of conflicting or socially threatening data—and they disliked the actor.[64] Studies of courtroom behavior yield similar results, finding that criminal defendants who display inappropriate emotions such as joy are more likely to be convicted.[65]

In fact, research shows that Dark Triad individuals can actually experience positive affect when confronted with sad emotions in others, and psychopaths can experience positive affect when confronted with fearful and angry expressions.[66] Conversely, both psychopaths and Machiavellianists have been shown to feel negative affect toward expressions of happiness.[67]

While you are likely to perceive such emotional inconsistency instinctively, being aware of these warning signs can assist you in perceiving danger sooner rather than later.

7

The Ax Murderer Next Door

Familiarity Breeds Contentment

The airport shuttle drops you off one block from your hotel, late at night. As you cross the street, you intentionally avoid a homeless man ranting and raving, punching his fists at the air. When you are far enough away, you look back and see a petite blond woman leave an office building and begin to walk toward the man. Afraid for her safety, you continue to watch, and see her walk *right past* the man, less than one foot away . . . and say hello. *What?*

The petite blond woman has been walking past that man twice a day for fifteen years. What is unfamiliar and frightening to you is not to her. She is not afraid of him because he is *familiar*. She might even describe him as "harmless." Why? Because she knows him personally? No. Because she sees him every day.

She should be more careful. That is the point.

Favoring the Familiar Face

One of the more memorable con men I prosecuted was a party crasher with goals beyond scoring a couple of free drinks. Purporting to be "in the entertainment business," he was a familiar face at Hollywood galas, often having slipped in without a ticket. Seeking wealthy women to befriend (and exploit financially), he had succeeded in making himself a recognizable presence. Ironically, with his movie star shades and trendy attire, he looked like an actor.

A few astute women, however, noticed that this handsome young man never seemed to know anyone at the party, and only focused on introducing himself to *older* women, even though these show business galas were filled with beautiful women his own age (twenty-five). These preliminary observations blew his cover. He never did find a woman to exploit.

I ran into him not long after he pled guilty to trespassing—his larger goal having been thwarted by the observant A-listers. He sold me my popcorn at the local movie theatre. That was the perfect job for him in the "entertainment business," because he was not a good actor.

The Pleasure of Recognition

Familiarity looks good. We tend to like people we see frequently.[1] This can include neighbors, coworkers, or even community members we encounter on a regular basis at the grocery store or coffee shop. You may have never spoken to these people, but you recognize them. Sometimes you even wave hello. In reality, however, you know next to nothing about them.

Although familiarity can increase the assessment of beauty through perceived similarity,[2] familiarity is different from similarity because people you see frequently do not need to be similar to you in any way to become attractive. Familiarity generates attraction on its own.[3] Mere exposure to the same person repeatedly, without anything more, can increase liking.[4] While in some cases, repeated contact may increase preexisting feelings whether favorable or unfavorable,[5] familiarity is more likely to breed contentment than contempt.[6]

How does familiarity produce positive feelings? Through generating predictability, reassurance, comfort,[7] and attraction.[8]

The danger, however, is that despite the positive feelings, what is familiar is not always safe.

Familiarity Breeds Complacency

The best stories about how quickly defendants become familiar come from my days as a public defender, when I was accustomed to going alone into a jail holding tank filled with over twenty men. In that warm, malodorous, and overcrowded space, I would sit and try to talk with one client while another was urinating in a toilet less than four feet away, and eighteen others were shuffling around, all talking at once.

While my mixture of emotions at the time included discomfort and sometimes disgust, one thing I never felt was fear. If you knew what some of those guys were charged with you might wonder, *why not?* The answer was that I saw men like this every day. I dreaded the revolting stench and crowded conditions, but not the clients themselves.

Now a prosecutor, I recognize that letting your guard down around criminal defendants can be dangerous. You would think we don't need to be reminded of this. But we do. Because repeated exposure generates familiarity, which can breed complacency. And it doesn't take long.

In the courtroom, even with the scariest-looking defendants, we get used to seeing the same guy sitting there day after day, and our guard goes down. This even happens with defendants whose increased risk of danger is indicated through specially colored wristbands or certain colors of jail-issued clothing.

While we don't go near the defendant's chair at first, as the days pass, even in first-degree murder trials, some prosecutors find themselves walking *right behind* him to get to the clerk's desk, passing within arm's length of someone who didn't think twice about killing in cold blood. Why? Because he has become familiar.

Who else becomes familiar? The defendant's family and friends who are sitting in the audience watching the trial. As time goes on, lawyers find themselves speaking freely in front of them. They talk about their personal lives, where they live, and even their children, *including their names and the schools they attend.*

Sometimes it takes a wake-up call to jolt everyone back to their senses. This occurred in a courtroom down the hallway from where I was trying a case, when one of the lawyers, having become complacent like everyone else, walked directly behind the defendant's chair to get to the clerk's desk.

This time, as he got close enough, the defendant lunged out of his chair with a shank (homemade knife) he had been concealing, waiting for the right time to strike. Thankfully, the bailiff intervened and the assault was thwarted.

You can bet the rest of us kept our distance from the defendant's chair after that. But only for a while. Eventually, some people started to slip back into the same routine.

Relaxing in Familiar Surroundings

One sight that is sure to spoil the mood (and your appetite) during a romantic picnic in the park is a flasher in a trenchcoat who shows up to give you an eyeful. Disgusting! But have you noticed the stranger sitting on a park bench in the distance by the swing set? He is there every day, and is far more dangerous than the bold exhibitionist that just ruined your meal.

Perhaps you never noticed him because he has become familiar. In all types of settings, familiarity causes us to lower our guard, which can cause us to miss red flags. Consider how different our usual level of perception is from a person trained to be alert for signs of danger or distress at all times.

The lifeguard sits in his tower monitoring the beach when literal red flags are posted on the shoreline due to a dangerous rip current. As he scans the waters edge, he observes hundreds of people splashing around, enjoying the day.

Nonetheless, because of his attention and training, he hones in on one person who is flailing about in the waves not because he is playing, but because he is drowning. Immediately, the lifeguard leaps out of his chair to save a life.

The accuracy of the lifeguard's interpretation of the behavior he observes in the water can mean the difference between life and death. So can the length of the delay between his perception and his decision to act on what he sees.

Good thing I am not a lifeguard, you might think to yourself. Nonetheless, there are times when you might find yourself in a situation that requires a heightened state of awareness. Walking at night to catch the bus in an unfamiliar city, for example, you might find your antenna is up and you are paying attention to your surroundings. Startled by an unusual noise in the middle of the night, you are more likely to reach for a flashlight (or a weapon) than your iPhone. If you do reach for your phone, it will be to call 911, not to check e-mail.

For most of us, however, this heightened state of awareness does not characterize a day spent within familiar surroundings. Far from it. Within comfortable surroundings, our antenna goes down. We tie up our physical senses with a cup of coffee in one hand, smart phone in the other, earphones in our ears, and sunglasses on our eyes.

In this state of distraction, we wave hello to the guy on the metro (about to commit an armed robbery) who has become familiar because we have seen him so many times. This time, we fail to see the knife handle protruding from his waistband.

Familiarity Through Self-Disclosure:
When an Open Book Is Fiction

We are more likely to believe others who are familiar, and are partial to friends and family members over strangers.[9] But be cautious of people who make themselves familiar too quickly through self-disclosure.

Consider the case of an intelligent businesswoman who discloses too much financial information to a man she meets on the subway—presenting a textbook example of the "strangers on a train" phenomenon—where we feel comfortable sharing intimate details with a stranger we don't expect to see again.[10]

The woman in this case, however, is also motivated to self-disclose by the man's own self-revelations—making himself familiar through disclosing circumstances that were similar to her own. Over the course of an hour, he presents an emotional life story about losing both of his parents to cancer, as well as a valiant story of overcoming cancer himself. After hearing all this, the woman is moved with compassion and shares some of the details of her own battle with cancer. Unfortunately, she also shared her credit card number in order to make a donation to the charity this man claimed to support.

That was a mistake. Because while this man came across as an open book, he was actually a tear-jerking novel. Using a *psychopathic fiction*,[11] he fabricated the whole story. He already knew about her battle with cancer as well as her resources, as she was a prominent, wealthy advocate for cancer research. That is why he targeted her in the first place.

Self-disclosure is one of the most effective rapport-building strategies, especially when it involves revealing emotion.[12] Self-revelations are also fueled by the *clicking model*, where people engage in a higher level of self-disclosure more rapidly with other individuals with whom they "click."[13]

Unfortunately, although the man on the train made himself seem familiar quickly, the woman could not determine this man's true colors by examining his FLAGs because she didn't have any honest information with which to work. Strangers on a train are still strangers.

Online, ironically, strangers are called "friends" and "connections." If you don't think this is true, ask someone who has collected hundreds of Facebook friends to describe who these people are. While they will not be able to tell you about all of them, they will probably claim that the "friends" they don't recognize "look familiar."

Online acquaintances can become familiar quickly based on frequency of contact, even when they have never met in person. This superficial familiarity can lead to heightened self-disclosure—which many people already find easier online given the relative anonymity of cyberspace.[14]

In fact, people report liking others *more* after interacting with them online, and feel they know them better than when interacting in person.[15] These feelings often fuel the desire to move the relationship offline,[16] where I end up with the case when it turns out that familiar does not equal safe.

Defending Familiar Territory:
Relational Maintenance Through Misperception

Familiarity doesn't just dull our senses in public and online, it can even cloud perception within long-term romantic relationships, causing people to remain involved with unsuitable partners.

"But we have been through so much together!" my victim exclaims when, in examining the multiple cigarette burns inflicted by her partner, I suggest that she consider leaving this man, as the bloom appears to be off the rose.

Her response is typical, considering the circumstances under which I meet these women. Although the first act of physical aggression should have been a game changer, domestic violence victims often suffer through years of abuse without ever calling foul.

Many people choose to remain in relationships because they are familiar, rather than venture back into the jungle of single life—something they may not have experienced in decades, and the thought of which creates unbearable anxiety. How do they cope? Through cultivating a distorted, positive view of their partner. Here is how it happens.

As relationships develop, reality is often replaced by positive illusions.[17] While positive illusions are not necessarily bad, and may in some cases actually improve relationships,[18] they also explain why people ignore or downplay unpleasant or damaging information in order to maintain a positive view of their partner.[19]

Positive illusions are particularly prevalent where there is relational investment.[20] A person who has poured considerable effort and time into a relationship is motivated to avoid having to begin all over again with a new partner.[21] In order to maintain the relationship, they view their partner's weaknesses in a fashion that allows them to continue to view their partner in a positive light.[22]

However, while minimizing negative experiences within intimate relationships may improve relational satisfaction with some couples, it can also damage relationships by decreasing the motivation to address problems, which can worsen over time.[23]

Some people even develop selective amnesia. Have you ever listened to a friend describing her partner in such glowing, positive terms that you begin to wonder if she has a new paramour you haven't met? You have to fight back the urge to interrupt her, "Wait, who are we talking about?" You wonder if she is losing her memory. She may be. *Selectively.*

The desire to maintain a relationship can result in biased memories of a partner's behavior.[24] Termed *wishful memory of responsiveness*, the desire to bond with a partner can distort memories about the level of a partner's responsiveness, leading to memories of a partner's past behavior as more favorable than it really was.[25]

But it gets worse. In order to diffuse threats to the stability of a relationship, some people will actually construct stories about their partners, turning faults into virtues in order to cast them in a positive light.[26] People are able to incorporate even the most negative evidence into narratives with happy endings.[27] For example, stubbornness becomes integrity rather than egocentrism, in order to diminish the threat.[28]

Storytelling results in complex narratives that integrate different aspects of the relationship in a fashion that sustains positive convictions.[29] As with any good work of fiction, loose ends are tied up by transforming a partner's negative traits, or denying their existence.[30] This allows the person spinning the story to retain confidence in the relationship.[31]

This brings us to a relational maintenance strategy I see frequently when cross-examining character witnesses: see no evil, hear no evil—the belief that what you avoid can't hurt you.

Protecting Your Investment:
Willful Blindness

I stand to cross-examine the young lady on the witness stand who is serving as a character witness for the defendant. Having dated him for over a year, she has just explained to the jury how honest, upstanding, and wonderful he is. My first question is "Are you aware of his criminal record?" She immediately discredits the value of her testimony in one fell swoop as she closes her eyes, puts her hands over her ears, and shakes her head, stating "I don't want to know."

We are all familiar with the clichés "knowledge is power" and "ignorance is bliss." Can both statements be true? Some women who turn both a blind eye and a deaf ear to negative information about their significant other would say "yes." Having become comfortable in a relationship with the wrong type of guy, they wear emotional blindfolds to intentionally limit the amount of new information they learn about their significant other in order to maintain relational satisfaction. This is usually because they are reasonably sure the new information would not be positive.

They are not alone. Despite the advantages of knowledge, there are many circumstances under which people choose to remain ignorant.[32] People resist learning that someone got a better deal on an expensive purchase, that they gained weight over the holidays, or the details of a medical diagnosis.[33] People also resist acquiring information about others that is inconsistent with their beliefs, and avoid information that could threaten existing relationships.[34]

Avoiding information allows people to maintain their beliefs, relationships, and behavior patterns, and prevent negative emotions.[35] Avoiding learning about a partner's indiscretions, for example, spares people the emotions of shame and anger associated with the discovery.[36] In fact, even the anticipation of unpleasant or negative relationship information increases the desire for informational avoidance.[37]

Familiarity Through Proximity:
The Ax Murderer Next Door

We are all familiar with the words of the serial killer's next-door neighbor: "But he seemed like such a nice guy!" What gave the neighbor that impression? Usually the answer is simple familiarity, due to proximity.

The neighbor may have waved to the ax murderer as they pulled out of their respective driveways every morning. Perhaps she chatted with him while they fueled their vehicles at the local gas station—never wondering what was under the tarp of his pickup truck. She may have wheeled her shopping cart past this homicidal maniac at the grocery store, comforted that they bought the same brand of milk—while not thinking twice about the coil of rope in his cart.

In other words, when neighbors of serial killers are questioned in depth about their interactions with the murderer, we usually find that they really did not know the person at all. They thought he was "nice" simply because he was familiar.

You might feel the same way about your neighbor, until the day his mail is accidentally delivered to your house by mistake. Although he is a sixty-five-year-old man who lives alone, he has subscriptions to *Glamour* and *Seventeen* magazines. Can you think of an innocent explanation?

People become familiar through proximity, which increases the potential and likelihood of forming relationships.[38] The *proximity effect* links physical distance and liking, and was generated from findings that university students identified their closest friends as those who lived close to them, with whom they associated most frequently.[39]

Proximity also generates attraction.[40] This may occur because proximity increases exposure, which in turn increases liking.[41] Even seeing the faces of strangers on a regular basis can increase liking.[42] In fact, research even shows we are more likely to marry people who are in close proximity.[43]

Proximity, however, does not equal safe. Consider one of the most heinous examples of this in recent years.

Hiding in Plain Sight

Neighborhood watch programs don't work if no one is looking. The challenge, however, is knowing what to look for. Sometimes the monster is hiding in plain sight.

The late Ariel Castro kept three young women hostage in his Cleveland home for over a decade while publicly leading a seemingly normal life as a bus driver, friendly neighbor, and bass player in a local band. How did he get away with it? The same way the ax murderer does. By hiding in plain sight behind a façade of familiarity.

Castro was a familiar face to his neighbors. Neighbor Charles Ramsey saw Castro every day. In his words "He just comes out to his backyard, plays with the dogs, tinkers with his cars and motorcycles, goes back in the house."[44] Castro even offered neighborhood children rides up and down the block on his bicycle or four-wheeler.[45]

That was his public persona. The lifestyle he led behind closed doors would have revealed the monster behind the façade. Castro's home was described as a "house of horrors." That is why he focused on keeping people out of it.

One of his relatives explained that Castro was very private and only socialized outside his home. "He'd never have anyone come over," the relative explains. "He'd never had [a] social life unless they were outside on the porch or something, as far as I know."[46]

Castro's daughter, Angie Gregg, who had described her father before his horrific crime was revealed as a "friendly, caring, doting man,"[47] recalls that Castro never wanted to be away from the house for very long— not even to visit her, as she lived out of state.[48] Adding to this obsessive focus on his home, when she was inside, Gregg remembers her father disappearing during dinner without explanation.[49]

Even though she was one of the few people who was allowed inside, she was still restricted in the parts of the house she could access. She recalls that Castro kept the house tightly locked up, including the basement, which was always kept locked.[50] When she asked to see her childhood bedroom, which was upstairs, Castro dissuaded her, claiming there was too much "junk" up there.[51]

In addition, Gregg recalls that Castro delayed answering the door when she came over—often signaling through a window for her to wait, and then waving her around to the rear of the house to let her in.[52] She remembers the music was usually turned up loud, although at the time she assumed this was normal behavior since Castro was a musician.[53]

In addition to all the observable red flags, Castro's lifestyle included a history of domestic violence toward his wife, and abducting his own daughters.[54] Perhaps we should not be surprised that he fulfilled his goal of replacing past victims with new victims.

Fortunately, the brave young women Castro kept hostage for all of those years have not only survived, but serve as role models for other young people who have suffered similar plights. Their ordeal also inspires us to keep our antennas up within our own neighborhoods and communities in order to assess whether people who are familiar are really as good as they look.

Historical Familiarity:
History Repeats Itself

Sometimes familiarity results from shared history. I have handled many child molestation cases where victims failed to reveal sexual abuse because the perpetrator was a family member or friend they have known all their lives.

Historical familiarity can be deceptive because history does not equal honesty. Many of us have known people for years only to discover the hard way that we never really knew them at all. This is because as people become familiar over time, our history with them can become a skewed barometer of character.

History power is a type of power created within an established relationship that includes shared experience, familiarity, and trust.[55] Virtual history power allows sexual predators to cultivate Internet relationships with unsuspecting victims, using the interaction to create the illusion of a positive relationship that often endures even after the victim finds out the truth about the perpetrator.[56] It also creates a sense of familiarity in many other circumstances, which can mask signs of deception.

History is best used for its predictive value because it exposes you to someone's FLAGs, which are often consistent over time. Nonetheless, I have handled fraud cases where victims are cheated by longtime friends who they knew cheated in school and cheated on girlfriends. They found out the hard way that a dishonest lifestyle is not likely to be confined only to certain areas.

The next time someone takes you to lunch to propose doing business together and intentionally fails to tell the server about an expensive item accidentally omitted from the bill, consider whether they would hesitate to cheat you out of future business profits just as easily.

FLAG-ing When Familiarity Is a Façade

Familiarity is a façade that can be fatal. This occurred in a baby homicide case I handled, where an infant died from what is known as *shaken baby syndrome*—where intentional shaking causes brain hemorrhaging, leading to death.

The suspect was the neighborhood babysitter who everyone used. While this woman was familiar within the community, believe it or not, no one knew much about her. Only a few of the parents had spent any amount of quality time with this woman one-on-one before trusting her with their children. Everyone hired her—because everyone else did.

Here is a good test: familiarity is a façade when you recognize someone, but do not know anything about the person's FLAGs. This indicates that while you may have become used to seeing them, you do not know anything about them.

In order to determine whether a familiar face is good or bad, consider *why* the person is familiar. The more information you know about them, the better. Do they walk the same hiking trail you do on weekends, attend the same classes at your university, or work at your company? Shared life-style, academic pursuits, or career goals indicate far more common ground than someone who merely happens to park in the space next to you at your apartment complex—which might indicate shared income bracket, but not much else.

Exploring the basis of familiarity is important because of how easily it can be manipulated. Pedophiles admit moving into neighborhoods where there are many children. Social climbers frequent locations where they are likely to interact with luminaries they want to meet.

I have handled cases where stalkers have eased their way into a vic-tim's comfort zone through strategically increasing their level of famil-iarity. Knowing where the victims lived, shopped, worked, or went to school, these men would spend time in the areas frequented by their vic-tims, making themselves a familiar face.

One of my more perceptive stalking victims noticed that when her stalker pulled into the gas station where she was fueling her car, his gas pump stopped after only a few minutes. This was a clue that he was not there because he needed gas. She recalled seeing the same man at the gro-cery store on several occasions, where he only had a few items in his cart. A chilling "coincidence"—all the same brands that she bought. Oh, if everyone were this perceptive.

THE FAÇADE OF FAMILIARITY

Focus: Beyond waving hello to someone every day, have you ever noticed where they focus their attention?

Lifestyle: Do you know how a person spends their time outside of the setting where you regularly see them?

Associations: Do you share common friends or acquaintances? Do you even know with whom they associate?

Goals: What do you know about the person's ambitions? Are they familiar be-cause you are both in the same political science class or yoga class?

8

Craving Excitement

The Call of the Wild

The receptionist calls and tells me my victim has arrived. I walk out into the crowded waiting area, but don't see her. I know what she looks like because I have the photographs from the crime scene. Deciding that perhaps she has gone to the restroom, I wait for a bit.

After another few minutes, I begin to worry that she may have gotten cold feet and left. Given the racy outfit she was wearing the night of the accident coupled with her status as a trespasser at the scene of the crime, I wonder if she has some outstanding arrest warrants and might have decided not to risk talking to a prosecutor.

I finally ask the receptionist if she knows where my victim has gone, at which point she gestures toward a demurely dressed woman in a business suit with a monogrammed briefcase who is sitting right in front of me.

Whoops. Although I know better, I had succumbed to stereotyping. I was looking for the sensation-seeking lawbreaker in ripped jeans and a red leather jacket I saw in the crime scene photos from the racetrack. I mistook the well-dressed woman sitting in front of me for either a defense attorney or an expert witness, not someone who willingly climbed into a race car with a man who had just pounded several beers for an illegal spin in the dark.

Taking a Drive on the Wild Side

The silver lining was that the case landed on my desk as a reckless driving with injury instead of a vehicular homicide. One of the questions I had for the victim was, under the circumstances, what in the world was an intelligent, educated woman like her doing in that car in the first place?

The victim, Jeanette, tells me the story. She met the defendant, Dane, ironically enough, at a red light. She heard him before she saw him as he rolled up in a Corvette painted like a race car, with an engine as loud as the music blaring from his car speakers.

Jeanette had never met anyone like Dane and was captivated by his accounts of life in the fast lane. She had always been fascinated with race cars, loved watching the video footage from his helmet cam, and wondered what it would be like to actually be out on the track. She found out sooner than she anticipated.

Where do you suppose Dane took her on their first date? To a nice restaurant? The opera? Nope. To a local speedway after hours, where a quick dinner of fried chicken and beer is followed by a terrifying spin in his race car, her screams drowned out by the heavy metal music blasting from his stereo. Notwithstanding the fear of the ride, or perhaps because of it, Jeanette agrees to see him again. And again. Until one night, his luck ran out.

On that fateful evening, Dane misjudged a corner of the track and rolled the car. Jeanette was injured when the seatbelt failed and she was thrown into the windshield. Dane later admitted that he knew the seatbelt was broken. Looking back, Jeanette recalls that he didn't even ask her to fasten it.

When a Checkered Flag Is a Red Flag

Jeanette's case demonstrates that there is nothing about being successful, intelligent, or well educated that immunizes people from exercising bad judgment once they become emotionally involved.

In deciding whether or not Dane was relationship material, Jeneatte could have placed more weight on the FLAGs he was flying—and not just the checkered flags. Although he was a talented driver (when he wasn't drinking), and talent is attractive,[1] there wasn't much more to Dane than a stimulating exterior. He was not focused on getting to know Jeanette personally, because he viewed her simply as a playmate, not a soul mate.

Dane was committed to a lifestyle of sensation seeking, enjoying activities proven to be both stimulating and dangerous such as speeding,[2] racing,[3] and other high-risk sports.[4] Not team sports, however, because he was a lone wolf both personally and professionally—preferring competition over collaboration. He hadn't fixed the seatbelt because lacking any close associations, he rarely drove with a passenger.

Given Dane's self-focus, what steps did he take to ensure Jeanette's safety? I will answer that question in court by offering the broken seatbelt into evidence as Prosecution's Exhibit Number One.

Good People Gone Wild:
The Allure of the Extreme

There is nothing quite like preparing to submit a case to the jury and having a witness burst through the back door of the courtroom carying a pair of bloody tennis shoes, announcing that she has found the murder weapon. I can tell you from experience, that moment is now the most memorable part of the trial.

People enjoy excitement.

Most of us can relate to the occasional hankering for a bit of adventure. And I don't mean ordering something new on the menu at the corner deli. Nor does it have to be something as extreme as celebrating your eightieth birthday by parachuting out of a perfectly good airplane. Many people are simply attracted to the idea of adding a little stimulation to their lives.

Some prefer to experience excitement vicariously. The popularity of television shows about undercover cops, secret agents, or the quest for the "deadliest catch" illustrates the enjoyment of vicarious thrills. Who can forget the world's captivation with the beloved "Crocodile Hunter" Steve Irwin, before he was tragically killed by a stingray in 2006? We are enthralled by brave risk takers and enjoy living vicariously through their exploits.

For some people, experiencing danger secondhand isn't good enough. These people pursue excitement through everything from risky occupations to sports to incredibly dangerous activities such as the Running of the Bulls in Spain.[5]

Other individuals, however, are attracted not to activities, but to *people* who are exciting. Seeking sensation seekers who like to live on the edge, many people are enthralled with a man who parachuted into an active volcano or wrestled with a Bengal tiger in the wild and lived to tell the tale.

Some of my victims in the passion-filled-adventure-gone-wrong cases that I have met over the years, however, will tell you that becoming involved with these guys isn't that cool. Reading the FLAGs behind the fun can help to separate those who enjoy dangerous activities from those who are *dangerous*.

Detecting the Dark Side of Sensation Seeking

For some people, risky behavior is a lifestyle. One study found that air traffic controllers, thought to be one of the riskiest professions, were likely to engage in thrill-seeking sports or physical activities outside of work.[6] People who volunteer for risky job assignments, such as may occur in a military environment, also tend to be high sensation seekers, especially in the area of thrill and adventure seeking.[7]

While there are plenty of wholesome, safe sensation seekers in the world, sensation seeking is not always a positive trait. It is linked with risk taking and dangerous activities, ranging from extreme sports to unsafe sexual practices,[8] engaged in in order to achieve the desired level of stimulation.[9]

Sometimes, sensation seeking is linked with criminal behavior. And I am not just talking about streaking at a ballgame. Sensation seeking is linked with theft, vandalism, reckless driving, and substance abuse.[10]

The highest amount of sensation seeking is found in people with antisocial personalities.[11] Even highly arousing music preferences such as rock and heavy-metal (Dane's music of choice) are associated with sensation seeking and antisocial personality traits.[12]

Sensation seeking is also linked to impulsivity, which can be manifest through focus of attention.[13] People in an impulsive state are influenced by information that attracts their attention,[14] and are often unable to resist temptation, which can lead to risky behavior.[15]

To distinguish between the two concepts, sensation seeking is defined as seeking novel stimulation and the willingness to engage in risky behavior in order to achieve it, while impulsivity involves acting without considering the consequences.[16] Thus, while sensation seekers may pursue a wide array of conduct ranging from skydiving to trying a new restaurant, such behavior is only impulsive when it is performed without regard to potential costs.[17]

Both impulsivity and sensation seeking are linked with Dark Triad personality.[18] Psychopaths present themselves as fun and exciting,[19] and sure enough, the need for excitement is characteristic of psychopathy.[20] In fact, some have identified a subtype of psychopathy that results in the enjoyment of risk taking simply for the thrill of it, as opposed to as a means to gain attention or recognition.[21]

On the other hand, *status-driven risk taking*, also linked to Dark Triad personality, is risk taking that is motivated by social and financial gain, and is distinguished from engaging in risky behavior merely for the thrill of it.[22] It involves engaging in highly dangerous activity in pursuit of power and wealth.[23]

Racing with a passenger whom you know has a broken seatbelt is consistent with the fact that psychopaths not only crave excitement and are impulsive, but they also shirk responsibility.[24]

The bottom line is that regarding relationship potential, guys like Dane pack a double whammy. They are better suited for a fling than a relationship because both sensation seeking and Dark Triad personality are linked with short-lived romance.[25]

Separating Sensation from the Source:
Transferred Arousal

As Jeanette realized after the accident, part of her attraction to Dane stemmed from the excitement she felt when she was with him. This is because feelings of romantic, sexual interest can stem from a misattribution of physical arousal.[26]

Intense physical arousal may provoke feelings of romantic love for an attractive person who happens to be nearby.[27] *Excitation transfer theory* describes how arousal from one incident generates arousing emotions such as passion in a subsequent setting.[28]

Research suggests that we can experience heightened sexual attraction during states of high anxiety.[29] One study involved an attractive female interviewer making contact with men on one of two bridges in Canada: a fear-arousing suspension bridge, and a "control" bridge without any dangerous attributes.[30] The interviewer had subjects fill out a questionnaire that included a request to write a short dramatic story prompted by a picture of a young woman.[31]

The results? The men contacted on the fear-arousing suspension bridge included more sexual content in their stories, and were more likely to attempt future contact with the female interviewer than the control group.[32]

Have you ever been attracted to someone you saw at the gym? Research also establishes a link between exercise-induced arousal and attraction. In one study, male subjects ran in place for a period of time, then were led into a dark room and showed a videotape of either an attractive or unattractive woman.[33]

The subjects were then asked to rate the woman, believing they would meet her immediately after the experiment.[34] The study found that males who had just exercised were more attracted to the attractive woman and less attracted to the unattractive woman as compared with subjects who had not just exercised.[35]

You might even be more attracted to your date if the two of you watch an arousing movie together. This same study examined arousal induced by listening to three different taped selections: selected passages from *A Wild and Crazy Guy* starring Steve Martin designed to elicit positive arousal, a graphic mob killing and mutilating of a missionary in front of his family designed to elicit negative arousal, and a textbook scene of the circulatory system of a frog designed to provide a neutral control selection.[36]

The results of the tape-selections experiment mirrored the exercise experiment in the sense that arousal, both negative and positive, produced more attraction to the good-looking woman and less attraction to the unattractive woman when compared to the control group.[37] (So if you want to set the mood for romance, skip the documentary.)

Beware of the Bad Influence:
Making It Look Good to Look Bad

Contrasting Jeanette's image in court with what I saw in the crime scene photos, I had to ask out of sheer curiosity, *what was with that outfit?* I still remember her blushing admission. Having embarked on one of the most exhilarating dating adventures of her life, she explained that she got a thrill out of dressing the part.

Jeanette is not alone. In the dating world, one of the unfortunate consequences of being attracted to the "bad boy" (or girl) is the possibility of adopting the negative qualities of a romantic interest.[38] Researchers studying this phenomenon cite the example of "good girl" Sandy in the movie *Grease* deciding to trade in her wholesome image at the end of the movie for one of rebellion, where she is transformed into a cigarette-smoking vision in black leather—a rebellious counterpart to her love interest Danny.[39]

Some people adopt negative attributes of a romantic interest into their own self-concept in a desire to become closer to the object of their affection.[40] This is especially true when the romantic interest is self-accepting of the negative qualities.[41]

Even wholesome people can be led astray by people who make it look good to look bad. Some of the victims in my human trafficking cases were college girls with good grades, yet were lured into a life of vice by a stimulating, flamboyant suitor—who turned out to be a pimp. Sex workers explain that a pimp lures women by "looking good, smelling good, flashing his possessions, and presenting himself as someone who can counter boredom with both adventure and excitement."[42]

The extent to which these girls have abandoned their wholesome image is demonstrated when they are arrested. Their cell phones are often filled with photos of themselves, not in lettered college sweatshirts, but posing in skimpy outfits with Gucci bags and wads of one hundred dollar bills, demonstrating the level of indoctrination into the glamorized subculture of vice.

Inviting Excitement:
The Life of the Party

Some people are exciting to be with not because they take you on death-defying adventures or make a deviant lifestyle look alluring, but because they are a blast to hang out with. Sociable, funny, and energetic, they are on everyone's party invitation list because they can spice up the most mundane event and stimulate any crowd.

But these lively partygoers do not end up with lampshades on their heads. Their attraction stems from the way they focus on other people. While many of these friendly socialites genuinely love their neighbors as themselves, others harbor darkness beneath the disguise.

For example, let me know if you have met this guy. At happy hour he is outgoing, outspoken, and out for a good time. While not the best-looking man in the bar, women are drawn to him like bees to honey. Once he gets their attention, his gregarious nature and charisma take him as far as he wants to go. You have seen women you know leave the bar with him with a smile on their face.

That might be as much as you observe, but I often hear more of the story when some of the women who left the bar with him report that he wanted to go farther than they did and didn't take no for an answer. Unfortunately, I don't hear the whole story because these women often drank so much they are unable to recall everything that happened.

In many such instances, I am prevented from issuing charges because despite believing the victim, I know I cannot prove the crime. Not only do witnesses who observed the pair earlier in the evening describe them as affectionate, the bar's security cameras often reveal that "affectionate" is an understatement.

Wouldn't it be great if women could detect signs of danger *before* deciding to leave the bar with a guy like this? Here are a few things to look for.

Detecting the Dark Side of Extraversion

I ask the man on the witness stand, "What do you fantasize about when you masturbate?" Most men would drop their jaw if I asked that question. Not the sexual predators I prosecute. Without missing a beat, he looks over at the jury box and proceeds to share the lurid images, making eye contact with individual jurors as he describes the salacious details.

Despite their discomfort, the jury has to listen to this testimony in order to decide if he should be committed as a sexually violent predator. What often surprises them more than the lewd details themselves, is the defendant's bold willingness to share them.

This is an extreme example. Most of the time, extraversion is linked with a variety of positive qualities and traits, reflecting the reality that most extraverts are upstanding individuals with magnetic personalities and magnanimous goals. Some people however, use extraversion to mask a dark side. This is an effective façade, because extraverts are perceived as physically attractive,[43] confident, adventuresome, sociable, and enthusiastic.[44] In addition, compared to introverts, extraverts are more competitive and ambitious, spend more time socializing, and pursue fame.[45]

Are they relationship material? In general, extraverts tend to have more sexual partners[46] and prefer short-term mating.[47] Regarding gender differences, extraversion is linked with less relational commitment in women.[48] One study examining British adults showed that extraverted women were more likely to leave existing partners for new ones, while male extraversion was linked with promiscuity.[49]

But wait a minute, you might be thinking, I have plenty of outgoing friends who prefer short-term relationships. Does that necessarily mean they have a dark personality? Absolutely not. There are a variety of reasons people avoid intimacy. Let's look at some of the traits of concern.

High extraversion mixes with low agreeableness to link Dark Triad personality traits with short-term mating styles.[50] Consider how all three Dark Triad traits are involved.

Some extraverts are narcissists, whose desire for the spotlight drives them to be outgoing and attention seeking.[51] Narcissists, however, come across as not only extraverted, but also charming and entertaining.[52] They are able to engage others quickly and make positive first impressions.[53] Functionally impulsive and eager, they thrive in short-term social settings[54] where their self-confidence and charisma generates energy that fascinates other people.[55]

However, look at the FLAGs. Because although up front, narcissists can sizzle with a myriad of positive qualities, including confidence, excitement, and charisma,[56] their lifestyle might provide more accurate clues.

Seeking to uncover behavioral patterns of narcissists in everyday life rather than in a laboratory setting, researchers had college students wear digital audio recorders programmed to record intermittently throughout the day.[57] Results revealed that narcissists were not only more extraverted (talking about friends for example), they were also disagreeable (swearing), and used more sexual language—which may help to explain the link between narcissism and promiscuous short-term sexual strategies.[58]

Relevant to the date rape example, extraversion is also linked with Machiavellianism—which is associated with hostile attitudes about sex and promiscuity,[59] as well as sexually coercive behavior.[60] Machiavellians are willing to obtain sex by force as well as through deceptive sexual tactics such as cheating, insincere expressions of love, betraying confidences, and procuring sex by inducing intoxication.[61] And an evening with a Machiavellian is unlikely to involve sensitivity or warmth, because Machiavellians are emotionally cold.[62]

Rounding out the Dark Triad, extraversion can also be linked with psychopathy.[63] The bottom line is to look further than superficial gregariousness in order to uncover the true motives of that life-of-the-party stranger your friend just met, *before* she leaves the bar with him.

Everyone Loves a Good Mystery:
Infatuation by Intrigue

Some people avoid commitment because they are simply not interested in a relationship. Ironically, some of the strategies they use to avoid intimacy actually serve to *increase* their desirability. Here is how it happens.

A friend of mine named Jill meets Justin, an FBI agent. They meet at a dive bar where he is out with coworkers—a factor that is more revealing in retrospect than it was at the time. Having grown up watching every episode of the *X-Files*, Jill is wildly curious about the life of a real federal agent, and the fact that Justin is evasive about his job description only makes him more alluring.

They go on a few casual dates, but he is not opening up. When she asks questions about his personal life, he plays the artful dodger nonresponsive and evasive. He is also slow in responding to her e-mails and voice mail messages. *He must be busy,* she thinks. When they run into some of his colleagues at a sports bar one night, he does not introduce her. Again, she gives him the benefit of the doubt. *Probably slipped his mind.*

When Jill's friends warn her that Justin's nonchalant attitude signals disinterest, she contends that he is just being cautious. After all, given the work that he does, he probably just wants to move slowly. Actually, Justin doesn't want to move at all—and it has nothing to do with his job.

For men like Justin, dating relationships are casual and the focus is purely physical. They intentionally avoid incorporating sexual partners into their life, preferring to associate with colleagues without significant others.

Justin's relational style demonstrates a tactical avoidance of commitment.[64] Indications of this type of short-term relationship strategy include inaction, such as failing to return messages or ignoring a partner, avoiding physical intimacy such as "cuddling," and failing to introduce a partner to family and friends.[65] In order to increase their chances of hooking up with like-minded partners, many of these guys patronize dive bars— just like the one where Jill met Justin in the first place.

Less Is More:
The Appeal of Uncertainty

As a general rule, secrets are relationship saboteurs. They breed distrust and inhibit intimacy. So how did Jill became so infatuated with Justin in a relationship that was both secretive and a superficial? It is because in a dating context, sometimes less is more. When a person does not know very much about a prospective romantic partner, the uncertainty can be alluring.[66] Some women find men to be more attractive when the man's affections are uncertain.[67]

This phenomenon, illustrated through the "he loves me he loves me not" routine of picking petals off a flower, demonstrates the fact that uncertainty regarding a person's affections may cause us to think about them more intently—and more favorably.[68]

Truth be told, Jill's fascination with Justin was also heightened by her ignorance of his actual job responsibilities, which allowed her imagination to run wild. She imagined him, as an FBI agent, spending his days chasing fugitives and engaging in gun battles like the ones she has seen on TV. Having worked with many FBI agents, I knew there was a better chance that he was sitting at his desk returning phone calls and writing crime reports. But who was I to ruin a good fantasy?

Spotting the Short-Timer

Justin was not interested in a relationship because he was young, handsome, and enjoyed variety. Like many people his age, he was drawn to a string of different partners simply because they were *new*.

A study researching the attractiveness of opposite-sex faces revealed that men prefer new faces over familiar faces—demonstrating an attraction to novelty in considering possible sexual partners.[69] This result is believed to indicate men's preference for new sexual partners, compared to women's.[70]

Experiments show that male rats that are satiated with their sexual partner will regain their libido when the partner is replaced with a new one.[71] Clearly, we don't want to automatically generalize these results to humans, although such a correlation is possible.[72]

Men around the world admit to wanting sexual variety. Out of a sample of 16,000 people across ten world regions, men expressed a higher desire to experience sexual variety than women.[73] Further, when researchers investigating gender differences in the willingness to have casual sex approached people on a college campus and asked if they would have sex with them, 72 percent of the men agreed, compared to none of the women.[74]

With these results in mind, warning FLAGs of a serial first dater include a focus on attractive alternatives instead of on a current partner, a lifestyle that includes frequently associating with potential romantic interests in social settings, and goal-directed behavior in pursuit of meeting new people.

Some people who prefer short-term relationships simply seek variety. Others have darker traits. All three Dark Triad traits are correlated with a preference for short-term relationships, a goal often pursued through strategies of intimacy avoidance to prevent "entangling commitments."[75] The fact that men with Dark Triad personalities use short-term mating strategies might explain why they often have lower standards in selecting romantic partners.[76]

Regarding relational preferences, narcissists prefer "friends with benefits" and one-night stands, while psychopaths prefer "booty-calls."[77] Machiavellianism is linked with promiscuity.[78]

Not only do people with Dark Triad personality employ game-playing love styles,[79] they also engage in mate poaching.[80] In the end, a short-term relationship with a dark personality might be for the best, since all three Dark Triad traits are linked with conflict in long-term relationships and marital dissatisfaction due to low agreeableness.[81]

Star Struck:
Blinded by the Limelight

It is a chaotic scene outside the courthouse when a celebrity is arriving for his or her first court appearance. Scores of onlookers crowd around the roped off press area where the "perp walk" is scheduled to occur. Some hold up handmade signs of support, while others have brought photos or other items that they hope the accused will autograph. Some hold their phones in the air, eager to catch a snapshot of their favorite celebrity during the walk of shame.

One of the most interesting aspects of such events, considering the occasion, is the fact that most of the people in attendance are not gathered to throw stones. They are gathered to show support. Regardless of the crime, I always hear loyal voices above the fray. "We love you!" "We know you are innocent!" Sometimes I hear young women squealing with delight as the defendant finally arrives and walks past them, sometimes waving and smiling, flanked by his lawyers.

I sometimes ask supporters if they know what crime a particular celebrity defendant is charged with having committed. I receive a range of answers. Some are brutally honest: "No." Others guess: "Some type of white-collar crime?" Still others demonstrate the blinding effect of celebrity power: "I don't care—that guy is my hero!"

These people are blinded by the limelight. Famous people bring positive excitement that overshadows negative information. Here is how it happens.

The Fascination of Fame:
Seeing Past the Spotlight

Society has long been fascinated with famous people.[82] We are fascinated by their lives, successes, and failures, and hunger for information provided through programs such as *Access Hollywood* and *Entertainment Tonight*.[83]

While most people do not mingle with Hollywood luminaries, they do know people of prominent status within a smaller social community. These big fish in small ponds include everyone from city mayors and local newscasters to church pastors and prolific university professors. Many of these local personalities are exciting to spend time with because of the stimulation they provide, offering a rousing break from the normal routine.

Unfortunately, however, some people tend to mentally airbrush the already sanitized image that many of these people project, which can cause them to miss signs that their favorite local celeb is not as great as they appear in the spotlight. Because unlike the bright house lights in a bar at closing time, the bright lights of fame do not accentuate flaws, they hide them. That is why when trying to detect the FLAGs of people of prominence, we have to look more closely.

For example, I know this is going to really surprise you, but one of the risks of being famous, whether on a large scale or small scale, is having "star power" go to your head. The result? Celebrity narcissism.

Acquired situational narcissism describes the phenomenon where people in positions of high power, such as celebrities, acquire narcissistic traits by virtue of their position.[84] Studies show that celebrities have more narcissistic traits than the general public,[85] and female celebrities exhibit more narcissistc traits than their male counterparts.[86]

Celebrity narcissism is not only problematic from a bad-looks-good perspective; it can be contagious. The general public can be influenced by celebrity narcissism, glamorizing self-indulgent behavior as the new normal, and something to be emulated.[87] For example, one study found that people who watched narcissistic behavior on reality television programs exhibit more narcissistic behavior themselves than people who watched drama.[88]

Reality TV personalities exhibit the greatest number of narcissistic traits, followed by comedians, actors, and musicians.[89] In fact, the success of Reality TV stars is believed to stem from the initial appeal of their narcissistic persona, which prompts producers and agents to hire them, while their enduring success may be due to the narcissistic tendency to provide entertainment through creating drama.[90]

So before you roll out the red carpet, how can you be sure your favorite local celebrities are truly as good as they look? Consider their FLAGs in examining the way they use their money, status, and influence. Many public figures spend their free time focused on charitable causes and philanthropic pursuits, while embracing a lifestyle of healthy, responsible living. They donate money, volunteer at charity events, and are spokespeople for societal and environmental causes.

Famous people also reveal their true colors through their preferred associations. Some of them mentor young people, are family-oriented, and endear themselves to fans by attending awards ceremonies with a spouse or sibling instead of bringing a controversial date as a publicity stunt. You can also learn much from the way someone in the limelight treats their friends and acquaintances—especially those who can do nothing to further their career.

Naturally, the goals people hold speak volumes about their character. Your observations may assist you in determining whether a politician is running for office out of a sincere desire to improve the standard of living for the citizens in his or her district, or with self-focused goals of power or fame.

The Seduction of Sensationalism

Some people generate excitement through creating a scene—wherever they go. I prosecuted one man for starting a series of public riots. He was an animal rights activist, protesting in front of stores that sold animal fur. He was loud, animated, and wildly energetic, and really knew how to rile up a crowd.

At the scenes of the riots he caused, he would usually end up on the roof of the building, wearing a cape and lit up like a Christmas tree with ropes of flashing lights, shouting on a bullhorn as the voices of his supporters gained volume.

He had the same effect in the courtroom, where after furiously whirling in like the Tasmanian devil, his flamboyance and histrionics provided far more amusement than the facts of his case. He was also *pro per*, representing himself. While self-representation normally means you either have a "fool for a lawyer" or a "fool for a client" (usually both), it also means the defendant and the prosecutor have to communicate directly. Every time this guy called me, I have to admit—it was usually the most entertaining conversation I had all day.

Interesting people provide welcome stimulation. In many cases, the more unusual the better. When I am conducting research on the Internet and observe a link to the profile of someone who has compiled a statistical analysis of sex offenses in Western countries, I won't go near it unless I absolutely must, even though the analysis is relevant to my profession. However, as busy as I am, I might click on a link that teases: "See Lady Gaga's weirdest outfits yet!"

Some call it morbid curiosity. Given the "normal" (some would say mundane) lives many people lead, unusual people are fascinating—particularly when they possess a mixed bag of traits. One of the most alluring traits in that colorful grab bag is talent. While talent can be enormously attractive,[91] it sometimes mixes with self-destructive tendencies to produce notorious characters who become even more well known as their fame evolves into infamy.

In fact, over time, some people become better known for their flamboyant, destructive behavior than for the talent with which they originally rose to fame. Nonetheless, sometimes, especially when they are behaving badly, fallen stars continue to capture headlines around the world. They also usually manage to maintain a loyal following even *after* their fall from grace.

You might be thinking, who would want to become involved with someone merely because they are unusual or different? Instinctively, this does not sound like a good match, and it usually isn't. However, people do it all the time—often leading to what are known as fatal attractions.

Fatal Attraction:
How to Avoid Getting Burned by the Flame

Some people are hopelessly attracted to and excited by unusual people and begin relationships with these oddballs despite an almost complete lack of common ground. Not surprisingly, such fascination often fizzles, and qualities that were initially attractive become irritating or even repulsive. Described as *fatal attraction,* the moth getting too close to the flame analogy occurs when romantic partners go from "nice to passive" and "strong to stubborn," "outgoing to over the top," and "exciting to scary."[92]

Fatal attractions are found more frequently when initially attractive characteristics include extreme traits, whether unique or different.[93] Although becoming involved with a partner who is different in some way can make a person feel special, it can lead to trouble down the road.[94] When partners are different from each other, or from the average person, such as when one partner is unusual or extreme in some sense, it can generate disillusionment over time.[95]

Examples of this "enchantment to disenchantment" dynamic include the woman drawn to an aloof partner because of his carefree attitude toward life, who over time ends up viewing him as immature.[96] Or the man who is attracted to a woman of strong character who ends up irritated with her behavior, describing her as "domineering" and "pushy."[97]

Some people present an incompatible mix of traits that should certainly have signaled trouble from the beginning. Researchers provide the example of a woman who is a "bookworm" in one setting and a "college girl gone wild" in another as likely to be viewed as unreliable and therefore an undesirable partner.[98] A partner's different identities can also hinder relational success when they are inconsistent emotionally (enemy or friend) or logically (Republican or Democrat).[99]

We can take steps to avoid fatal attractions by examining FLAGs at the outset, instead of sugarcoating undesirable qualities because we find the person to be stimulating, or disregarding signs of incompatibility.

For example, interesting people who are flamboyant and attention seeking are frequently self-focused, instead of being concerned with the welfare of others. Regarding compatibility, because fatal attractions often involve fascination with a person's *unfamiliar* lifestyle, consider whether you are interested in adapting to the other person's routine, and if so, how you would fit in.

Do you have any friends in common? Would you want to? How often does the person you find so interesting associate with people like you? Are you anxious about how you are going to introduce the person to your family and friends?

Finally, if you become involved with someone who walks to the beat of a different drum, consider what goals and objectives the person is pursuing in adopting an image and lifestyle that is so drastically different from the mainstream—and whether you want to run the risk of being judged guilty by association.

SEPARATING SINCERITY FROM STIMULATION

Focus: Well-adjusted adrenaline junkies focus on more than thrill seeking. They are also focused on work, family, and safety.

Lifestyle: The extent to which a sensation seeker's lifestyle revolves around his or her passion indicates availability, amenability, and interest in personal relationships. Die-hard scuba divers often live near the ocean. Mountain climbers and expert skiers live thousands of feet above sea level. Consider whether these people will compromise, or expect partners to acclimate.

Associations: Healthy extreme sports enthusiasts often join clubs to meet like-minded athletes, demonstrating a desire to bond with others In their quest for adventure. Antisocial risk takers prefer solo sensation seeking.

Goals: Long-term goals often distinguish well-rounded thrill seekers from those who are merely chasing the next endorphin fix.

9

Forbidden Fruit

The Temptation of Taboo

The photo goes viral within the hour. The well-known politician, married with children, posing with a scantily clad, tattooed, exotic dancer. Apparently, they have been having an affair for over a year.

What? Why would an elected official with a family begin a relationship that could ruin both his marriage and his career? There might be multiple reasons. He might be bored, sexually preoccupied, looking for adventure, or seeking new experiences. However, one of the possible reasons is counterintuitive: he might be aroused by the fact that under the circumstances, his choice of a partner is *wrong*.

The Appeal of Wrong

In my line of work, I not only see bad people doing bad things, I also see *good* people doing bad things. This results from indulging the one drive I see more often than most people—the desire to engage in behavior because it is *wrong*. This explanation is baffling, yet I see it repeatedly.

A pilot takes a selfie in the cockpit during a flight with a pretty blond passenger—who posts it on Facebook. A couple of straight *A* students drink to excess and then drag race on the freeway in the middle of the night. We shake our heads in disbelief.

While we don't always know what prompts such mischief, sometimes we do. Because while most people are not motivated *solely* by the desire to misbehave, in some of the cases I have handled, people admit that the wrongfulness of their actions was part of the allure.

I have listened to pyromaniacs express the excitement, sometimes even sexual arousal that sparked their desire, so to speak, to set fires. I have watched video footage adult men sent to underage girls showing them masturbating in front of the camera while their wives can be seen sleeping in bed in the background. Incredible, right? Yet corroborated by research.

In *Seductions of Crime: Moral and Sensual Attractions in Doing Evil*, in a chapter aptly entitled "Sneaky Thrills," Jack Katz uses an example of two rich boys driving around in a new red Firebird one of them had just received for his sixteenth birthday, stealing a pizza from a delivery boy's car.[1] Despite the fact that they weren't hungry—one of the thieves described it as the best pizza they had ever tasted.[2]

Some of you may remember when actress Winona Ryder was convicted of shoplifting from Saks Fifth Avenue. Could she not afford to pay for the merchandise? While her motivation was not determined, some shoplifters steal for the thrill of committing the crime and to enjoy the sensation of risk and game-playing, rather than because of a desire for the stolen items themselves.[3]

Sometimes people expose themselves to things they know they shouldn't be looking at, such as nudity. In some of my cases, I have to display blown-up photographs of a perpetrator's penis because a distinguishing characteristic was described by the victim. Although they understand it is necessary to prove identity, many jurors are visibly uncomfortable conducting this examination.

Not everyone, however, experiences this discomfort. Researchers studying voyeurism discovered that a significant percentage of people surveyed admitted they would watch an attractive person undressing if they knew they wouldn't be caught.[4] Some people (more men than women) admitted they would watch two attractive people having sex if they knew they wouldn't be detected.[5]

The Fascination of the Forbidden

Individuals often look more attractive when they are "off limits." This can occur because things can appear more arousing when people know they are not supposed to be looking at them. Sometimes *especially* when they know they should not be looking. When someone takes a step toward pursuing the prohibited object of his or her affection, the excitement can become overpowering.

Some people who work for companies that prohibit dating other employees joke that this prohibition (which is violated all the time) only increases the perceived attractiveness of coworkers, even those whom they might not look twice at on the street.

From this relatively tame example, it gets much worse. A woman with a loving family begins an extramarital affair with her son's Harley-riding guitar teacher. A successful businessman takes a detour on the way home to buy thirty minutes from a prostitute, then sprays himself with cologne before going home to greet his wife and children. And stereotypical "good girls" around the world continue to fall for "bad boys" with reputations to match.

Whether they involve infidelity, indecency, inappropriateness, or illegality such as liaisons with underage girls, good people sometimes seek bad relationships. Paradoxically, the allure is not compatibility, but impropriety.

Popular films have romanticized unsuitable relationships, portraying characters caught in love triangles with archetypes of both appropriate and inappropriate partners. Men must choose between the Madonna and the Whore; women are torn between the Prince and the Scoundrel, or the Hero and the Villain.[6] Unlike in the movies, however, people caught in real life love triangles do not always make the right choice.

Some people can be wrong based on the situation. Just like the song

"Jesse's Girl" by Rick Springfield, expressing the singer's obsession with another man's paramour, someone might be a great person with positive FLAGs, but dating your best friend.

Other partners are wrong because of social conventions and taboos. The pastor of the local church should not be dating a stripper, nor should the city mayor, or the local elementary school principal. Professional ethics prohibit certain types of relationships as well, such as between a psychiatrist and a patient, or a lawyer and a client. And the list goes on.

As a prosecutor, I am kept busy with cases involving people who stray off the path in pursuit of relationships that are illegal. Unfortunately, however, it happens far more often than we can detect. Contrary to the wide-eyed professions of men on television caught in underage sting operations that this is their "first time," it probably isn't.

Why do people persist in pursuing things that are prohibited? Let us begin by examining the appetizing allure of forbidden fruit.

The Sweet Aroma of Forbidden Fruit

We have long recognized the enhanced appeal of the forbidden. This phenomenon has been demonstrated empirically in many different situations. From certain types of foods[7] to warning labels on violent television programming[8] and video games[9] to cigarette smoking,[10] research shows that some things are more attractive when they are restricted or prohibited.

Let's start literally. Forbidden fruit not only looks good, it often smells and tastes good too. Whether our weakness is freshly baked doughnuts, ballpark hot dogs, or ice-cold Dr. Pepper, we are not inclined to avoid these delicacies because we know they are unhealthy. To the contrary, their lack of nutritional value often makes them more appealing because they become *temptations*.

And when we are on a diet, all bets are off. Forbidden fruit is almost *irresistible*. Research shows that people on a diet are selectively attentive to appetizing food cues.[11] Even chronic dieters overindulge when presented with desired foods.[12]

The same phenomenon is observed with alcohol, cigarettes, and other addictive substances.[13] Regular users pay more attention to drug-related cues, especially when they are trying to abstain or are battling cravings, resulting in increased motivation to use the drug.[14]

In the case of warning labels on violent films, studies show that films were perceived as more attractive when the U.S. Surgeon General was the source, compared to labels with no source.[15] With violent video games, the more restrictive the age label on the game, the more attractive it was judged to be.[16] With smoking, its status as taboo clothed it with positive arousal, pleasure, and excitement.[17] With food restrictions (parents: listen to this), researchers discovered that children would eat more of the restricted foods—whether the food was candy or fruit![18]

The desire for forbidden fruit is explained by *reactance theory*, where our desire to engage in prohibited behavior is heightened by restricting our freedom to do so.[19] *Commodity theory* holds that something perceived as unavailable or hard to get is viewed as more coveted. [20]

Forbidden fruit theory also explains the allure of forbidden relationships. For adolescents, forbidden friends may become forbidden fruit—leading to an increased desire to spend time with deviant peers.[21] Parental disapproval and prohibition of adolescent friendships have been found to predict *more* contact with deviant peers one year later, and indirectly predict increased adolescent delinquency two years later.[22]

It is suggested that the desire to spend time with "bad" friends in adolescence stems from suppressed autonomy imposed by restrictive parents, which can increase both the frequency and the intensity of adolescent contact with delinquent peers.[23]

Forbidden relationships often include participating in forbidden behavior, such as sexual activity. Predators exploit this desire by catering to the curiosity of preteens who know they are too young to be experimenting, which often makes the temptation even greater.

The Wolf in Sharp Clothing

The temptation to prematurely engage in sexual activity is heightened when proposed by the already *wrong* type of boyfriend. Especially a handsome, *older* boyfriend with a fancy car. Bad men know this. Consider how pimps and human traffickers seduce their victims.

Vanessa is initially startled when the shiny red Corvette convertible pulls up beside her as she is walking to school. The handsome young man behind the wheel rolls down the window, flashing a smile as bright as his car.

He immediately tells her how "hot" she looks and asks if she has a boyfriend. Vanessa keeps walking, trying to obey the instructions of her parents not to talk to strangers. But she answers his questions because she is flattered by his attention, and impressed by his flamboyant good looks. She is especially impressed by his car. A block later she climbs in.

The man tells Vanessa his name is Rock Star, and he asks to see her the following day . . . and the day after. Before long they are spending time together every day. At school, Vanessa has become quite the rock star herself. Previously an unknown, she is now the envy of her peers when her "older" boyfriend rolls up in his flashy car to pick her up from school.

Then there are the presents. Rock Star buys her sexy clothes and a *real* Gucci bag, which she proudly shows to her increasing number of friends, but hides from her parents. He even gives her a cell phone so they can communicate without her parents finding out—which only adds to the excitement of the secret relationship.

Here comes the catch. Rock Star's attention does not come for free. Although Vanessa was a virgin, Rock Star convinces her to have sex with him. While a twenty-three-year-old, he is ten years her senior, she agrees because she is in love with him and believes that as soon as she is old enough, they will get married.

After about a month, Rock Star drops the bomb. He tells Vanessa she is so good at sex he would like her to sell it for him—so he can start putting the money aside for their future together. At first she is shocked.

Rock Star calmly explains, however, that if she doesn't do it, he will find another girl who will. That would mean a breakup—which to young Vanessa would be devastating.

Reluctantly, Vanessa agrees. Once she services her first "customer," there is no turning back.

Infatuation Masks Exploitation:
The Focus Beneath the Flash

By the time I meet girls like Vanessa they are well past their first customer—but not past the delusional notion that their boyfriend-turned-pimp cares about them.

Sadly, her case is not unusual; this sort of thing happens every day. I have prosecuted many young men like Rock Star for human trafficking, pimping, and pandering, and am familiar with the relational dynamics that facilitate the progression from boyfriend to pimp. Unlike documentary portrayals of human trafficking victims bound by physical chains, most victims are bound by emotional chains, which while invisible, are much stronger. By the time we finally make an arrest, many of these girls have already become entrenched in the lifestyle; some have even tattooed the names of their pimp on their bodies, sometimes including the words "property of."

While many people suffer from the "not in my backyard" delusion that trafficking activity only occurs in other countries, the Rock Stars of the world are not only in your backyard, they are in your front yard as well.

Hunting in packs, they boldly cruise school yards, bus stops, movie theatres, and other locations where young women are likely to be hanging out without their parents. One of their most popular hunting grounds is the shopping mall food court—where they know adults feel comfortable dropping off teenagers to spend time with friends. How do you spot these predators? Their focus is not on the selection of pizza, but the selection of prey.

Like a pedophile in a playground, they assess potential victim receptivity. Once they select a target, they approach girls the same way Rock

Star approached Vanessa. They come on strong, showering victims with attention and gifts while showcasing a flashy lifestyle of money and power. These men are incredibly dangerous sharks in the water and are coming soon to a mall near you, if they aren't already there.

One of the warning signs Vanessa might have seen was Rock Star's shift in focus from her—to how she could make money for him. In his own words, she was his cash cow. Young and energetic, she can meet with up to twenty customers a day. How much of the money she makes does she give to Rock Star? Believe it or not, *all of it.*

The money was used to support Rock Star's lifestyle, which involved living out of motel rooms, shared with other pimps and young girls like Vanessa. In fact, he even asked Vanessa if she had any friends who she could introduce to him.

What was Rock Star's goal? Not marriage, but money. This is the glorified single-minded ambition of the pimping subculture. These individuals are not working toward finding legitimate employment or obtaining a college degree. They are looking for a quick profit through exploiting women.

Here is another challenge presented by the forbidden fruit phenomenon. Had Vanessa's parents found out about Rock Star and tried to forbid the relationship, it might have been even more appealing.

Fanning the Flames:
Forbidden Romance

Most people are familiar with the story of Tony and Maria in *West Side Story*, as well as *Romeo and Juliet*. Scholars studying what they termed the "Romeo and Juliet Effect" sought to explore the mythological beliefs about forbidden love—that is, "The more the flame is covered up, the hotter it burns." [24] As expected, they discovered that parental interference in a romantic relationship intensified the romantic feelings.[25]

C. Nathan DeWall and coauthors (2011) tested the forbidden fruit theory within adult relationships.[26] Rationalizing that overt attempts at constraining a person's consideration of attractive alternatives (such as through a jealous partner) would likely increase the attractiveness of those alternatives through classic reactance theory, they chose to implicitly constrain attention to alternatives through distraction.[27]

The results? They found that implicitly preventing people from paying attention to desirable romantic alternatives decreased perceived satisfaction and commitment within existing relationships, and increased positive attitudes toward infidelity.[28] It also increased attention paid to romantic alternatives, as well as memory of the alternatives.[29]

The topic of relational alternatives brings us to one of the most common types of forbidden relationships: the affair. While people engage in affairs for many reasons, there are some common themes. Researchers suggest that the "thrilling significance" of affairs stems from the fact that they provide a break from ordinary mundane existence, instead involving "hotels, resorts, conferences, fast cars, back rooms, snatched moments of meretricious bliss separated from the context of an orderly, predictable and repetitive life."[30]

Other affairs embody the often used sentiment about "wrong feeling so right." Some people satisfy appropriate feelings through inappropriate partners who make them feel vibrant, alive, young, and sexy. The temptation to indulge can be further enhanced within a relationship that is supposed to be purely professional—a complication that often adds an additional layer of stimulation. When faced with this type of forbidden fruit, some people, against their better judgment, decide to take a bite.

Virtual Fruit Looks Just as Good

The cases that land on my desk involve more than infidelity. They involve illegality. Imprudent, clandestine pairings between teenage girls and older men that flourish from the privacy of a teenager's iPhone, right under the noses of her parents.

How does it happen? A thirteen-year-old girl describes the attraction of her secret relationship with her thirty-one-year-old online paramour: "He cared about me. That's what our relationship was about. He was a positive influence in my life, and I enjoyed being the only one from my world who knew Mark. He listened to my feelings about the people and circumstances around me. And he always supported me with encouragement and advice."[31] In time, this young girl found out that this man had lied about not only his age, but even his name.[32]

In another case, a woman characterizes her secret, online relationship as a teenager with a thirty-seven-year-old married man as an *addiction*.[33] Thinking about this man, whom she had never met, monopolized her time and disrupted her concentration.[34] In order to avoid the withdrawal symptoms she would suffer when he seemed to be losing interest, she would e-mail him sexually explicit photos of herself in order to regain his attention.[35] In fact, she would send photos or engage in provocative conversation just to hear him call her "honey" or "sweetie."[36]

In addition to the inappropriate nature of such relationships, there is often the added stimulation of secrecy.

The Seduction of Secret

Secrecy fuels the appeal of clandestine relationships.[37] Just ask the young teenager who has to sneak around with her outlaw boyfriend. Or the young business executive who is dating her boss in a company where such fraternization is forbidden. Some relationships are arousing specifically because they have to be kept under wraps.

Even the initiation of these relationships is a thrill. Two people with the same group of friends who shouldn't become involved because they are dating other people spend all evening talking at a party, leading to the exchange of private cell phone numbers.

Over the course of the next two weeks, the pair exchange an increasing number of text messages, unable to harness their budding mutual attraction. When they are in public amid their social group, they are giddy with exhilaration as they exchange furtive glances, unable to suppress the silly smiles that accompany the game.

Even child molestation victims admit being attracted to the secrecy of their relationship with the offender. The perpetrator's instructions not to tell anyone about the relationship because it is "our secret" can cause victims to feel special and loved.[38]

Secrecy appears to enhance arousal in connection with both past and current relationships. Research participants reported that they were more likely to obsess over past relationships that were secret, and demonstrated more arousal to other study participants with whom they participated in the clandestine method of flirtation known as "footsie" under the table with others present.[39]

One consistent feature of secret relationships is the increased obsession that is generated by the attempted thought suppression associated with trying to keep a relationship under wraps.[40] Active thought suppression can lead to a rebound effect, causing increasing thinking about the thoughts that were suppressed.[41] This is especially true when the suppressed thoughts are secretive, exciting, and relationship related.[42]

While trying to suppress exciting thoughts can make them more exciting,[43] the arousal generated varies depending on the types of thoughts. Not surprisingly, research shows that more arousal is experienced when trying not to think about sex than dancing.[44]

Forbidden Fruit FLAGs Failure

The FLAGs flying within forbidden relationships are bright red in all four areas. This is because healthy relationships are not designed to be secret.

An individual's focus will be torn between his or her legitimate relationship and whomever they are seeing on the sly—likely causing relational distress with both partners. The strategy involved in leading a double life requires dishonesty, and reveals one of the major drawbacks of secret relationships: someone who is willing to sneak around with *you* might also sneak around behind your back. Relational dishonesty is rarely confined to only one relationship.

Stealth dating partners are unlikely to spend time with each other's friends or family, which prevents them from assessing the type and quality of their partner's respective associations. It also means that there is no opportunity to have a paramour vetted by trusted confidants, depriving both partners of the wisdom of multiple points of view.

What is the goal of spending time with someone who is "off limits"? Either the partners will outgrow the thrill of living under the radar and move on, or one of them will demand legitimacy. Either way, secret relationships usually are a waste of valuable time that people can never get back.

Seeking the Scoundrel

Why do women swoon over Johnny Depp's character Captain Jack Sparrow in *Pirates of the Caribbean*? Because some women are fascinated with intelligent, ruthless manipulators. Especially when they are handsome and charismatic.

I have handled cases where women pursued controversial public figures and infamous dethroned celebrities who engaged in deplorable misconduct. By their own admissions, they were aroused by the lurid details and scandalous nature of their partner's behavior. Unfortunately, they learned the hard way that their paramour was an equal opportunity offender who had no qualms about manipulating them as well.

While most women approach these ill-advised relationships with the belief that they are "the one" their man really loves, these unholy pairings usually result in the men behaving exactly the way they did in the past. From their perspectives, they haven't found "the one," but "the next one." The next victim, that is. Consider the following case.

The defendant's reputation preceded him. A petty criminal, his hustle was taking advantage of affluent women who were looking for an exciting, handsome man to spend time with. His low-level crimes were often hard to prove, but always included drama-filled story lines, attracting crowds of "court watchers"—members of the public who enjoyed watching trials, finding fact stranger than fiction.

Playing to his audience, this guy was an even better con artist in the courtroom than he was on the street. Handsome and witty, he spent most of the time on breaks joking around with the bailiff, his attorney, and the court staff. As hard as I tried to be the one serious face in the courtroom, I almost lost it one day when he burst into a *Saturday Night Live* skit that had the rest of his audience in stitches.

I prayed that no one would see my red face and watering eyes as I tried to hold back the laughter. Did I forget what this guy did? No. The defendant told me after the trial that he intentionally selected courtroom jokes he thought I would like.

As the trial continued, I found myself hoping he wouldn't testify. With his sense of humor and charisma, he would have the jury eating out of his hand by the time he was done. He did testify. And he walked.

The Man Your Mother Warned You About:
Detecting FLAGs of Darkness

This defendant was the proverbial man your mother warned you about. The most memorable thing about his case was that his latest victim was an attractive, successful real estate broker who went into the relationship with her eyes wide open. She knew all about his history—how feigning romantic interest in other women was his modus operandi to exploiting their resources.

His relational background is exactly what intrigued her. Like the court watchers, she was curious. Fascinated, actually. Unfortunately, she allowed her fascination to overcome her judgment.

What are some of the red flags that an attentive suitor has a dark personality? Psychopaths are usually focused on themselves, and on the present. They lead a lifestyle of irresponsibility, impulsivity, and the absence of meaningful goals.[45]

Like the petty criminal in my case, many psychopaths live as parasites.[46] It is estimated that almost 90 percent of women who have become involved with psychopaths have slid from six figure incomes to financial ruin due to the psychopath's parasitic lifestyle.[47] In fact, psychopaths live off the profits of others even when they don't need the money.[48]

A psychopath's interpersonal associations are often superficial.[49] The quest for novelty and continual stimulation keeps him moving between relationships to avoid boredom.[50] And having never really become emotionally attached, a psychopath will forget about past partners quickly. This was painfully evident in my case during the trial, where this despicable man, who performed as the courtroom clown during breaks, never even glanced at his latest victim/ex-fiancé when she testified with tears in her eyes that she was still in love with him.

As to goals, sure he had one. To find the next woman to manipulate—which apparently didn't take him long. I saw him at a swanky restaurant downtown about a month after the trial, out with a new attractive woman. Unabashed when he saw me, he smiled broadly, and waved.

FLAGING THE FORBIDDEN

Focus: Is the person focused on you or the thrill of sneaking around with you? Are they interested in spending time with you in public or only in private?

Lifestyle: Is the person comfortable leading a clandestine lifestyle and is that part of the attraction? If your relationship became legitimate, would you still be interested?

Associations: Would you fit in with your partner's peer group and vice versa? Do you want to be seen with your partner in public, or would you be afraid of what other people would think?

Goals: Does your paramour intend to have an honest relationship with you? When?

Looking for Love in All the Wrong Places

"Where did you meet your husband?" I ask a woman who I am considering calling as a character witness in trial. "At work," she explains. Because

I know that until recently she worked as a correctional officer at a prison, I make a joke about the hectic lives of law enforcement couples.

"Well, he didn't *work* at the prison," she says. We stare at each other awkwardly for a minute, until I get it. Now I remember that she resigned from her job as a prison guard *in order to* get married. While she met her husband in the workplace, he was on the wrong side of the bars.

Let me tell you how this sort of thing happens. In my former career as a criminal defense attorney, I frequently went into the jail to talk with my clients. While there are strict rules regarding what a visitor can bring into a custodial setting, one thing never left at the door is vulnerability to manipulation. Criminals know this, and the smart ones know how to exploit it.

A gang member in prison describes his method of seducing a female correctional officer. He begins with a wink, progresses to conversation and cleverly thought-out letters, and gradually initiates sexual contact.[51] When the two are caught having sex, the officer is terminated and prosecuted.[52] Is she horrified in retrospect at her shocking lapse in judgment? No. To the contrary, she is still in love with him and writes him letters.[53]

Statistically, most cases of correctional staff sexual misconduct involve women becoming involved with male inmates.[54] Sometimes they not only engage in sexual relationships with these men, but they also tattoo their names on their bodies and bear their children.[55]

For those of you who think that all of this is beyond the pale, let me take it one step further. Some of these women reveal that they were *looking* for romance among the convicted felons on their ward. And like other cases of forbidden fruit, the wrongfulness of their conduct only served to increase the temptation.

The Wrong Place at the Right Time

Sometimes, when we give in to temptation we have only ourselves to blame. We ate the ice cream because it was in the freezer. We know we shouldn't keep it in the house, forcing ourselves to decide when the craving hits, whether it is worth driving all the way to the grocery store. (I keep my car keys by the front door.)

From this relatively harmless example, sadly, it gets much worse. Some people intentionally put themselves in positions to "run into" someone they know they should not be seeing. "I'm just looking," some of them say. But willful exposure to temptation is the first step.

Good people make sure they are not tempted to pick forbidden fruit by avoiding the tree. In the same way that a recovering alcoholic will stay out of a bar, a person experiencing inappropriate thoughts will stay away from the object of their misplaced desire. Instead of strategizing ways to cross paths with the person, they will avoid him or her like the plague.

Someone who won't give you the time of day while they are committed to someone else will make a much better partner should circumstances change than the person who flirts with you notwithstanding their relationship status.

Faithful partners focus on maintaining the quality of their current relationships, not investigating who might be around the corner, whether in an online chat room for swingers or at the local singles bar after work. They don't spend time associating with others to whom they are attracted, on- or offline. They lead a lifestyle designed to minimize exposure to temptation with the goal of preserving healthy, honest relationships.

In order to stay the course, good people will also avoid associating with individuals who might lead them down the wrong path—no matter how desirable that path might appear. A recovering addict will avoid associating with people who are still using drugs. A married man will politely decline an invitation to join his bachelor friends who are meeting a group of women at a nightclub.

Believe it or not, some convicted child molesters express the desire to remain in custody to protect the community. I have handled cases where pedophiles have admitted that because they are still fantasizing about children, they want to remain incarcerated to ensure they don't act on their deviant thoughts and fantasies.

Whatever the temptation, avoidance is a much safer strategy than willing exposure. A person's FLAGs reveal which course they have chosen.

10

Seeking the Wolf

When Dangerous Is Desirable

I t is always interesting to learn where people met their spouses. Blind date? High school sweethearts? Online dating site?

I can tell you about one woman who married a man after saving his life. *How romantic,* you might think. But before you call her a heroine, let me explain. She didn't pull him from a burning car or revive him after he was fished out of a swimming pool. This woman met her husband in the courtroom, where she saved his life by refusing to vote for the death penalty with the other jurors, after convicting him for first-degree murder.[1] Five months later, they were married.[2]

Unbelievable, right? But true. Some jurors become fascinated with criminal defendants due to the "strange intimacy" created between the participants in a criminal trial.[3] They sit there often for days or weeks on end listening to endless details about a defendant's life, and over time, may develop romantic feelings.[4]

Having observed the courtroom-to-the-bedroom phenomenon for years, I am not phased. I had one juror after the trial express interest in contacting a defendant whose crimes were so gruesome that another juror had raised her hand mid-testimony to ask to take a break so she could go throw up.

A far cry from the lesson of the Little Red Riding Hood story—don't talk to strangers; in what I describe as the seeking-the-wolf phenomenon, some people pursue others who look good *because they look bad*.

Bad Is the New Good:
The Rise of the Dark Hero

The most popular character in the movie *The Dark Knight* was not Batman; it was The Joker, in the legendary performance of the late Heath Ledger. His malevolent character as a villain of pure evil captivated audiences and stole the show.

Some people view criminals as "folk heroes," living in the fantasy world of "badness" that law-abiding citizens only dream of.[5] Examples of criminals in this genre include characters such as Thelma and Louise and Bonnie and Clyde.[6] There is also cultural fascination with "antiheros" such as James Bond[7] who perform heroic deeds, yet have dark personalities.

In romantic literature, the desirability of "dark heroes" for short-term relationships demonstrates a preference for features that indicate superior genetic quality.[8] But dark heroes are not just literary fiction. There are many documented cases of women becoming involved with real-life dark heroes.

Sheila Isenberg, in *Women Who Love Men Who Kill*, explains that some women love convicted murderers because similar to the heroes in romance novels, they view these men as presenting an appealing mix of passion, violence, and tenderness.[9] One woman, married to a man convicted of kidnapping, rape, and murder, describes her husband as "sensitive to the tiniest of animals."[10] Other women view their convict mates as thoughtful, caring human beings, as their knights in shining armor, and as their salvation.[11]

The Dark Hero and the Dark Triad

Unfortunately, as attractive as they are, dark heroes often exhibit Dark Triad personality, which is linked with a myriad of antisocial personality traits such as criminality and aggressiveness.[12] Dark Triad traits are often revealed through the creation of a volatile, drama-rich environment—which satisfies a Dark Triad individual's desire for stimulation and impulsivity.[13]

Psychopaths can have hot tempers, isolate victims from their support system as predators isolate their prey in the wild, and even isolate their victims from outside interests, seeking to cultivate total dependence.[14] Demonstrating the value of soliciting multiple exposures, friends and family of the victim are key to recognizing this toxic relational progression. Because despite making a good first impression, psychopaths ultimately alienate their victim's support system—causing them to notice the offender's negative behavior, as well as the victim's negative personality changes.[15]

Notwithstanding the negative traits, the Dark Triad personality is attractive to women.[16] One explanation for the female attraction to the Dark Triad suggests that women may fall for men's attempt to sell themselves as well as their desired sexual strategy.[17] Another explanation is that women are attracted to "bad boys" who are prone to risk taking and exude hard-headedness and confidence.[18]

And confidence is sexy. As are men who behave in ways that demand respect. No one wants a man who is a welcome mat. Guys who are "too nice" are not appealing. In fact, research demonstrates that men are perceived to be more attractive when they do not appear to be happy.[19] When shown photos of men displaying emotions of happiness, shame, pride, and neutral expressions, men were judged to be most attractive when expressing pride, and least attractive when expressing happiness.[20] Researchers note that these results are consistent with evolutionary and gender-based principles linking pride with high-status,[21] and recognize that expressions of pride may transmit enhanced masculinity.[22]

The Dark Knight in Shining Body Armor

Some men are attractive because of the dangerous work they do through careers in law enforcement, the military, martial arts, or other jobs involving the potential use of deadly force. Many women are drawn to these men because dangerousness often signals the ability to defend and protect.

I have met countless women over the years who intentionally select partners with dangerous, authoritarian-type jobs that involve carrying a weapon and knowing how to use it. Some of these men make wonderful husbands who defend and protect their family. Others end up with their actions summarized in a domestic violence police report on my desk.

What makes the difference? The desire of some women to be cared for and protected leads them to place undue emphasis on the value of dangerous qualities, while downplaying darker personality traits. Consider the case of a woman who believes she has met her assertive, dominant knight in shining armor.

Richard makes a strong impression on his first date with Jessica at an expensive restaurant where he has reserved the best table. As the leader of the local SWAT team, he entertains Jessica throughout dinner with war stories and vivid descriptions of his work.

Jessica is not only impressed by his job, she is also impressed by his assertiveness. Not only does he order for both of them and select the wine, but also he demands that the waiter send back Jessica's steak when it is prepared incorrectly. Jessica perceives Richard's taking charge of the situation as comforting because it demonstrates that he can take care of her needs.

As their relationship develops, Richard quickly establishes himself as Jessica's sole source of support. He takes over paying the rent for her apartment and convinces her to quit her job because his income can support them both.

Richard doesn't, however, like to share. He insists on doing things as a couple, refusing to double date or meet Jessica's family for fear of being judged. While she is disappointed, Jessica tries to see his point of view.

When Richard proposes marriage, Jessica agrees, envisioning a life of stability, something she has always wanted. Richard arranges an exclusive destination wedding in Tahiti—a ceremony that is sparsely attended due to the exorbitant cost and remote location.

In less than a year, Richard's care has turned into control, and his protection has turned into possessiveness. Or were those negative traits there all along? Richard's professional life is on the rocks as well, as a result of several citizen complaints about his use of excessive force—something Jessica learns has been an ongoing pattern. She blames his flare-ups at home on job-related stress, reminding herself that the danger and unpredictability of law enforcement work must be taxing.

The last straw for Jessica comes when two police officers show up at their house in response to a 911 call from a neighbor who heard Richard screaming at her, accusing her of flirting with another man. Although Jessica tries to protect Richard by telling the officers the argument was all her fault, they notice the side of her face is swollen where he just slapped her, and he is arrested.

Jessica is devastated. Given his position within the law enforcement community, she explains that she did not anticipate his destructive, violent behavior. The few friends and family who have met Richard want to know—why not?

When What Growls Like a Wolf Is a Wolf

Some dangerous people are as scary as they look. Richard wasn't flying red flags at half-mast. To the contrary—the warning signs indicating his dangerousness seemed loud and clear. So how did Jessica get carried away?

Therapists are familiar with the reality that many women who are initially swept away by romantic bliss continue to defend abusive partners once the honeymoon is over.[23] Susan Forward and Joan Torres in *Men Who Hate Women and the Women Who Love Them* note that women in unhealthy relationships often focus on their partner's attractive traits, while dealing with unattractive traits through minimization and rationalization.[24]

I have observed this dynamic for years in working with victims of domestic violence. Intimate relationships present a mix of love and aggression[25] that is widespread and pervasive.[26] Believe it or not, however, relational aggression does not always result in relational dissatisfaction.[27] In fact, a significant percentage of recipients of aggression interpret it as evidence of the perpetrator's love.[28]

In the same way that a wife may be able to maintain a globally positive view of her marriage by blaming her husband's lack of emotional support on the stress of his job,[29] so victims of abuse make similar excuses. Not only do they "forgive and forget," they frequently externalize violence by blaming it on something outside the relationship,[30] as Jessica did.

Other domestic violence victims remain in abusive relationships because they misconstrue abuse as love, or attribute the abuse to something other than lack of care or concern.[31] A woman in an abusive relationship may thereby expose herself to risk of further abuse by excusing harmful behavior through benevolent attributions, and choosing to remain in the relationship.[32] Such failure to perceive the negative intentions of her partner may make it easier for her to forgive his behavior and remain emotionally attached.[33]

Unfortunately, such misperception can be a fatal mistake. While some men kill their partners in a jealous rage, others require no such provocation. I prosecuted one man who stabbed his wife to death because she was "running her mouth." Whatever the circumstances, we wonder if the capacity to commit such senseless violence could have been detected earlier.

HOW BAD LOOKS GOOD IN ABUSIVE RELATIONSHIPS

- Possessive looks protective.
- Controlling looks comforting.
- Aggressive looks assertive.
- Violent looks passionate.
- Rude looks direct.
- Condescending looks confident.
- Paranoid looks careful.

When Red Signals Danger, Not Passion

Violence is often predictable. A man initiating sexual activity with a woman he picked up at a bar reacts with viscious brutality as soon as he goes far enough to realize his partner is actually another man. The case lands on my desk within a matter of hours due to the severity of the victim's injuries. Yet I have seen equally violent reactions stemming from arguments over alleged cheating during a game of pool. The most predictive factor was not the provocation, but the predisposition.

Violent disposition is most frequently overlooked within romantic relationships. In the case of Richard and Jessica, Jessica was caught up in the romantic drama of becoming involved with a dangerous man. Yet her passion for his dominance was misplaced. We need look no further than the FLAGs Richard was flying on their first date to detect Richard's true colors.

From the beginning of the evening, Richard was focused on himself and on controlling his environment. Demonstrating brazen disregard for social etiquette, he monopolized the conversation, berated the servers, and even dictated Jessica's order. While a man ordering for a woman in a restaurant is not terribly unusual, in most cases the man has some indication of his date's preferences. Is she a vegetarian? A Vegan? Regarding the wine, how did Richard know Jessica wasn't a recovering alcoholic? Can you imagine?

Richard also failed "The Waitress Test."[34] The rude manner in which he demanded Jessica's steak be sent back to the kitchen was a sneak preview of the way *she* would be treated down the road.[35]

Richard lived a lifestyle of dominance and control—through violence if necessary. His heavy-handed method of upholding the law was documented through citizen complaints. And Richard was not a situational bully; he was an equal opportunity offender. As a result, he didn't associate with many people other than Jessica because his adversarial personality alienated his coworkers as well as his family members—all of whom were estranged.

Why didn't Jessica's friends and family step in? Because they were unaware of the severity of the problem. Many women fail to disclose domestic abuse to friends, family, or law enforcement because they are ashamed, blame themselves, or fear the reactions of others.[36]

They also didn't know what was going on because Richard was pursuing his goal of cultivating Jessica's dependence by isolating her from outside support. Even his selection of Tahiti for the wedding, which might be viewed as romantic under other circumstances, was designed to minimize attendance by Jessica's friends and family.

It turned out that Richard married his first wife in Tahiti as well. At the same resort. For the same reasons.

Separating the Dangerous from the Virtuous

Having worked with law enforcement officers every day for my entire career, I can tell you the vast majority of them are wonderful, upstanding people who cherish their partners and treat them like gold. They are not violent, aggressive, or ill-tempered at home simply because they have stressful jobs.

There are, however, exceptions to every rule. Bad apples in every orchard. While most peace officers are drawn to the job by an honorable desire to protect society, some have ulterior motives.

Risky vocations such as law enforcement are often linked with high sensation seeking.[37] And according to personnel specialists, being a police officer is ranked as one of the riskiest occupations a person can have.[38] High sensation seeking is linked with antisocial personality[39] and Dark Triad personality traits.[40]

But before we run down that trail, stepping back and examining the FLAGs of people with dangerous jobs can help us separate the good from the bad, because people vary widely in terms of how they view their profession.

Many law enforcement officers are focused on protecting the public, not on flaunting their status as armed and dangerous. Some of the brave men and women who embody the mission *to protect and to serve* frequently volunteer to work undercover in order to keep people safe, particularly at schools, public gatherings, and charity events.

Regarding lifestyle, some people with dangerous jobs relish the chance to stay home and relax when they are off the clock. For others, their personal life is an extension of their professional career and includes risky sports, dangerous adventures, and other activities designed to replicate the adrenaline rush of a police chase.

Some law enforcement officers are never off duty. This can be good or bad. For example, some officers always remain vigilant for signs of criminal activity out of habit and genuine concern for the welfare of their community. These are the guys you see in restaurants with their families who are never sitting with their back to the door. Others imprudently brandish their weapons during arguments off the clock, demonstrating underlying aggressive tendencies that might be problematic on the job as well.

Also note preferred company. When a shift is over, some law enforcement officers enjoy associating with colleagues in order to swap stories and cop talk. However, be cautious of those who *only* associate with colleagues due to a perceived inability to relate to people outside of the profession.

Other law enforcement officers head straight home after work to spend time with their family. Having survived another day, they do not want to miss a single moment of their children's lives.

Regarding goals, we want to know why someone chose a dangerous profession and what role it plays in their lives. For many people, a job is a way to put food on the table and kids through college. These people work to live, instead of live to work. For others, their job is the focus of their entire existence. More than a way to make money, some people are *defined* by their careers.

For the latter group, the reason someone chose a dangerous profession is far more revealing of their character than their job descriptions. For example, some people seek jobs in law enforcement in order to carry weapons for arrogant, selfish reasons. Others genuinely desire to protect society. Some people join the military to boost their ego and gain status and power; others desire to protect their country and its citizens—even if it means sacrificing their own lives.

> **DANGEROUS OR VIRTUOUS?**
>
> **Focus:** Protecting the neighbors or intimidating the neighborhood?
>
> **Lifestyle:** Relaxes with family after work or always on duty?
>
> **Associations:** Coworkers or criminals?
>
> **Goals:** Solving crime or seeking status?

The Wolf in Wolf's Clothing:
The Attraction of Bad

Like the gruesome crime scene photographs I have to show the jury in a murder case, sometimes we just can't sugarcoat the facts. Here it is: some women are attracted to men because they are *bad*.

This counterintuitive phenomenon is well documented. Sheila Isenberg in *Women Who Love Men Who Kill* reveals the stories of numerous women in love with murderers.[41] What kind of women? Defying stereotype, they come from a variety of backgrounds, professions, and income levels.[42]

Described as the dark side of romance, some women are excited by the brutality of the crime their lover has committed, and consider dangerous criminals to be the ultimate in male dominance and machismo.[43] Isenberg notes that "In our patriarchal culture, murderers are often viewed as more than male: the most macho, strong, violent, and brutal of all men. In a majority of movies and televisions shows, the violent mystique of the murderer—or the cop, spy, undercover agent, and so on—is the erotic centerpiece." [44] To become involved with such a man is a thrill to some women, particularly to those who are seeking excitement and passion.[45]

Women turned on by danger may be classified as experiencing *hybristophilia*—where arousal stems from having a partner known to have committed a violent crime such as murder.[46] They are attracted to these men because they are killers—finding their crime and the motivating bloodlust to be "enormously sexual and erotic." [47] Hybristophilia can even entice some women to commit homicide with their lovers.[48]

Other women co-offend out of an attraction to the "fast life" and "bad boys," and still others participate in crimes initiated by their male partners, including murder, out of fear of abandonment or to "maintain the thrill and excitement" of the relationship.[49]

Notorious serial killers consistently rack up swarms of groupies, particularly when their crimes are sexual in nature.[50] Examples of criminals who have engendered this type of cult following include Ted Bundy, John Gacy, and Richard Ramirez—also known as the "Night Stalker."[51] Each of these men had a supportive woman at his side eager to marry him *after* he was convicted.[52]

Why do serial killers hold such fascination for many women? Psychiatrist Park Dietz notes that "[p]articularly notorious inmates attract prison groupies." [53] He explains that "relationships with these men can give women social significance, perhaps for the first time in their lives." [54] For other women, their fascination with serial killers has been described as hero worship and *erotomania*—pursuing criminal celebrities in order to share in their fame and notoriety.[55]

The appeal of the violent criminal might also include the pleasure of experiencing danger vicariously, and the desire to "save" the criminal—who may be perceived as simply a product of a bad childhood.[56]

The Erotic Combination:
Both Bad and Good

Some individuals present an enticing mix of qualities that are both bad and good. In *A Billion Wicked Thoughts: What the World's Largest Experiment Reveals About Human Desire*,[57] Ogas and Gaddam conducted research that helps understand this phenomenon.

They looked through a billion different Web searches, which included

500,000 personal search histories, and examined five million sexual solicitations posted in online classified sections.[58] They looked at thousands of romance e-novels, hunderds of online erotic stories, the forty thousand most-visited adult Web sites, and observed thousands of individuals revealing their desires online using message boards.[59]

Among their findings was the interesting concept of *erotic illusions*, described as combinations of arousing cues, which are appealing in a fashion similar to the combinations of sensory cues used to create cravable foods.[60] Fictional characters whose appeal is due to erotic illusions include attractive vampires such as *Twilight*'s Edward Cullen, who present a powerful combination of danger, masculinity, and strength with the softness of love.[61]

Other characters are similarly appealing because despite their negative traits, they render positive benefits. Popular media characters who fit this description, in addition to James Bond, include Batman as the Dark Knight,[62] Gregory House, M.D.—who embodies the appeal of a character who is portrayed as a smug, manipulative, successful jerk,[63] and Dexter—who kills people, but only those who deserve to die.[64]

These findings are consistent with research demonstrating the tendency to "want it all" in relationships.[65] People want someone who is both strong and gentle, and both aggressive and nice—despite the unlikelihood of such human flexibility.[66]

Having now examined the ten reasons bad people can look good, we move to the final chapter—ending on a high note, celebrating the reality that much of the time, what looks good really is.

Green Lights

When Appearances are Reality

Many people who exude attractive qualities and satisfy your needs and desires are genuine and trustworthy, and make wonderful companions and loyal partners. These people are positively distinguished by their FLAGs, which reveal authentic personality traits, as well as healthy motivations and goals. Here are some examples.

Virtual Attraction:
The Appeal of Authenticity

I am listening to the daughter of one of my law-school classmates, a talented pianist, gush about her new boyfriend. "How did you meet him?" I ask. "Online," she explains. *Wait, that is the way she met her ex—who turned out to be a creep.* "Ross is very different," she assures me. "You'll see."

Wow, was that true. Unlike the clean-shaven six foot two man built like an Olympic athlete she used to date, when I finally meet her new boyfriend I am intrigued. Slight of build, bearded, and soft spoken, he doesn't fit her type. She explains, however, that the more she got to know him, the more attractive he became.

Although she met him on the *same* dating site she met her ex, Ross had a markedly different focus of attention. While her ex-boyfriend expressed immediate interest in her sexual preferences, Ross was enchanted with Stacy's musical proficiency. This was very important to Stacy, because while many men she dated over the years were interested in her physically, they could not even remember which instrument she played, much less had they ever expressed a desire to watch her perform.

While the online profile of her ex-boyfriend was dominated with photos of himself posing like a Greek god, Ross had only a few photos, mainly of his family. All of them loved classical music and were longtime supporters of the arts.

After a few months of virtual communication, their relationship moved offline—where it blossomed. Ross attends all of Stacy's concerts, always sitting in the front row. Now, Stacy tells me that despite Ross not being her type physically, she frequently catches herself describing him to her friends as one of the most attractive men she has ever dated. Because to Stacy, he is.

The Changing "Face" of Physical Attraction

What happened here? Ross actually *became* better looking to Stacy the more she got to know him. Research provides several explanations for this phenomenon.

One explanation involves virtual relationship building. When someone has expended time and effort building an intimate online relationship, they are motivated to view their partner in a positive light offline, even when the partner's physical features are less than would otherwise be desired.[1]

Other research demonstrates that beauty is in fact often in the eye of the beholder, showing that couples in satisfying relationships often rate their partners as more physically attractive than they are in reality, and downplay the attractiveness of relational alternatives.[2] Other aspects of positive relationships that can affect assessments of a partner's attractiveness include manner of dealing with relationship issues and relationship satisfaction.[3]

The *interaction appearance theory* is the process through which our assessment of a person's attractiveness increases the more we interact with them.[4] With positive interaction, we actually begin to perceive someone as more attractive than we did when we first met them.[5]

Ross became better looking to Stacy through his positive FLAGs demonstrating consistent authenticity. He focused on Stacy as a person and as a musician. Appreciation of the arts was already a part of his lifestyle, a passion he shared with his closest associations—family members, not drinking buddies.

Ross's intentions were revealed through what Stacy considered to be one of the most satisfying parts of their relationship—his respect. Ross respected Stacy as a person and a musician, not just as an attractive woman. Not only is respect an important human need that we all share,[6] it is also a significant predictor of satisfaction within intimate relationships, and a key contributing factor to marital quality.[7]

As you might imagine, given all the ways in which Ross has demonstrated his sincerity and commitment, when Ross proposed to Stacy less than six months after I met him, Stacy's answer was a resounding "yes!" Now *that* was music to his ears.

Constructive Power:
The Ethical Tone at the Top

Many powerful people are as good as they look. They are encouragers and advisors, exercising their power in a fashion designed to benefit others.

The positive use of power is one of the topics I cover consistently in the business ethics class I teach at a local state university. It usually comes up in connection with corporate integrity, because whenever this topic makes the headlines, it is usually bad news.

However, the abundance of research on the *negative* characteristics of top-level executives has prompted researchers to explore the other side of the coin. Some results demonstrate that virtuous character strengths among the upper echelons of executive leadership are linked with higher performance ratings.[8] These character strengths included integrity, social intelligence, and bravery.[9]

A virtuous tone at the top is good news for subordinates. Because instead of sitting in their ivory tower corner offices, many corporate executives take advantage of the opportunity to use their position and years of experience to empower their troops.

During visits to company branch offices, they take the time to get to know new employees, acknowledging them as the future of the company. They provide advice, guidance, practical tips, and access to the wisdom they have gained through what is often a career's worth of experience working in the industry.

New employees absorb this priceless information like sponges, grateful for the opportunity to learn from the boss. And by using their experience to educate and empower less experienced employees, managers are able to enhance the workplace environment in a manner that no holiday bonus ever could.

The result? A collaborative corporate culture filled with motivated, confident, productive employees, on course to achieve professional success and company profitability.

How can you spot the benevolent leaders? Their FLAGs point in the same direction both professionally and personally. Their focus is on the company stakeholders, not just the shareholders, as they strive to exude transparency, ensure employee satisfaction, benefit their community, and promote a quality product.

Many people at the top of the food chain exercise transformative power as a personal lifestyle. They not only inspire and equip subordinates with encouragement and knowledge to help them succeed professionally, but they also provide the same type of empowerment in their personal endeavors.

Some corporate executives sit on boards of nonprofit charities and business development associations, strive to encourage young people to continue their education, and donate money for scholarships.

Positive Types of Power

Several examples of the benevolent use of power are particularly appeal- . ing because they incorporate other sources of attraction.

Attraction power is likability, independent of an existing relationship.[10] It can be generated through similarity or perceived authenticity, and can enhance all other sources of power.[11]

Referent power is identification with a power source viewed as similar, or as a role model.[12] Referent power is the process through which attractive people are inspirational and produce the desire for identification, as occurs through celebrity endorsements of consumer products.[13]

Informational power is used when someone with greater power persuasively teaches information to subordinates, who use the information.[14]

Character power is a person's enhanced ability to lead and influence others when he or she is perceived as trustworthy, honorable, and in possession of valuable traits of character.[15] Character power generates perceived credibility, and is foundational for all other sources of personal power.[16] Character power also involves perceived similarity with the power source, because we follow leaders who share our ambitions—thereby affirming our views and beliefs.[17]

Credibility:
When You Can Trust What You See

"F*** you!" the defendant screams at the judge, as I am handling the mental health court calendar. Without missing a beat the judge corrects the defendant. "That's f*** you, your Honor."

The courtroom breathes a collective sigh of relief, having been worried about how the judge was going to respond. His quick-witted comeback, however, elicits more than nervous laughter from the gallery. It also produces respect. The steady demeanor of this seasoned jurist demonstrates that he has the experience, confidence, and credibility to deliver justice in any case.

Some people who make you feel confident and safe are as qualified as they appear to be. Whether through credentials, experience, proficiency, or expertise, their credibility is authentic. You can take what these people say straight to the bank, and follow their advice with confidence.

One of the things that distinguish them from the false authorities of the world is the way they *use* their training, experience, and expertise. Without ulterior motives, they use what they have learned to assist and empower others. Whether explaining technical information, giving advice, or sharing the wisdom they have learned over the years, these people are worth their weight in gold. I have the privilege of knowing people like this, who are eager to put their knowledge and expertise to good use. They make great guest speakers.

Every semester I invite a successful businessman to speak to the business ethics class I teach at a local state university. Experienced, knowledgeable, and articulate, he begins to talk about his successful business ventures. This is of some interest to my students, as most of them are business majors, hoping to land good jobs after graduation. I always find it hard not to smile, however, as I anticipate what is coming.

I watch every head in the classroom suddenly snap up from their smart phones when he gets to the part about: ". . . and I am even more careful now that I am finally out of prison." At this point I can always tell from the students' expressions which ones have been paying attention. *What did he say?* That's right. This guy is the real deal. Who better to teach students why they should worry about business ethics than someone who has served time in prison for an ethical violation?

Needless to say the class is riveted for the rest of the hour. Many students abruptly abandon their covert text-a-thons and sit with their mouths hanging open for the rest of the class period, not wanting to miss a word.

Afterward, I am inundated with requests for this man's contact information, and consistently in my evaluations—when answering the question about what was the best part of the class, they say "the guest speaker." I don't take this personally, because I have to agree.

This man is pure credibility, having literally walked the walk. He speaks with the authority of someone who knows firsthand what can happen if you cut corners. Instead of becoming embittered, he chooses to use his experience to educate others so that they don't make the same mistakes, selflessly using his credibility to educate and empower the next generation.

Genuine Attention:
How Ordinary People Land Extraordinary Partners

Ben is a handsome, successful, motion picture executive. His wife, Claire, whom he adores, is a delightful woman with a big smile and a kind word for everyone she meets. Although she doesn't need to work, she enjoys supporting her husband's career through helping with his bookkeeping, scheduling, and maintaining their home.

Appearance wise, Claire is best described as plain. She wears very little makeup, dresses modestly, and does not color her hair, which is slowly turning gray. "Au natural," she jokes, flashing her trademark smile.

Some of Ben's colleagues in the industry are curious. Given Ben's long list of female admirers, how did Claire manage to pull this off? If you asked Ben, he would tell you it was easy, and it didn't take long. Here is how it happened.

Ben meets Claire at his health club, where they both do their morning workout, often on adjacent treadmills. Claire is fascinated with Ben's career in the motion picture world. She looks forward to Ben's stories in the morning—and Ben loves to tell them. She is the first person in a long time that has expressed genuine interest in the trade into which Ben pours his heart and soul.

Most of the beautiful women he meets in the course of his career seem to fall into one of two camps. They are incredibly shallow, preferring to talk about celebrity gossip rather than about Ben's career, or they are self-motivated, focused on Ben only in the hopes of landing a role in one of his movies. Most of these women make Ben feel unimportant and used.

Claire, on the other hand, rocks his world. Without big screen aspirations of her own, she lives vicariously through Ben's adventures. She listens, laughs, and looks forward to more. To Ben, Claire is a breath of fresh air. He can't wait to see her each morning. Not because of how she looks, but because of the way she makes him feel. As soon as he sees her bright smile and ponytail from across the room, he might as well have injected himself with a shot of morphine. The euphoric feeling is coming. Are you getting the picture?

The Transparency of True Love:
Spotting the Real Thing

Many people are driven by self-interest. They spend most of their time focused on themselves, thinking about their own lives, plans, and goals. The most popular people, however, are focused on others. Claire is one of those.

While other women Ben dated lived a lifestyle of social climbing in order to further their own careers, Claire's lifestyle revolves around her desire to cultivate and maintain a loving relationship. Unlike many of Ben's past girlfriends, who spent more time looking in the mirror than listening to him, Claire gives Ben her full attention.

With genuine goals and authentic admiration, Claire makes Ben feel like the most wonderful man in the world because she honestly thinks that he is. Her support inspires him to professional excellence in his career, and gives him a reason to look forward to coming home every night. Claire, in turn, has landed a wonderful, appreciative spouse who loves her exactly the way she is. Graying hair and all. What some might call an unlikely pairing has turned out to be a match made in heaven.

Now *that* is the kind of happy ending worthy of a motion picture worth seeing.

Affirmation Through Unconditional Acceptance

The tirade begins as soon as I enter the interview room to meet the domestic violence victim. As I extend my hand to greet her, she begins screaming at me, accusing me of "tearing apart" her family and "ruining her life" by having her husband arrested and charging him with mayhem for setting her on fire.

Although it is a warm day, the victim is wearing long pants and long sleeves to hide the fresh scars. Perhaps she doesn't know that I have already seen the ghastly hospital photos in order to decide the crimes with which to charge her husband.

As I sit down and open my case file she continues her rant, complaining about how unfairly her pyromaniac husband was treated by law enforcement, and how she has no interest in cooperating. I assure her that we understand she doesn't want to testify, but will make the process as bearable for her as we can.

After a period of time during which the victim's behavior progresses from bad to worse, it becomes apparent we are wasting our time. As I leave, I introduce her to a woman who is just arriving. "Another cop?" she asks. No, I explain, this is your victim advocate. Never having had an advocate of any kind in her life, she is confused. "What does she want from me?" "Nothing," I explain, "she wants to know what *she* can do for *you*. She is part of our team."

How does this woman like her new team? We have our answer when I call her as a witness one month later, where despite her antics during our initial meeting, she bravely takes the stand and testifies against her husband. The law allows a domestic violence victim to have a support person of her choosing sit next to the witness stand. Who does she choose? Not a friend or family member. Her victim advocate.

Just the Way You Are

Why would a victim choose someone she just met to sit with her during what is often one of the most traumatic experiences she has ever endured— testifying against a man who is sitting right in front of her in the court-room? Because the role of a victim advocate is to provide *unconditional* support. They don't pass judgment, and they don't criticize. They don't dispute or question the victim's feelings. They listen, empathize, and en-courage. Who wouldn't want a person like that around?

Naturally affirming people confirm the value and importance of others. Confirmation expresses validation and acceptance, and validation promotes emotional bonding.[18] Confirmation does not necessarily con-stitute approval, but acceptance and affirmation.[19]

I see the value of affirmation every day within the criminal justice system. Domestic violence victims who have been brainwashed by vio-lent offenders into believing they are worthless, insignificant, and some-how responsible for their plight are emboldened through affirmation of their value and worth to face their abusers in court. Individuals facing other types of physical, mental, or emotional challenges are empowered in the same fashion, through the affirmation of their importance.

The authenticity of naturally affirming people is evident through their FLAGs. These other-focused individuals lead a lifestyle driven by seeing the good in everyone they meet. They spend time with close friends and family, but also associate with a wide variety of acquaintances from all walks of life, because in humility, they do not look down on anyone. Their goals are altruistic, and they can find the silver lining in any situation because they always see the glass as half full.

Similarity Stimulates Support

Have you ever had someone who is observing you going through a dif-ficult time tell you "I know how you feel"—when you know they have no idea? How helpful is that? Whether in connection with losing a job, losing a spouse, or losing a house in a tornado, inauthentic support is more likely to generate resentment than relief.

Instead, what is most helpful in difficult times is support and encouragement from someone who has been through *the same thing*. The more difficult the circumstances, the more valuable the similarity. In this fashion, positive use of similarity is inspiring and empowering.

I see this every day in my profession. Human trafficking victims become survivors and use their experience to empower others. Brave young men and women who have withstood years of abuse bond with other victims who have been through the same thing in a way that the rest of us cannot.

Alcoholics and Narcotics Anonymous operate on a similar principle, pairing a person who is newly sober with a sponsor who has many years of sobriety. A recovering addict is likely to bond with someone who has been through the same challenges and struggles that accompany newfound sobriety.

Positive interaction with similar others can also help young people who are headed in the wrong direction get back onto the right path. Adults who have excelled in a young person's area of interest can be incredibly effective mentors and role models.

Similarity Breeds Success:
The Big Brother

A significant portion of my caseload over the years has involved juvenile offenders. Having been in charge of the juvenile Serious Habitual Offenders Unit, I am familiar with juvenile recidivism—and how to break the cycle. Young, impressionable, and lacking the wisdom of age, many teenagers are ripe for rehabilitation. The key is pairing them with an adult voice they will respect, and whose advice they will follow.

Sadly, for many of these troubled teens, that voice does not belong to either of their parents. This is particularly true when the parents are struggling with legal problems of their own. So we pair them with successful adults who have similar interests. Whether sports, fashion, or occupation, similarity can facilitate positive influence.

Successful athletes are great examples of this principle in action. To assist in the rehabilitation of juvenile offenders, many communities work with Big Brother programs that pair well-known local athletes with aspiring students who are struggling academically and running with the wrong crowd. The admiration these young men have for their Big Brothers sometimes borders on hero worship—which results in rapt attention to the Big Brother's instruction and advice—both on and off the football field, hockey rink, or basketball court.

Building upon similar interests and goals, the Big Brothers explain to their protégés how important it is for an athlete not only to be in great physical shape, but also to live a clean life in terms of nutrition, rest, spirituality, and family values. They share examples of great athletes whose lives and careers were derailed by harmful lifestyle choices such as drug addiction, criminal behavior, and violence.

These parings are success stories for many young men who take advantage of this opportunity. They express less anxiety about their future, and often for the first time in their young lives, they have an inspiring adult role model with whom they can relate.

Many types of informal mentoring relationships operate the same way. Protégés select mentors whom they view as role models, and mentors select protégés who remind them of themselves earlier in life.[20] Protégés who view their role models as similar may seek to increase similarity even further by imitating the role model, prompting positive behavior change.[21] In this fashion, similarity breeds success.

Recognizing When Familiar Is Safe:
Walking the Walk

Recognition alone doesn't equal safe. I recognize the defendant in the courtroom day after day when I am in trial, and the homeless guy yelling in front of the courthouse. However, I also recognize the same faces at the gym every day at the crack of dawn. It is these early risers who share my lifestyle of health and fitness who are more likely to be on the safe side.

While familiarity can mask danger or instill a false sense of security, many people who make us feel comfortable because they are familiar turn out to be as safe as they appear. Usually, it is because they are genuinely *similar* as well. We share the same profession, hobbies, interests, friends, and life goals. In other words, we share similar FLAGs.

Familiarity through similarity is much safer than mere exposure. Many manipulators claim to be involved in the same things as the people they want to target, but the true test of their authenticity is whether they are just talking the talk, or actually walking the walk. Watching someone in a spin class or sweating through a heat yoga class on a regular basis is better evidence of his or her lifestyle than simply observing a person loitering around your apartment building wearing a jogging suit.

Similarly, college students who recognize a familiar face on campus could be looking at a sexual predator scoping out potential victims. On the other hand, students who recognize each other because they have classes together and see each other frequently in the library can more safely rely on the perception that familiarity is good. This is because like-minded individuals who share a lifestyle of structure and discipline are likely to share other goals as well.

Familiar faces are also more likely to be safe when they share your associations. Unlike people who have become familiar because you see them at the bus stop every morning, people within the same social group interact with a frequency that affords the chance to perceive each other's FLAGs.

In all of these examples, familiarity is more likely to be as good as it looks, the more you know about the other person.

When Exciting Is Enriching:
Complementary Companionship

Exciting people are not only stimulating, many of them are also authentic. These adventurous individuals make good companions for those who want to experience vicarious stimulation, as well as those looking for a partner with whom to share the excitement.

Some people revel in the stories their adventurous partners bring home from exhilarating jobs, or enjoy the vicarious thrill of hearing the description of what it was like to snowboard down a death-defying double black diamond run while they sat and enjoyed a hot chocolate in the ski lodge.

One of my colleagues in the legal community was drawn to her partner, a professional ice hockey player, because of his fearless, aggressive performance in the rink. Now married for ten years, she is still his number-one fan, attending all his games. He has an admiring, supportive spouse, and she has an exciting, appreciative partner.

As with other areas of attraction, the FLAGs of exciting people reveal underlying character traits, lifestyle, and goals. Unlike adrenaline junkies who recklessly chase the hottest new sport for the thrill of it or for bragging rights, there are scores of talented sports fanatics who enjoy the same activities, but within the context of a healthy, safety-conscious lifestyle.

Sharing the Thrill:
The Hang Glider Built for Two

Smart thrill seekers often hook up with partners who share their passion. Whether seeking vicarious or actual stimulation, "meetup" groups and special interest clubs are geared to connecting like-minded individuals who often share similar FLAGs. From mountain climbing to cross-country skiing, associating with people who share the same focus, lifestyle, and goals can promote satisfying relationships.

Having common interests can increase relational satisfaction and quality. While a sunshine-loving white-collar executive engaged to a storm chaser might predict trouble on the horizon, so to speak, two storm chasers can leap into a weather van and drive off into the clouds.

When people satisfy their quest for adventure and excitement by associating with like-minded enthusiasts, it is helpful to remember that while some sensation seekers are experts in their sport, sensible and safety-minded, others are reckless, self-centered, and irresponsible. The key is being able to tell the difference.

Seasons Change:
When Forbidden Fruit Becomes Ripe

A good friend of mine met her husband when her son was dating his daughter. At the time, he was married to someone else. My friend married him several years later after he was widowed. Fast-forward another decade and her son ends up (finally) tying the knot with his daughter. I performed the wedding—officially pronouncing the groom both her son and her son-in-law. Confusing enough?

This scenario illustrates the reality that unlike other types of "bad" relationships that are harmful, some relationships are only taboo due to *situational* inappropriateness—which can change. What would have been an extramarital affair becomes a wholesome relationship once both parties are divorced or widowed. Having a crush on the boss can become a legitimate pursuit once a subordinate is transferred to a different division or takes a different job. And once a trial is over, lawyers on opposing sides who got along in court better than expected can pursue a different type of relationship—vowing never to try a case against each other again.

In the same fashion that certain foods or beverages which are "off limits" when a woman is pregnant or on a diet eventually become permissible again, attractive people can lose their forbidden fruit status as well. Changing seasons often bring changing circumstances.

When What Looks Bad Is Good:
Danger as Virtue

Many people who are dangerous are also *good*. There are scores of law enforcement agents, trained military personnel, professional boxers, and martial artists of every type of discipline whose hands are lethal weapons—who are honorable and righteous. These upstanding citizens would never use their deadly skills to do evil. To the contrary, many of these people are employed in positions with the primary responsibility of protecting society. While their dangerousness is still arousing, their skills are used benevolently rather than malevolently.

One of the most dangerous witnesses I ever put on the stand didn't carry a weapon. He didn't need to. This 250-pound wall of solid muscle was a security guard at a local department store. While never the aggressor, he had ample occasion to demonstrate the extent to which he would protect the store's merchandise by catching and detaining thieves for law enforcement.

He also attracted a fan club of young women who spent an excessive amount of time and money in the store, to the dismay of their parents and the delight of the merchants. In short, he was an ideal employee.

When he first entered the courtroom, some of the jurors shrank back in their seats. At first glance, this was one scary-looking dude. Did I mention his tattoos? While mostly covered up by his security uniform, this man even had tattoos on his face. Lightning bolts and barbed wire. Although he was also a born-again Christian, the large cross on his chest was unfortunately not visible in the courtroom.

It didn't take long, however, after this man started to testify about how he caught the defendant shoplifting, that the jurors were leaning forward and smiling. Dedicated to protecting store merchandise, this man took his job very seriously. His ominous physique was not the result of lifting weights in prison (as one of the jurors thought at first when she saw the barbed wire tattoos), but a lifestyle of health and fitness.

He didn't run with a gang; he lived with his parents. His goal was to own his own security company one day, in order to provide protection to stores and businesses in his community. The jurors are nodding by the time he is done testifying. This is a dangerous man you *hope* lives in your neighborhood.

There are many versions of this witness. From third-degree black belts who share their expertise by offering free self-defense classes for women and children to the local police chief, also an expert marksman, who is on a first-name basis with most of the residents in his small town.

Community members feel safe knowing these people live in their neighborhood. These individuals are desirable because they are dangerous—and virtuous. They look good, and they really are.

Reaching a Verdict

A Life Well Perceived

While the world is filled with loyal friends, adoring partners, and compassionate strangers, it also contains enough shrewd manipulators to keep people like me in business for an entire career.

Life is easier and much more rewarding when you can tell the good from the bad. I developed the FLAGs to help you tell the difference. Geared for use within any type of relationship, from the impersonal to the intimate, they are specifically designed to provide an enlightening, unique perspective that can reveal a person's true colors.

Reading red flags, however, is an ongoing process. Because sometimes, a person's colors change.

Going Green—When Bad Becomes Good
FLAGs of Change

At the beach, you feel safe venturing back into the waves once the red flags on the shoreline are removed because you trust that the dangerous rip current is gone. In the same way, there might be circumstances under which you feel safe re-engaging with someone who is no longer flying red flags because you believe the danger is gone.

This book would not be complete without recognizing that people change. Sometimes drastically. Who can forget Edward Norton's portrayal of reformed white power murderer Derek Vinyard in *American History X*? Many people who previously lived a lifestyle of crime, drugs, or dishonesty turn their lives around and become role models for others who are on the wrong track.

When someone claims to have turned over a new leaf, however, you don't have to take their word for it. You would be amazed how many criminals I prosecute claim to have made a fresh start between the date of conviction and the date of sentencing where the court will pronounce judgment.

Instead, just like the famous Scripture passage explaining how you can tell a good tree from a bad tree by the fruit it produces,[1] you can detect a person's true colors by the FLAGs they fly. When authentic change occurs, whether as a result of illness, tragedy, finding God, or getting sober, FLAGs of change appear.

People who were previously self-absorbed begin to focus on family, education, and caring for others. They make lifestyle changes, heading to the gym after work instead of the bar. They trade in harmful associations for wholesome friends. And they adopt an entirely different set of goals.

How often does this happen? Every day. I have spent my career not only separating bad from good, but also watching bad become good. Sometimes what looks good on the outside becomes just as good on the inside—making it safe to venture back into the water, trusting what you see.

Refocused Perspective:
Flags of Victory

At this point, I have submitted all the evidence to you. The FLAGs will help you analyze everyone in your life that exudes one or more of the ten sources of attraction, and reach a decision regarding their personality makeup, motivation, or marriage potential. The practical examples and psychological research were provided to breathe life into the FLAGs in order to illustrate what to look for, where to look, and how to interpret what you see.

Through examining why we give people the benefit of the doubt when they make us feel good, you hopefully have gained a heightened awareness of your own emotional needs, as well as those of the important people in your life. These revelations might prompt you to examine the FLAGs you are flying, in order to improve the quality of your current relationships, and can help you make smart decisions when embarking on new ones.

It has been my privilege to share with you a career's worth of experience, insight, and research, with the goal of enhancing your ability to separate the dangerous from the desirable. It is my sincere hope that as a result, you will reach the right verdict with everyone you meet, so that all of your relationships will have a happy ending.

And with that, I rest my case. Good luck!

Endnotes

Introduction: Why Bad Looks Good

1. Jo-Ellan Dimitrius and Wendy Patrick Mazzarella, *Reading People: How to Understand People and Predict Their Behavior—Anytime, Anyplace* (revision) (New York: Random House, 2008).
2. See generally, Wendy L. Patrick, *Using the Psychology of Attraction in Christian Outreach: Lessons from the Dark Side* (New York: Peter Lang, 2013).
3. The *theory of social exchange* holds that we are drawn toward people who make us feel good. See, e.g., Ann Demarais and Valerie White, *First Impressions* (New York: Bantam Books, 2004), 24.
4. Although the names of the three Dark Triad personality characteristics will be used throughout the book in order to be faithful to the literature cited, this usage is meant to cover both clinical diagnosis and subclinical manifestation of traits consistent with these disorders.
5. Paul Babiak and Robert Hare, *Snakes in Suits: When Psychopaths Go to Work* (New York: Regan Books, 2006), 124.
6. Peter K. Jonason, Norman P. Li, and Emily A. Teicher, "Who is James Bond? The Dark Triad as an Agentic Social Style," *Individual Differences Research* 8, no. 2 (2010): 111–20.
7. Peter K. Jonason, Katherine A. Valentine, Norman P. Li, and Carmelita L. Harbeson, "Mate-Selection and the Dark Triad: Facilitating a Short-Term Mating Strategy and Creating a Volatile Environment," *Personality and Individual Differences* 51 (2011): 759–63 (760), doi: 10.1016/j.paid.2011.06.025.
8. Gregory Louis Carter, Anne C. Campbell, and Steven Muncer, "The Dark Triad: Beyond a 'Male' Mating Strategy," *Personality and Individual Differences* 56 (2014): 159–64 (162). (Researchers examining large national sample found no sex distinction in Dark Triad personality characteristics.)
9. Gregory Louis Carter, Anne C. Campbell, and Steven Muncer, "The Dark Triad Personality: Attractiveness to Women," *Personality and Individual Differences* 56 (2014): 57–61 (57–58).

10. Peter K. Jonason, David P. Schmitt, Gregory D. Webster, Norman P. Li, and Laura Crysel, "The Antihero in Popular Culture: Life History Theory and the Dark Triad Personality Traits," *Review of General Psychology* 16, no. 2 (2012): 192–99 (192).

11. Adrian Furnham, Steven C. Richards, and Delroy L. Paulhus, "The Dark Triad of Personality: A 10 Year Review," *Social and Personality Psychology Compass* 7, no. 3 (2013): 199–216, doi: 10.1111/spc3.12018.

12. Peter K. Jonason and Gregory Webster, "A Protean Approach to Social Influence: Dark Triad Personalities and Social Influence Tactics," *Personality and Individual Differences* 52 (2012): 521–26, doi: 10.1016/j.paid.2011.11.023.

13. Some research says you can detect Dark Triad traits. In one experiment, participants looking at photographs of emotionally neutral faces successfully detected the Dark Triad composite of traits—especially when looking at pictures of women. Nicholas S. Holtzman, "Facing a Psychopath: Detecting the Dark Triad From Emotionally-Neutral Faces, Using Prototypes From the Personality Faceaurus," *Journal of Research in Personality* 45 (2011): 648–54.

14. Holtzman, "Facing a Psychopath," 45.

15. Peter K. Jonason, Sarah Slomski, and Jamie Partyka, "The Dark Triad at Work: How *Toxic* Employees Get Their Way," *Personality and Individual Differences* 52 (2012): 449–53, doi:10.1016/j.paid.2011.11.008.

16. John F. Rauthmann and Gerald P. Kolar, "The Perceived Attractiveness and Traits of the Dark Triad: Narcissists Are Perceived as Hot, Machiavellians and Psychopaths Not," *Personality and Individual Differences* 54 (2010): 582–86.

17. *Diagnostic and Statistical Manual of Mental Disorders*, 5th ed. (Washington, D.C.: American Psychiatric Publishing, 2013), 669.

18. Nicholas S. Holtzman and Michael J. Strube, "The Intertwined Evolution of Narcissism and Short-Term Mating: An Emerging Hypothesis," in *The Handbook of Narcissism and Narcissistic Personality Disorder: Theoretical Approaches, Empirical Findings, and Treatments*, eds. W. Keith Campbell and Joshua D. Miller (Hoboken: John Wiley & Sons, Inc., 2011), 210–20 (213).

19. Mitja D. Back, Stefan C. Schmukle, and Boris Egloff, "Why Are Narcissists So Charming at First Sight? Decoding the Narcissism-Popularity Link at Zero Acquaintance," *Journal of Personality and Social Psychology*, 98, no. 1 (2010): 132–45 (143). Other research shows that narcissists tend to be disliked over the course of long-term relationships. Back et al., "Why Are Narcissists So Charming at First Sight?" 133.

20. Back et al., "Why Are Narcissists So Charming at First Sight?" 143.

21. Ibid., 140–41.

22. Robert D. Hare, *Without Conscience: The Disturbing World of the Psychopaths Among Us* (New York: The Guilford Press, 1993), xi.

23. Hare, *Without Conscience*, xi.

24. Hervey Cleckley, *The Mask of Sanity* (New York: New American Library), 1982.

25. Hare, *Without Conscience*, 34–35.

26. Ibid., 34.

27. Clive Boddy, *Corporate Psychopaths: Organizational Destroyers* (New York: Palgrave Macmillan, 2011), 38

28. Babiak and Hare, *Snakes in Suits,* 178.

29. Jason R. Hall and Stephen D. Benning, "The 'Successful' Psychopath: Adaptive and Subclinical Manifestations of Psychopathy in the General Population," in *Handbook of*

Psychopathy, ed. Christopher J. Patrick (New York: The Guilford Press, 2006), 459–78 (460–61).

30. Sharon Jakobwitz and Vincent Egan, "The Dark Triad and Normal Personality Traits," *Personality and Individual Differences* 40 (2006): 331–39 (332), doi: 10.1016/j.paid.2005 .07.006.

31. Beth A. Visser, Julie A. Pozzebon, and Andrea M. Reina-Tamayo, "Status-Driven Risk Taking: Another 'Dark' Personality?" *Canadian Journal of Behavioral Science* (February 10, 2014): 1–12 (2), doi: 10.1037/a0034163.

32. Michael Wai and Niko Tiliopoulos, "The Affective and Cognitive Empathic Nature of the Dark Triad of Personality," *Personality and Individual Differences* 52 (2012): 794–99 (794), doi: 10.1016/j.paid.2012.01.008."

33. Jakobwitz and Egan, "The Dark Triad," 332.

34. Farah Ali, Ines Sousa Amorim, and Tomas Chamorro-Premuzic, "Empathy Deficits and Trait Emotional Intelligence in Psychopathy and Machiavellianism," *Personality and Individual Differences* 47 (2009): 758–62 (759), doi: 10.1016/j.paid.2009.06.016.

35. Elizabeth J. Austin, Daniel Farrelly, Carolyn Black, and Helen Moore, "Emotional Intelligence, Machiavellianism and Emotional Manipulation: Does EI Have a Dark Side?" *Personality and Individual Differences* 43 (2007): 179–89 (180), doi: 10.1016/j.paid.2006 .11.019.

36. Pamela J. Black, Michael Woodworth, and Stephen Porter, "The Big Bad Wolf? The Relation Between the Dark Triad and the Interpersonal Assessment of Vulnerability," *Personality and Individual Differences* (in press) (2013): 1–5, http://dx.doi.org/10.1016/j.paid.2013.10.026.

37. Black et al., "The Big Bad Wolf?" 4.

38. Ibid., 4–5.

39. Babiak and Hare, *Snakes in Suits*, 37.

40. Ibid., 38–39.

41. Ibid., 38.

42. Hare, *Without Conscience*, 148.

43. Ibid.

44. Stephanie S. Spielmann, Geoff MacDonald, Jessica A. Maxwell, Samantha Joel, Diana Peragine, Amy Muise, and Emily Impett, "Settling for Less Out of Fear of Being Single," *Journal of Personality and Social Psychology* (2013): 1–25 (1).

45. Spielmann et al., "Settling for Less," 20.

46. Mark A. Fine, Tina A. Coffelt, and Loreen N. Olson, "Romantic Relationship Initiation Following Relationship Dissolution," in *Handbook of Relationship Initiation*, eds. Susan Sprecher, Amy Wenzel, and John Harvey (New York: Psychology Press, 2008), 391–407 (391).

Reading Red FLAGs: Four Ways to Separate the Dangerous from the Desirable

1. Murray R. Barrick, Jonathan A. Shaffer, and Sandra W. DeGrassi, "What You See May Not Be What You Get: Relationships Among Self-Presentation Tactics and Ratings of Interview and Job Performance," *Journal of Applied Psychology* 94, no. 6 (2009): 1394–1411, doi: 10.1037/a0016532.

2. Janine Willis and Alexander Todorov, "First Impressions: Making Up Your Mind After a 100-Ms Exposure to a Face," *Psychological Science* 17, no. 7 (2006): 592–98.

3. Willis and Todorov, "First Impressions," 596–97.

4. Rainer Romero-Canyas and Geraldine Downey, "What I See When I Think It's About Me: People Low in Rejection-Sensitivity Downplay Cues of Rejection in Self-Relevant Interpersonal Situations," *Emotion* 13, no. 1 (2013): 104–17 (105, 117), doi: 10.1037/a0029786.

5. Valerian J. Derlega, Barbara A. Winstead, and Kathryn Greene, "Self-Disclosure and Starting a Close Relationship," in *Handbook of Relationship Initiation*, eds. Susan Sprecher, Amy Wenzel, and John Harvey (New York: Psychology Press, 2008), 153–74 (156) (discussing *predicted outcome value theory*, which predicts people will self-disclose more quickly within what they anticipate will be a positive relationship).

6. The opposite is true as well—some of my colleagues in other states point out that, in some jurisdictions, you can't tell the clients and lawyers apart because everyone looks like a client.

7. Anthony R. Pratkanis, "Social Influence Analysis: An Index of Tactics," in *The Science of Social Influence: Advances and Future Progress*, ed. Anthony R. Pratkanis (New York: Psychology Press, 2007), 17–82 (33) (citing Lefkowitz et al., 1955).

8. Miquelle A. G. March and Roos Vonk, "The Process of Becoming Suspicious of Ulterior Motives," *Social Cognition* 23, no. 3 (2005): 242–56 (242).

9. Tamas Bereczkei, Bela Birkas, and Zsuzsanna Kerekes, "The Presence of Others, Prosocial Traits, Machiavellianism: A Personality x Situation Approach," *Social Psychology* 41, no. 4 (2010): 238–45, doi: 10.1027/1864-9335/a000032.

10. See generally, Bereczkei et al., "The Presence of Others."

11. E. J. Horberg, Dacher Keltner, and Michael W. Kraus, "Pride Displays Communicate Self-Interest and Support for Meritocracy," *Journal of Personality and Social Psychology* 105, no. 1 (2013): 24–37, doi: 10.1037/a0032849.

12. Simine Vazire and Samuel D. Gosling, "E-Perceptions: Personality Impressions Based on Personal Websites," *Journal of Personality and Social Psychology* 87, no. 1 (2004): 123–32 (124), doi: 10.1037/0022-3514.87.1.123.

13. Vazire and Gosling, "E-Perceptions," 124.

14. Ibid.

15. Ibid.

16. Ibid.

17. William B. Swann, Jr. and Jennifer K. Bosson, "Identity Negotiation: A Theory of Self and Social Interaction," in *Handbook of Personality: Theory and Research*, 3rd ed., eds. Oliver P. John, Richard W. Robins, and Lawrence A. Pervin (New York: The Guilford Press, 2008), 448–71 (458).

18. David John Hughes, Moss Rowe, Mark Batey, and Andrew Lee, "A Tale of Two Sites: Twitter vs. Facebook and the Personality Predictors of Social Media Usage," *Computers in Human Behavior* 28 (2012): 561–69, doi: 10.1016/j.chb.2011.11.001.

19. Hughes et al., "A Tale of Two Sites," 567.

20. Eric Tucker, "Social Networking Puts the Bite on Defendants," *The Associated Press* (July 22, 2008), http://www.lawtechnologynews.com/id=1202423145595/Social-Networking-Puts-the-Bite-on-Defendants?slreturn=20140230001425.

21. Sarah Ganim, "Jerry Sandusky, Former Penn State Football Staffer, Subject of Grand Jury Investigation," *The Patriot-News* (March, 31, 2011), http://www.pennlive.com/midstate/index.ssf/2011/03/jerry_sandusky_former_penn_sta.html.

22. Sarah Ganim, "Report: Former Coach Jerry Sandusky Used Charity to Molest Kids," *The

Patriot News (November 6, 2011) www.pennlive.com/midstate/index.ssf/2011/11/report _former_coach_jerry_sand.html.

23. Glenn D. Reeder, "Perceptions of Goals and Motives in Romantic Relationships," in *Handbook of Relationship Initiation*, eds. Susan Sprecher, Amy Wenzel, and John Harvey (New York: Psychology Press, 2008), 499–514 (501).

24. See, e.g., Kira O. McCabe, Nico W. Van Yperen, Andrew J. Elliot, Marc Verbraak, "Big Five Personality Profiles of Context-Specific Achievement Goals," *Journal of Research in Personality* 47 (2013): 698–707.

25. Wiebke Bleidorn, Christian Kandler, Ute R. Hulsheger, Rainer Riemann, Alois Angleitner, and Frank M. Spinath, "Nature and Nurture of the Interplay Between Personality Traits and Major Life Goals," *Journal of Personality and Social Psychology* 99, no. 2 (2010): 366–79, doi: 10.1037/a0019982.

26. See generally, Oliver C. Schultheiss, "Implicit Motives," in *Handbook of Personality: Theory and Research*, 3rd ed., eds. Oliver P. John, Richard W. Robins, and Lawrence A. Pervin (New York: The Guilford Press, 2008), 603–33.

27. Beth A. Visser and Julie A. Pozzebon, "Who are You and What Do You Want? Life Aspirations, Personality, and Well-Being," *Personality and Individual Differences* 54 (2013): 266–71, http://dx.doi.org/10.1016/j.paid.2012.09.010.

28. Visser and Pozzebon, "Who are You and What Do You Want?" 266.

29. Ibid.

30. Jack J. Bauer and Dan P. McAdams, "Growth Goals, Maturity, and Well-Being." *Developmental Psychology* 40, No. 1 (2004): 114–27 (123), doi: 10.1037/0012-1649.40.1.

31. Daniel N. Jones and Delroy L. Paulhus, "Differentiating the Dark Triad Within the Interpersonal Circumplex," in *Handbook of Interpersonal Psychology: Theory, Research, Assessment, and Therapeutic Interventions*, eds. Leonard M. Horowitz and Stephen Strack (Hoboken: John Wiley & Sons, 2011), 249–67 (259–60).

32. Jones and Paulhus, "Differentiating the Dark Triad," 260.

33. Glenn D. Reeder, Marla J. Ronk, Roos Vonk, Jaap Ham, and Melissa Lawrence, "Dispositional Attribution: Multiple Inferences About Motive-Related Traits," *Journal of Personality and Social Psychology* 86, no. 4 (2004): 530–44 (530), doi: 10.1037/0022-3514.86.4.530.

34. Reeder et al., "Dispositional Attribution," 530.

35. Ola Nordhall and Jens Agerstrom, "Future-Oriented People Show Stronger Moral Concerns," *Current Research in Social Psychology* (2013): 52–59 (57), http://www.uiowa.edu/~grp proc/crisp/crisp.html.

36. Nordhall and Agerstrom, "Future-Oriented People," 54.

37. Jones and Paulhus, "Differentiating the Dark Triad," 254.

38. Thomas A. Widiger and Donald R. Lynam, "Psychopathy and the Five-Factor Model of Personality," in *Psychopathy: Antisocial, Criminal, and Violent Behavior*, eds. Theodore Millon, Erik Simonsen, Morten Birket-Smith, and Roger D. Davis (New York: The Guilford Press, 1998), 171–87 (176–77).

39. Paul Babiak, Craig S. Neumann, and Robert D. Hare, "Corporate Psychopathy: Talking the Walk," *Behavioral Sciences and the Law* 28 (2010): 174–93 (191), doi: 10.1002/bsl.925.

40. Widiger and Lynam, "Psychopathy and the Five-Factor Model," 176–77.

1. The Power of Attraction

1. Marsha B. Jacobson, "Effects of Victim's and Defendant's Physical Attractiveness on Subjects' Judgments in a Rape Case," *Sex Roles* 7, no. 3 (1981): 247–55.

2. Laura K. Guerrero and Kory Floyd, *Nonverbal Communication in Close Relationships* (Mahwah: Lawrence Erlbaum Associates, 2006), 60.

3. Edward P. Lemay Jr., Margarite A. Bechis, Jessamine Martin, Angela M. Neal, and Christine Coyne, "Concealing Negative Evaluations of a Romantic Partner's Physical Attractiveness," *Personal Relationships* 20 (2013): 669–89 (669), doi: 10.1111/pere.12007.

4. Eugene W. Mathes and Linda L. Edwards, "Physical Attractiveness as an Input in Social Exchanges," *The Journal of Psychology* 98 (1978): 267–75.

5. David M. G. Lewis, Judith A. Easton, Cari D. Goetz, and David M. Buss, "Exploitative Male Mating Strategies: Personality, Mating Orientation, and Relationship Status," *Personality and Individual Differences* 52 (2012): 139–43, doi: 10.1016/j.paid.2011.09.017.

6. Lewis et al., "Exploitative Male Mating Strategies." Lewis et al. Note that men with this combination of characteristics may be more likely to perceive women in general as sexually exploitable. Lewis et al., "Exploitative Male Mating Strategies," 142–43.

7. Babiak and Hare, *Snakes in Suits*, 20.

8. Ibid., 27.

9. Ibid.

10. Viren Swami and Adrian Furnham, *The Psychology of Physical Attraction* (London: Routledge, 2008), 11.

11. Guerrero and Floyd, *Nonverbal Communication*, 58.

12. Judith H. Langlois, Lisa Kalakanis, Adam J. Rubenstein, Andrea Larson, Monica Hallam, and Monica Smoot, "Maxims or Myths of Beauty? A Meta-Analytic and Theoretical Review," *Psychological Bulletin* 126, no. 3 (2000): 390–423.

13. Robert B. Cialdini and Brad J. Sagarin, "Principles of Interpersonal Influence," in *Persuasion: Psychological Insights and Perspectives*, 2nd ed., eds. Timothy C. Brock and Melanie C. Green (Thousand Oaks: SAGE Publications, 2005) 143–69 (156).

14. Judee K. Burgoon, Laura K. Guerrero, and Kory Floyd, *Nonverbal Communication* (Boston: Allyn and Bacon, 2010), 83.

15. Frank W. Schneider, Jamie A. Gruman, and Larry M. Coutts, *Applied Social Psychology: Understanding and Addressing Social and Practical Problems* (Thousand Oaks: SAGE Publications, 2005), 82.

16. Burgoon et al., *Nonverbal Communication*, 83.

17. Swami and Furnham, *The Psychology of Physical Attraction*, 11.

18. Ibid.

19. Cialdini and Sagarin, "Principles of Interpersonal Influence," 156.

20. Guerrero and Floyd, *Nonverbal Communication*, 58.

21. Schneider et al., *Applied Social Psychology*, 82.

22. Barrick et al., "What You See," 1405.

23. Ibid., 1406.

24. Rebecca J. Brand, Abigail Bonatsos, Rebecca D'Orazio, and Hilary DeShong, "What is Beautiful is Good, Even Online: Correlations Between Photo Attractiveness and Text Attractiveness in Men's Online Dating Profiles," *Computers in Human Behavior* 28 (2012): 166–70.

25. Brand et al., "What is Beautiful is Good, Even Online."

26. Katelyn Y. A. McKenna (Yael Kaynan), "MySpace or Your Place: Relationship Initiation and Development in the Wired and Wireless World," in *Handbook of Relationship Initiation*, eds. Susan Sprecher, Amy Wenzel, and John Harvey (New York: Psychology Press, 2008), 235–47 (241).

27. McKenna, "MySpace or Your Place," 241.

28. Rafaele Dumas and Benoit Teste, "The Influence of Criminal Facial Stereotypes on Juridic Judgments," *Swiss Journal of Psychology* 65, no. 4 (2006): 237–44 (238).

29. Swami and Furnham, *The Psychology of Physical Attraction*, 13 (citing Darby and Jeffers, 1988; Kulka and Kessler, 1978; Solomon and Schopler, 1978).

30. Monica J. Harris and Christopher P. Garris, "You Never Get a Second Chance to Make a First Impression: Behavioral Consequences of First Impressions," in *First Impressions*, eds. Nalini Ambady and John J. Skowronski (New York: The Guilford Press, 2008), 147–68 (154) (citing Mazella and Feingold, 1994).

31. Cialdini and Sagarin, "Principles of Interpersonal Influence," 156 (citing Stewart, 1980).

32. Sheila Isenberg, *Women Who Love Men Who Kill* (New York: Simon & Schuster, 1991), 100–101.

33. Isenberg, *Women Who Love Men Who Kill*, 101.

34. Ibid., 103.

35. Ibid.

36. Ibid., 104–5.

37. Nicholas S. Holtzman and Michael J. Strube, "People With Dark Personalities Tend to Create a Physically Attractive Veneer," *Social Psychological and Personality Science* 4, no. 4 (2012): 461–67.

38. Holtzman and Strube, "People With Dark Personalities." While all three Dark Triad traits are linked with dressing to enhance attractiveness, the strongest correlation was found for psychopathy—considered to be the "darkest" trait. Holtzman and Strube, "People With Dark Personalities," 464–65.

39. Simine Vazire, Laura P. Naumann, Peter J. Rentfrow, and Samuel D. Gosling, "Portrait of a Narcissist: Manifestations of Narcissism in Physical Appearance," *Journal of Research in Personality* 42 (2008): 1439–47.

40. Vazire et al., "Portrait of a Narcissist," 1439–40.

41. Ibid., 1439.

42. Back et al., "Why are Narcissists so Charming at First Sight?" 141.

43. Holtzman and Strube, "The Intertwined Evolution," 214.

44. Harold Sigall and Nancy Ostrove, "Beautiful but Dangerous: Effects of Offender Attractiveness and Nature of the Crime on Juridic Judgment," *Journal of Personality and Social Psychology* 31, no. 3 (1975): 410–14.

45. Sigall and Ostrove, "Beautiful but Dangerous," 412.

46. Catherine Hakim, *Erotic Capital: The Power of Attraction in the Boardroom and the Bedroom* (New York: Basic Books, 2011), 10–15.

47. Hakim, *Erotic Capital*, 10.

48. Johannes Honekopp, "Once More: Is Beauty in the Eye of the Beholder? Relative Contributions of Private and Shared Taste to Judgments of Facial Attractiveness," *Journal of Experimental Psychology* 32, no. 2 (2006): 199–209, doi: 10.1037/0096-1523.32.2.199.

49. Viren Swami, Stefan Stieger, Tanja Haubner, Martin Voracek, and Adrian Furnham, "Evaluating the Physical Attractiveness of Oneself and One's Romantic Partner:

Individual and Relationship Correlates of the Love-Is-Blind Bias," *Journal of Individual Differences* 30, no. 1 (2009): 35–43 (36), doi: 10.1027/1614-0001.30.1.35.

50. Michael R. Cunningham and Anita P. Barbee, "Prelude to a Kiss: Nonverbal Flirting, Opening Gambits, and Other Communication Dynamics in the Initiation of Romantic Relationships," in *Handbook of Relationship Initiation*, eds. Susan Sprecher, Amy Wenzel, and John Harvey (New York: Psychology Press, 2008), 97–120 (102) (citing Wong and Cunningham, 1990).

51. Cunningham and Barbee, "Prelude to a Kiss," 102 (citing Wong and Cunningham, 1990).

52. Andrew J. Elliot and Daniela Niesta, "Romantic Red: Red Enhances Men's Attraction to Women," *Journal of Personality and Social Psychology* 95, no. 5 (2008): 1150–64.

53. Elliot and Niesta, "Romantic Red."

54. Andrew J. Elliot, Tobias Greitemeyer, Richard H. Gramzow, Daniela Niesta Kayser, Stephanie Lichtenfeld, Markus A. Maier, and Huijun Liu, "Red, Rank, and Romance in Women Viewing Men," *Journal of Experimental Psychology: General* 139, no. 3 (2010): 399–417.

55. Elliot et al., "Red, Rank, and Romance," 400–402, 411–12.

56. Julie Fitness, Garth Fletcher and Nickola Overall, "Interpersonal Attraction and Intimate Relationships," in *The Sage Handbook of Social Psychology*, eds Michael A. Hogg and Joel Cooper (London: SAGE Publications, 2003), 258–78 (259–60)

57. Viren Swami, Adrian Furnham, Tomas Chamorro-Premuzic, Kanwal Akbar, Natalie Gordon, Tasha Harris, Jo Finch, and Martin J. Tovee, "More Than Just Skin Deep? Personality Information Influences Men's Ratings of the Attractiveness of Women's Body Sizes," *The Journal of Social Psychology* 150, no. 6 (2010): 628–47 (629).

58. Viren Swami, Corina Greven, and Adrian Furnham, "More Than Just Skin-Deep? A Pilot Study Integrating Physical and Non-Physical Factors in the Perception of Physical Attractiveness," *Personality and Individual Differences* 42 (2007): 563–72 (565).

59. Swami et al., "More Than Just Skin Deep? Personality Information," 629.

60. Swami et al., "More Than Just Skin Deep? A Pilot Study," 565.

61. Sampo V. Paunonen, "You Are Honest, Therefore I Like You and Find You Attractive," *Journal of Research in Personality* 40 (2006): 237–49.

62. Swami and Furnham, *The Psychology of Physical Attraction*, 142–44.

63. Ronald E. Riggio, Keith F. Widaman, Joan S. Tucker, and Charles Salinas, "Beauty is More Than Skin Deep: Components of Attractiveness," *Basic and Applied Social Psychology* 12, no. 4 (1991): 423–39 (424).

64. Swami et al., "More Than Just Skin Deep? Personality Information," 629–30.

65. Ibid., 628–47.

66. Kevin M. Kniffin and David Sloan Wilson, "The Effect of Nonphysical Traits on the Perception of Physical Attractiveness: Three Naturalistic Studies," *Evolution and Human Behavior* 25 (2004): 88–101 (98–99).

67. Barbara May Gayle and Raymond W. Preiss, "An Overview of Dyadic Processes in Interpersonal Communication," in *Interpersonal Communication Research: Advances Through Meta-Analysis*, eds. Mike Allen, Raymond W. Preiss, Barbara Mae Gayle, and Nancy A. Burrell (Mahway: Lawrence Erlbaum Associates, 2002), 111–23 (113).

68. Gayle and Preiss, "An Overview of Dyadic Processes," 113.

69. Cunningham and Barbee, "Prelude to a Kiss," 104.

70. Ibid.

71. Ibid.

72. Jerry M. Burger, "Fleeting Attraction and Compliance with Requests," in *The Science of*

Social Influence: Advances and Future Progress, ed. Anthony R. Pratkanis (New York: Psychology Press, 2007), 155–66 (155–59).

73. Robert Levine, *The Power of Persuasion: How We're Bought and Sold* (Hoboken: John Wiley and Sons, 2003), 56.

74. Levine, *The Power of Persuasion*, 56.

75. Peter A. Andersen, "Influential Actions," in *Perspectives on Persuasion, Social Influence, and Compliance Gaining*, eds. John S. Seiter and Robert H. Gass (Boston: Pearson Education Inc., 2004), 165–80 (166) (citing Cialdini, 1984).

76. See generally, Robert Helmreich, Elliot Aronson, and James LeFan, "To Err is Humanizing—Sometimes: Effects of Self-Esteem, Competence, and a Pratfall on Interpersonal Attraction," *Journal of Personality and Social Psychology* 16, no. 2 (1970): 259–64.

77. Margaret S. Clark, Sherri P. Pataki, and Valerie H. Carver. "Some Thoughts and Findings on Self-Presentation of Emotions in Relationships," in *Knowledge Structures in Close Relationships: A Social Psychological Approach*, eds. Garth J. O. Fletcher and Julie Fitness (Mahwah: Lawrence Erlbaum Associates, 1996), 247–74 (249–50).

78. See, e.g., Judee K. Burgoon and Aaron E. Bacue. "Nonverbal Communication Skills," in *Handbook of Communication and Social Interaction Skills*, eds. John O. Greene and Brant R. Burleson (New York: Lawrence Erlbaum Associates, 2003), 179–219 (188).

79. Burgoon and Bacue, "Nonverbal Communication Skills," 188.

80. Barry M. Staw, Robert I. Sutton, and Lisa H. Pelled, "Employee Positive Emotion and Favorable Outcomes at the Workplace," *Organization Science* 5, no. 1 (1994): 51–71 (56) (citing Fiske and Taylor, 1991).

81. Clark et al., "Some Thoughts and Findings," 253–54.

82. Carla Van Dam, *Identifying Child Molesters: Preventing Child Sexual Abuse by Recognizing the Patterns of the Offenders* (New York: The Haworth Maltreatment and Trauma Press, 2001), 146.

83. Van Dam, *Identifying Child Molesters*, 146.

84. Ibid. (referencing Hare's (1993) description of the psychopath).

85. Leslie A. Zebrowitz and Joann M. Montepare, "First Impressions from Facial Appearance Cues," in *First Impressions*, eds. Nalini Ambady and John J. Skowronski, (New York: The Guilford Press, 2008), 171–204 (184).

86. Paul. D. Cherulnik, Kristina A. Donley, Tay Sha R. Wiewel, and Susan R. Miller, "Charisma is Contagious: The Effect of Leaders' Charisma on Observers' Affect," *Journal of Applied Social Psychology* 31 (2001): 2149–59 (2157).

2. Follow the Leader: The Attraction of Power

1. Dacher Keltner, Deborah H. Gruenfeld, and Cameron Anderson, "Power, Approach, and Inhibition," *Psychological Review* 110, no. 2 (2003); 265–84 (267).

2. Markus Brauer and Richard Y. Bourhis, "Social Power," *European Journal of Social Psychology* 36 (2006): 601–616 (608–9).

3. Brauer and Bourhis, "Social Power," 609.

4. Peter M. Blau, *Exchange and Power in Social Life* (Oxford: Transaction Books, 1986), 65–67.

5. Paul W. Eastwick, Brian M. Wilkey, Eli J. Finkel, Nathaniel M. Lambert, Grainne M.

Fitzsimons, Preston C. Brown, and Frank D. Fincham, "Act With Authority: Romantic Desire at the Nexus of Power Possessed and Power Perceived," *Journal of Experimental Social Psychology* 49 (2013): 267–71, http://dx.doi.org/10.1016/jesp.2012.10.019.

6. Laura K. Guerrero, Peter A. Andersen, and Walid A. Afifi, *Close Encounters: Communication in Relationships,* 2nd ed. (Los Angeles: SAGE Publications, 2007), 235.

7. Eastwick et al., "Act With Authority," 270.

8. Brian P. Meier and Sarah Dionne, "Downright Sexy: Verticality, Implicit Power, and Perceived Physical Attractiveness," *Social Cognition* 27, no. 6 (2009): 883–92.

9. Meier and Dionne, "Downright Sexy." The evolutionary theory of desirability that was tested in this experiment holds that women are perceived as more attractive when they are seen as powerless—which translates into faithfulness and youth. Hence the photo placement at the bottom of the screen. Meier and Dionne, "Downright Sexy."

10. See, e.g., Eastwick et al., "Act With Authority."

11. See, e.g., Meier and Dionne, "Downright Sexy," 884–85.

12. John Levi Martin, "Is Power Sexy?" *American Journal of Sociology* 111, no. 2 (September 2005): 408–46, www.jstor.org/stable/10.1086/432781.

13. While research demonstrates the attractiveness of social advantage, an interesting study revealed the attractiveness of the unfairly disadvantaged. See Kenneth S. Michniewicz and Joseph A. Vandello, "The Attractive Underdog: When Disadvantage Bolsters Attractiveness," *Journal of Social and Personal Relationships* 30, no. 7 (2013): 942–52.

14. Martin, "Is Power Sexy?" 411.

15. Ibid., 439.

16. William G. Graziano and Jennifer Weisho Bruce, "Attraction and the Initiation of Relationships: A Review of the Empirical Literature," in *Handbook of Relationship Initiation,* eds. Susan Sprecher, Amy Wenzel, and John Harvey (New York: Psychology Press, 2008), 269–95 (279).

17. Angela D. Bryan, Gregory D. Webster, and Amanda L. Mahaffey, "The Big, the Rich, and the Powerful: Physical, Financial, and Social Dimensions of Dominance in Mating and Attraction," *Personality and Social Psychology Bulletin* 37, no. 3 (2011): 365–82.

18. Ogi Ogas and Sai Gaddam, *A Billion Wicked Thoughts: What the World's Largest Experiment Reveals About Human Desire* (New York: Dutton, 2011), 96.

19. Graziano and Bruce, "Attraction and the Initiation of Relationships," 279.

20. Zebrowitz and Montepare, "First Impressions," 184.

21. Martin, "Is Power Sexy?" 411. Martin's study, however, found that both men and women find men who have power over them to be sexy. Martin, "Is Power Sexy?" 439.

22. Nancy C. M. Hartsock, *Money, Sex, and Power: Toward a Feminist Historical Materialism* (New York: Longman, 1983), 6.

23. Hartsock, *Money, Sex, and Power,* 6.

24. Ibid., 157–58.

25. Ibid., 157–61.

26. Martin, "Is Power Sexy?"

27. Laurie A. Rudman, and Julie E. Phelan, "The Interpersonal Power of Feminism: Is Feminism Good for Romantic Relationships?" *Sex Roles* 57 (2007): 787–99.

28. Ibid.

29. Reeder, "Perceptions of Goals and Motives," 501.

30. Ibid.

31. Lord Acton, *Letter to Bishop Mandell Creighton, 1887.*

32. Jonathan W. Kunstman and Jon K. Maner, "Sexual Overperception: Power, Mating Motives, and Biases in Social Judgment," *Journal of Personality and Social Psychology* 100, no. 2 (2010): 282–94 (282), doi: 10.1037/a0021135.

33. Kunstman and Maner, "Sexual Overperception," 282.

34. Ibid.

35. Ibid.

36. John J. Sosik, William A. Gentry, and Jae Uk Chun, "The Value of Virtue in the Upper Echelons: A Multisource Examination of Executive Character Strengths and Performance," *The Leadership Quarterly* 23 (2012): 367–82 (367), doi: 10.1016/j.leaqua.2011.08.010.

37. Samuel P. Oliner, *The Nature of Good and Evil: Understanding the Many Acts of Moral and Immoral Behavior* (St. Paul: Paragon House, 2011), 1.

38. Barbora Nevicka, Annebel H. B. De Hoogh, Annelies E. M. Van Vianen, and Femke S. Ten Velden, "Uncertainty Enhances the Preference for Narcissistic Leaders," *European Journal of Social Psychology* 43 (2013): 370–80, doi: 10.1002/ejsp.1943.

39. Nevicka et al., "Uncertainty Enhances the Preference for Narcissistic Leaders," 371.

40. Sarah Francis Smith, Scott O. Lilienfeld, Karly Coffey, and James M. Dabbs, "Are Psychopaths and Heroes Twigs Off the Same Branch? Evidence from College, Community, and Presidential Samples," *Journal of Research in Personality* 47 (2013): 634–46, http://dx.doi.org/10.1016/j.jrp.2013.05.006.

41. Smith et al., "Psychopaths and Heroes," 635.

42. Babiak et al., "Corporate Psychopathy," 188–89.

43. Scott O. Lilienfeld, Irwin D. Waldman, Kristin Landfield, Ashley L. Watts, Steven Rubenzer, and Thomas R. Faschingbauer, "Fearless Dominance and the U.S. Presidency: Implications of Psychopathic Personality Traits for Successful and Unsuccessful Political Leadership," *Journal of Personality and Social Psychology* 103, no. 3 (2012): 489–505, doi: 10.1037/a0029392.

44. Lilienfeld et al., "Fearless Dominance and the U.S. Presidency," 498.

45. David T. Lykken, "Psychopathic Personality: The Scope of the Problem," in *Handbook of Psychopathy*, ed. Christopher J. Patrick (New York: The Guilford Press, 2006), 3–13 (11).

46. John F. Rauthmann and Gerald P. Kolar, "How 'Dark' are the Dark Triad Traits? Examining the Perceived Darkness of Narcissism, Machiavellianism, and Psychopathy," *Personality and Individual Differences* 53 (2012): 884–89 (885).

47. Rauthmann and Kolar, "How 'Dark' are the Dark Triad Traits?" 884–85.

48. Jakobwitz and Egan, "The Dark Triad," 332.

49. Benoit Leclerc, Jean Proulx, Patrick Lussier, and Jean-Francois Allaire, "Offender-Victim Interaction and Crime Event Outcomes: Modus Operandi and Victim Effects on the Risk of Intrusive Sexual Offenses Against Children," *Criminology* 47, no. 2 (2009): 595–618 (598).

50. Louanne Lawson, "Isolation, Gratification, Justification: Offenders' Explanations of Child Molesting," *Issues in Mental Health Nursing* 24 (2003): 695–705 (702). Sandfort opines that extra-familial pedophile relationships are more symmetrical than relationships involving incest. Theo Sandfort, *Boys on Their Contacts with Men: A Study of Sexually Expressed Friendships* (Elmhurst: Global Academic Publishers, 1987), 90–91.

51. James A. Vela-McConnell, *Unlikely Friends: Bridging Ties and Diverse Friendships* (Lanham, Plymouth: Lexington Books, 2011), 20.

52. Cosimo Schinaia, *On Paedophilia* (London: Karnac, 2010), 194–95.

53. Christiane Sanderson, *The Seduction of Children: Empowering Parents and Teachers to Protect Children from Child Sexual Abuse* (London: Jessica Kingsley Publishers, 2004), 171.

54. Frances P. Reddington and Betsy Wright Kreisel, *Sexual Assault: The Victims, the Perpetrators, and the Criminal Justice System,* 2nd ed. (Durham: Carolina Academic Press, 2009), 260.

55. Eric Leberg, *Understanding Child Molesters: Taking Charge* (Thousand Oaks: SAGE Publications, 1997), 41.

56. Celia Williamson and Terry Cluse-Tolar, "Pimp-Controlled Prostitution: Still an Integral Part of Street Life," *Violence Against Women* 8, no. 9 (2002): 1074–92.

57. Williamson and Cluse-Tolar, "Pimp-Controlled Prostitution," 1080.

58. Sara Swann, "Helping Girls Involved in 'Prostitution': A Barnardos Experiment," in *Home Truths About Child Sexual Abuse: Influencing Policy and Practice: A Reader,* ed. Catherine Itzin (London: Routledge: 2000), 277–89 (278–79).

59. Swann, "Helping Girls," 278–79.

60. Lisa Goldblatt Grace, "Understanding the Commercial Sexual Exploitation of Children," *The Link* 7, no. 2 (Fall 2008/ Winter 2009): 1, 3–6 (4).

61. Van Dam, *Identifying Child Molesters,* 150–51.

62. Ibid., 150.

63. Ibid., 170.

64. Esther Van Leeuwen and Susanne Tauber, "The Strategic Side of Out-Group Helping," in *The Psychology of Prosocial Behavior: Group Processes, Intergroup Relations, and Helping,* eds. Stefan Sturmer and Mark Snyder (Chichester: John Wiley and Sons, 2010), 81–99 (88).

65. Leeuwen and Tauber, "The Strategic Side of Out-Group Helping," 91.

66. Van Dam, *Identifying Child Molesters,* 171.

67. Ibid.

68. Ibid.

69. Leeuwen and Tauber, "The Strategic Side of Out-Group Helping," 82–83.

70. Ibid., 83 (citing Nadler and Halabi, 2006).

71. Blau, *Exchange and Power,* 118.

72. Van Dam, *Identifying Child Molesters,* 150.

73. Ibid., 170.

74. Ibid., 151.

75. Marchand and Vonk, "The Process of Becoming Suspicious," 242–43.

76. Ibid., 243.

77. Ibid.

78. Ibid.

79. Ibid.

80. Joey T. Cheng, Jessica L. Tracy, Alan Kingstone, Tom Foulsham, and Joseph Henrich, "Two Ways to the Top: Evidence that Dominance and Prestige are Distinct Yet Viable Avenues to Social Rank and Influence," *Journal of Personality and Social Psychology* 104, no. 1 (2013): 103–25.

81. Cheng et al., "Two Ways to the Top," 105.

82. Ibid., 103.

83. Ibid.

84. Ibid., 105.

85. Ibid.

86. Ibid., 106–7.

87. Ibid.

88. Ibid., 107. Cheng and coauthors chose the term *prestige* because status is defined differently within other disciplines such as personal psychology, where it indicates influence, agency, control, and dominance, as opposed to admiration or respect. Cheng et al., "Two Ways to the Top," 107.

89. Ibid.

90. Ibid., 107–8.

91. Bogdan Wojciszke and Anna Struzynska-Kujalowicz, "Power Influences Self-Esteem," *Social Cognition* 25, no. 4 (2007): 472–94 (475).

92. Boddy, *Corporate Psychopaths*, 64.

93. Clive R. Boddy, "Corporate Psychopaths, Bullying and Unfair Supervision in the Workplace," *Journal of BUSINESS Ethics* 100 (2011): 367–79, doi: 10.1007/s10551-010-0689-5.

94. Boddy, "Corporate Psychopaths," 368.

95. John C. Turner, "Explaining the Nature of Power: A Three-Process Theory," *European Journal of Social Psychology* 35 (2005): 1–22 (18).

96. Guerrero et al., *Close Encounters*, 234.

97. See, e.g., Sheng Wang, Edward C. Tomlinson, and Raymond A. Noe, "The Role of Mentor Trust and Protégé Internal Locus of Control in Formal Mentoring Relationships," *Journal of Applied Psychology* 95, no. 2 (2010): 358–67 (358).

98. Kathy Ehrensperger, *Paul and the Dynamics of Power: Communication and Interaction in the Early Christ-Movement* (London, New York: T&T Clark International, 2009), 31.

99. Thomas E. Wartenberg, *The Forms of Power: From Domination to Transformation* (Philadelphia: Temple University Press, 1990), 183–84.

100. Wartenberg, *The Forms of Power*, 183–84.

101. Ibid., 108–9.

102. Ibid.

103. "Scarface: The Quotes," www.jgeoff.com/scarface/quotes.html (with spelling corrections).

104. Ogas and Gaddam, *A Billion Wicked Thoughts*, 101.

105. Nicolas Gueguen and Lubomir Lamy, "Short Research Note: Men's Social Status and Attractiveness: Women's Receptivity to Men's Date Requests," *Swiss Journal of Psychology* 71, no. 3 (2012): 157–60, doi: 10.1024/1421-0185/a000083.

106. Matthew 6:21.

3. Perceiving is Believing: The Comfort of Credibility

1. Anna C. Salter, *Predators: Pedophiles, Rapists, and Other Sex Offenders: Who They Are, How They Operate, and How We Can Protect Ourselves and Our Children* (New York: Basic Books, 2003), 26–28.

2. Salter, *Predators*, 27.

3. Ibid.

4. Ibid., 26.

5. James B. Stiff and Paul A. Mongeau, *Persuasive Communication*, 2nd ed. (New York: Guilford Press, 2003), 107.

6. Charles C. Self, "Credibility," in *An Integrated Approach to Communication Theory and Research*, 2nd ed., eds. Don W. Stacks and Michael B. Salwen (New York: Routledge, 2009), 435–56 (435).

7. Richard M. Perloff, *The Dynamics of Persuasion: Communication and Attitudes in the 21st Century*, 4th ed. (New York: Routledge, 2010), 167.

8. Pratkanis, "Social Influence Analysis," 30.

9. O'Keefe, *Persuasion Theory and Research*, 182–83; Robert H. Gass and John S. Seiter, *Persuasion, Social Influence, and Compliance Gaining*, 4th ed. (Boston: Allyn & Bacon, 2011), 77–78.

10. Wartenberg, *The Forms of Power*, 108.

11. Bertram H. Raven, "The Bases of Power and the Power/Interaction Model of Interpersonal Influence," *Analyses of Social Issues and Public Policy* 8, no. 1 (2008): 1–22 (3).

12. Karen S. Cook, Russell Hardin, and Margaret Levi, *Cooperation Without Trust?* (New York: Russell Sage Foundation, 2005), 27–28.

13. Cook et al., *Cooperation Without Trust?* 27–28.

14. Ibid., 28.

15. Gass and Seiter, *Persuasion, Social Influence, and Compliance Gaining*, 78–79.

16. Gary C. Woodward and Robert E. Denton, Jr., *Persuasion and Influence in American Life*, 5th ed. (Long Grove: Waveland Press, Inc., 2004), 111.

17. Perloff, *The Dynamics of Persuasion*, 168.

18. Alison R. Fragale, Jennifer R. Overbeck, and Margaret A. Neale, "Resources Versus Respect: Social Judgments Based on Targets' Power and Status Positions," *Journal of Experimental Social Psychology* 47 (2011): 767–75 (767).

19. Erik W. de Kwaadsteniet and Erik van Dijk, "Social Status as a Cue for Tacit Coordination," *Journal of Experimental Social Psychology* 46 (2010): 515–24 (516).

20. De Kwaadsteniet and Dijk, "Social Status," 515.

21. Andersen, "Influential Actions," 172.

22. Pratkanis, "Social Influence Analysis," 31.

23. Ibid., 32–33.

24. Ibid., 33.

25. Ibid., 39.

26. Ibid.

27. See, e.g., Van Dam, *Identifying Child Molesters*, 100–103.

28. Eric Beauregard, Jean Proulx, Kim Rossmo, Benoit Leclerc and Jean-Francois Allaire, "Script Analysis of the Hunting Process of Serial Sex Offenders," *Criminal Justice and Behavior* 34, no. 8 (August, 2007): 1069–84 (1080); Leclerc et al., "Modus Operandi," 192.

29. See, e.g., Sandfort, *Boys on Their Contacts With Men*, 58.

30. Kenneth V. Lanning, *Child Molesters: A Behavioral Analysis: For Law-Enforcement Officers Investigating the Sexual Exploitation of Children by Acquaintance Molesters*, 4th ed. (Alexandria: National Center for Missing and Exploited Children, 2001), 60.

31. Clancy, *The Trauma Myth*, 42–43.

32. Leclerc et al., "Modus Operandi," 192.

33. Horberg et al., "Pride Displays," 25.

34. Ibid.

35. Stanley Milgram, "Behavioral Study of Obedience," *Journal of Abnormal and Social Psychology* 67, no. 4 (1963): 371–78.

36. Milgram, "Behavioral Study of Obedience," 376.

37. Burgoon et al., *Nonverbal Communication*, 358.

38. Andersen, "Influential Actions," 172 (citing Bickman, 1971).

39. Ibid. (citing Unger, 1972).

40. Ibid. (citing Kleinke, 1977).
41. Also known as *new religious movements*.
42. Steven Hassan, *Combating Cult Mind Control* (Rochester: Park Street Press, 1988), 41.
43. Raphael Aron, *Cults, Terror, and Mind Control* (Point Richmond: Bay Tree Publishing, LLC, 2009), 15.
44. See, e.g., Katherine Ramsland and Patrick N. McGrain, *Inside The Minds Of Sexual Predators* (Santa Barbara: Praeger, 2010), 145 (describing a serial rapist dubbed the "classified ad rapist" due to his pretense of showing up at women's homes looking respectable in a suit, in response to posted advertisements).
45. "Nurses Remain Most Trusted Professionals in America, Gallup Survey Says," National News, *Advance Healthcare Network* (December 5, 2012), http://nursing.advanceweb.com/News/National-News/Nurses-Remain-Most-Trusted-Professionals-in-America-Gallup-Survey-Says.aspx.
46. Kristine M. Kuhn, Timothy R. Johnson, and Douglas Miller, "Applicant Desirability Influences Reactions to Discovered Resume Embellishments," *International Journal of Selection and Assessment* 21, no. 1 (2013): 111–20.
47. Kuhn et al., "Applicant Desirability." Interestingly, when the favored applicants claimed to have a college degree (a requirement for the position) when they were actually several units short, their perceived trustworthiness and likability was lowered more than the less favored applicants who made the same false claim. Kuhn et al., "Applicant Desirability," 119.
48. Kuhn et al., "Applicant Desirability," 119.
49. Paul Babiak, "From Darkness into the Light: Psychopathy in Industrial and Organizational Psychology," in *The Psychopath: Theory, Research, and Practice*, eds. Hugues Herve and John C. Yuille (Mahway: Lawrence Erlbaum Associates: 2007), 411–28.
50. Babiak and Hare, *Snakes in Suits*.
51. Babiak, "From Darkness into the Light," 417–18.
52. Babiak and Hare, *Snakes in Suits*, 88.
53. Boddy, *Corporate Psychopaths*, 64.
54. Kevin Dutton, *The Wisdom of Psychopaths: What Saints, Spies, and Serial Killers Can Teach Us About Success* (New York: Scientific American/ Farrar, Straus and Giroux, 2012), 21.
55. Dutton, *The Wisdom of Psychopaths*, 21.
56. Clive Boddy, *Corporate Psychopaths: Organizational Destroyers* (New York: Palgrave Macmillan, 2011), 8, 42.
57. Boddy, *Corporate Psychopaths*, 42.
58. Babiak, "From Darkness into the Light," 413–14. The individuals studied were identified through their scores on the Hare Psychopathy Checklist—Revised (PCL-R; Hare, 1991). Babiak, "From Darkness into the Light," 412–13.
59. Babiak, "From Darkness into the Light," 413–14.
60. Smith et al., "Psychopaths and Heroes," 634.
61. Ibid.
62. Ibid.
63. Hare, *Without Conscience*, 113.
64. Lykken, "Psychopathic Personality," 11.
65. Smith et al., "Psychopaths and Heroes," 635.
66. Ibid., 643.
67. Babiak, "From Darkness into the Light," 414.

68. Babiak and Hare, *Snakes in Suits*, 96.
69. Boddy, "Corporate Psychopaths," 368.
70. Boddy, *Corporate Psychopaths*, 24.
71. Babiak, "From Darkness into the Light," 416–17.
72. Ibid., 417.
73. Ibid., 414.
74. Babiak and Hare, *Snakes in Suits*, 38.
75. Babiak, "From Darkness into the Light," 414.
76. Babiak et al., "Corporate Psychopathy," 189–90.
77. Babiak and Hare, *Snakes in Suits*, 38.
78. Ibid.
79. Hall and Benning, "The 'Successful' Psychopath," 460.
80. Jones and Paulhus, "Differentiating the Dark Triad," 259–60.
81. Babiak et al., "Corporate Psychopathy," 192.
82. Ogas and Gaddam, *A Billion Wicked Thoughts*, 102–3.
83. Ibid.
84. Burgoon et al., *Nonverbal Communication*, 357.
85. Vazire and Gosling, "E-Perceptions," 124.

4. Suddenly Smitten: The Pleasure of Positive Attention

1. Swami and Furnham, *The Psychology of Physical Attraction*, 139–40.
2. James Knoll, "Teacher Sexual Misconduct: Grooming Patterns and Female Offenders," *Journal of Child Sexual Abuse* 19 (2010): 371–86 (373) (citing Ramirez, 2007) (33-year-old married teacher flattered at attention of her 15-year-old male student announces their affair while intoxicated).
3. Knoll, "Teacher Sexual Misconduct," 375–76.
4. Ibid., 373.
5. Paul W. Eastwick, Eli J. Finkel, Daniel Mochon, and Dan Ariely, "Selective Versus Unselective Romantic Desire," *Psychological Science* 18, no. 4 (2007): 317–19.
6. Eastwick et al., "Selective Versus Unselective Romantic Desire," 318.
7. Ibid.
8. Elaine Walster, G. William Walster, Jane Piliavin, and Lynn Schmidt, "'Playing Hard to Get'" Understanding an Elusive Phenomenon," *Journal of Personality and Social Psychology* 26, no. 1 (1973): 113–21.
9. Walster et al., "'Playing Hard to Get,'" 118–19.
10. Charles Derber, *The Pursuit of Attention: Power and Ego in Everyday Life*, 2nd ed. (Oxford: Oxford University Press, 2000), 12–13.
11. Graziano and Bruce, "Attraction and the Initiation of Relationships," 281.
12. Swami and Furnham, *The Psychology of Physical Attraction*, 139–40.
13. Arthur Aron, Helen E. Fisher, Greg Strong, Bianca Acevedo, Suzanne Riela, and Irene Tsapelas, "Falling in Love," in *Handbook of Relationship Initiation*, eds. Susan Sprecher, Amy Wenzel, and John Harvey (New York: Psychology Press, 2008), 315–36 (324–25).
14. Aron et al., "Falling in Love," 324.
15. Ibid.
16. Jon K. Maner, Matthew T. Gailliot, D. Aaron Rouby, and Saul L. Miller, "Can't Take My

Eyes Off You: Attentional Adhesion to Mates and Rivals," *Journal of Personality and Social Psychology* 93, no. 3 (2007): 389–401 (398), doi: 10.1037/0022-3514.93.3.389.

17. Maner et al., "Can't Take My Eyes Off You," 390.

18. Ibid., 398.

19. Ibid.

20. Kory Floyd, *Communicating Affection: Interpersonal Behavior and Social Context* (Cambridge: Cambridge University Press, 2006), 1.

21. Floyd, *Communicating Affection*, 1.

22. Ibid., 88.

23. Ibid., 95.

24. Ibid., 4–5.

25. Kory Floyd and Perry M. Pauley, "Affectionate Communication Is Good, Except When It Isn't: On the Dark Side of Expressing Affection," in *The Dark Side of Close Relationships II*, eds. William R. Cupach and Brian H. Spitzberg (New York: Routledge, 2011), 145–73 (147).

26. Floyd and Pauley, "Affectionate Communication," 147.

27. Floyd, *Communicating Affection*, 134–38.

28. Sandra L. Brown, *Women Who Love Psychopaths: Inside the Relationships of Inevitable Harm with Psychopaths, Sociopaths, and Narcissists* 2nd ed. (Penrose: Mask Publishing, 2009), 190.

29. Brown, *Women Who Love Psychopaths*, 190.

30. Ibid.

31. Claudia Moscovici, *Dangerous Liaisons: How to Recognize and Escape from Psychopathic Seduction* (Lanham: Hamilton Books, 2011), 21.

32. Moscovici, *Dangerous Liaisons*, 21.

33. Brown, *Women Who Love Psychopaths*, 189.

34. Moscovici, *Dangerous Liaisons*, 58.

35. Brown, *Women Who Love Psychopaths*, 189.

36. Babiak and Hare, *Snakes in Suits*, 57.

37. Moscovici, *Dangerous Liaisons*, 82.

38. W. Keith Campbell, "Narcissism and Romantic Attraction," *Journal of Personality and Social Psychology* 77, no. 6 (1999): 1254–70 (1255).

39. W. Keith Campbell and Craig A. Foster, "Narcissism and Commitment in Romantic Relationships: An Investment Model Analysis," *Personality and Social Psychology Bulletin* 28, no. 4 (2002): 484–95 (484).

40. Campbell and Foster, "Narcissism and Commitment," 485.

41. Amy B. Brunell and W. Keith Campbell, "Narcissism and Romantic Relationships: Understanding the Paradox," in *The Handbook of Narcissism and Narcissistic Personality Disorder: Theoretical Approaches, Empirical Findings, and Treatments*, eds. W. Keith Campbell and Joshua D. Miller (Hoboken: John Wiley & Sons, Inc., 2011), 344–50 (345).

42. Brunell and Campbell, "Narcissism and Romantic Relationships," 345.

43. Campbell and Foster, "Narcissism and Commitment," 485.

44. Mitja D. Back, Albrecht C. P. Kufner, Tanja M. Gerlach, Michael Dufner, John F. Rauthmann, and Jaap J. A. Denissen, "Narcissistic Admiration and Rivalry: Disentangling the Bright and Dark Sides of Narcissism," *Journal of Personality and Social Psychology* 105, no. 6 (2013): 1013–37 (1014), doi: 10.1037/a0034431 (discussing the agency model of narcissism).

45. Seung Yun Lee, Aiden P. Gregg, and Seong Hoon Park, "The Person in the Purchase:

Narcissistic Consumers Prefer Products that Positively Distinguish Them," *Journal of Personality and Social Psychology* 105, no. 2 (2013): 335–52, doi: 10.1037/a0032703.

46. Lee et al., "The Person in the Purchase," 336.
47. Ibid., 347.
48. Campbell and Foster, "Narcissism and Commitment," 486.
49. Back et al., "Narcissistic Admiration and Rivalry," 1014 (discussing the dynamic self-regulatory processing model of narcissism).
50. Campbell, "Narcissism and Romantic Attraction"; David R. Collins and Arthur A. Stukas, "Narcissism and Self-Presentation: The Moderating Effects of Accountability and Contingencies of Self-Worth," *Journal of Research in Personality* 42 (2008): 1629–34 (1629).
51. Campbell and Foster, "Narcissism and Commitment."
52. Jonason et al., "The Dark Triad: Facilitating a Short-Term Mating Strategy in Men," 7.
53. Campbell and Foster, "Narcissism and Commitment," 485.
54. Jean M. Twenge and W. Keith Campbell, *The Narcissism Epidemic: Living in the Age of Entitlement* (New York: Atria, 2013), 214.
55. Twenge and Campbell, *The Narcissism Epidemic*, 214.
56. Ibid., 215.
57. Arlette E. Greer and David M. Buss, "Tactics for Promoting Sexual Encounters," *The Journal of Sex Research* 31, no. 3 (1994): 185–201.
58. Melanie Booth-Butterfield and Michael R. Trotta, "Attributional Patterns for Expressions of Love," *Communication Reports* 7, no. 2 (Summer 1994): 119–29 (126).
59. Carrie A. Bredow, Rodney M. Cate, and Ted L. Huston, "Have We Met Before? A Conceptual Model of First Romantic Encounters," in *Handbook of Relationship Initiation*, eds. Susan Sprecher, Amy Wenzel, and John Harvey (New York: Psychology Press, 2008), 3–28 (16).
60. Cunningham and Barbee, "Prelude to a Kiss," 109.
61. Ibid.
62. Bredow et al., "Have We Met Before?" 16.
63. Ibid.
64. Cunningham and Barbee, "Prelude to a Kiss," 109.
65. Bredow et al., "Have We Met Before?" 11.
66. Ibid.

5. The Not-So-Secret Admirer: The Allure of Affirmation

1. Abraham H. Maslow, *Motivation and Personality*, 3rd ed. (New York: HarperCollins Publishers, 1987), 6.
2. Maslow, *Motivation and Personality*, 15–26.
3. Ibid., 17.
4. A. H. Maslow, "A Theory of Human Motivation," *Psychological Review* 50, no. 4 (1943): 370–96 (381).
5. Maslow, "A Theory of Human Motivation," 381–82.
6. Stefan C. Dombrowski, John W. LeMasney, C. Emmanuel Ahia, and Shannon A. Dickson, "Protecting Children from Online Sexual Predators: Technological, Psychoeducational, and Legal Considerations," *Professional Psychology: Research and Practice* 35, no. 1 (2004): 65–73 (66–67).

7. Van Dam, *Identifying Child Molesters*, 151–52.
8. Peter A. Andersen and Laura K. Guerrero, "The Bright Side of Relational Communication: Interpersonal Warmth as aSocial Emotion," in *Handbook of Communication and Emotion: Research, Theory, Applications, and Contexts*, ed. by Peter A. Andersen and Laura K. Guerrero (San Diego: Academic Press, 1998) 303–29 (311).
9. Peter Briggs, Walter T. Simon, and Stacy Simonsen, "An Exploratory Study of Internet-Initiated Sexual Offenses and the Chat Room Offender: Has the Internet Enabled a New Typology of Sex Offender?" *Sexual Abuse: A Journal of Research and Treatment* 23, no. 1 (2011): 72–91 (87).
10. Roger Gaspar and Peter Bibby, "How Rings Work," in *Organized Abuse: The Current Debate*, ed. Peter C. Bibby (Aldershot, Hants: 1996), 49–58 (52–53).
11. Andersen and Guerrero, "The Bright Side of Relational Communication," 311.
12. William B. Swann and Brett W. Pelham, "The Truth About Illusions: Authenticity and Positivity in Social Relationships," in *Handbook of Positive Psychology*, eds. C. R. Snyder and Shane J. Lopez (Oxford: Oxford University Press, 2002) 366–81 (367).
13. Babiak and Hare, *Snakes in Suits*, 74–75.
14. Elaine Chan and Jaideep Sengupta, "Insincere Flattery Actually Works: A Dual Attitudes Perspective," *Journal of Marketing Research* 47 (February 2010): 122–33.
15. Ibid.
16. Cialdini and Sagarin, "Principles of Interpersonal Influence," 157.
17. See, e.g., Roos Vonk, "Self-Serving Interpretations of Flattery: Why Ingratiation Works," *Journal of Personality and Social Psychology* 82, no. 4 (2002): 515–26, doi: 10.1037//0022-3514.82.4.515.
18. Elliot Aronson, "The Power of Self-Persuasion," *American Psychologist* (November, 1999): 875–46 (879). One possibility is that people enjoy flattery, but do not care much for flatterers or those who provide favors. Aronson, "The Power of Self-Persuasion," 879.
19. Fitness et al., "Interpersonal Attraction," 259.
20. Demarais and White, *First Impressions*, 75.
21. Jana Hackathorn and Amanda Brantley, "To Know You Is (Not) to Want You: Mediators Between Sociosexual Orientation and Romantic Commitment," *Current Psychology* (January 10, 2014) doi: 10.1007/s12144-013-9199-9.
22. Hackathorn and Brantley, "To Know You Is (Not) to Want You."
23. Jackie Turton, *Child Abuse, Gender and Society* (New York: Routledge, 2008), 76–77.
24. Ronald B. Adler, Lawrence B. Rosenfeld, and Russell F. Proctor II., *Interplay: The Process of Interpersonal Communication* (Oxford: Oxford University Press, 2010), 317–18.
25. Hare, *Without Conscience*, 35.
26. Ibid.
27. Ibid., 148.
28. Ibid.
29. Ibid., 148–49.
30. John W. McHoskey, "Machiavellianism and Sexuality: On the Moderating Role of Biological Sex," *Personality and Individual Differences* 31 (2001): 779–89 (779).
31. Swami and Furnham, *The Psychology of Physical Attraction*. Interestingly, research shows that we like people most who dislike us initially but then grow to like us, and dislike most those who display the opposite pattern of (waning) affection. Swami and Furnham, *The Psychology of Physical Attraction*, 140 (citing Aronson and Linder, 1965).
32. Babiak and Hare, *Snakes in Suits*, 44.

33. Ibid.

34. Ibid.

35. Meliksah Demir and Metin Ozdemir, "Friendship, Need Satisfaction and Happiness," *Journal of Happiness Studies* 11 (2010): 243–59 (245).

36. Demir and Ozdemir, "Friendship," 243.

37. Steve Duck, *Friends, for Life: The Psychology of Close Relationships* (Brighton, Sussex: The Harvester Press Limited, 1983), 25.

38. Nancy L. Collins, Maire B. Ford, and Brooke C. Feeney, "An Attachment–Theory Perspective on Social Support in Close Relationships," in *Handbook of Interpersonal Psychology: Theory, Research, Assessment, and Therapeutic Interventions*, eds. Leonard M. Horowitz and Stephen Strack (Hoboken: John Wiley & Sons, 2011), 209–31 (209).

39. Floyd, *Communicating Affection*, 34–36.

40. C. David Mortensen, *Optimal Human Relations: The Search for a Good Life* (New Brunswick, London: Transaction Publishers, 2008), 147.

41. Mortensen, *Optimal Human Relations*, 151.

42. Bereczkei et al., "The Presence of Others."

43. Tamas Bereczkei, Bela Birkas, and Zsuzsanna Kerekes, "Public Charity Offer as a Proximate Factor of Evolved Reputation-Building Strategy: An Experimental Analysis of a Real-Life Situation," *Evolution and Human Behavior* 28, no. 4 (2007): 277–84.

44. Adam M. Grant and Francesca Gino, "A Little Thanks Goes a Long Way: Explaining Why Gratitude Expressions Motivate Prosocial Behavior," *Journal of Personality and Social Psychology* 98, no. 6 (2010): 946–55 (947).

45. Grant and Gino, "A Little Thanks," 947.

46. Researchers refer to these as *face needs*. See, e.g., Stephen W. Littlejohn, *Theories of Human Communication*, 7th ed. (Belmont: Wadsworth/ Thompson Learning, 2002), 109.

47. Roelof Hortulanus, Anja Machielse, and Ludwien Meeuwesen, *Social Isolation in Modern Society* (London: Routledge, 2006), 15.

48. Maslow, "A Theory of Human Motivation," 381.

49. This is known as *competence face*. Sandra Metts and Erica Grohskopf, "Impression Management: Goals, Strategies, and Skills," in *Handbook of Communication and Social Interaction Skills*, eds. John O. Greene and Brant R. Burleson (Mahway: Lawrence Erlbaum Associates, 2003), 357–99 (361).

50. Van Dam, *Identifying Child Molesters*, 153.

51. Ibid., 152–53.

52. Daniel J. Howard, Charles Gengler, and Ambuj Jain, "What's in a Name? A Complimentary Means of Persuasion," *Journal of Consumer Research* 22 (September, 1995): 200–11 (200).

53. L. Crocker, L. Clare, and K. Evans, "Giving Up or Finding a Solution? The Experience of Attempted Suicide in Later Life," *Aging & Mental Health* 10, no. 6 (November 2006): 638–47.

54. Marchand and Vonk, "The Process of Becoming Suspicious," 243–44.

55. Ibid., 244 (citing Fein, Hilton, and Miller, 1990).

56. Ibid.

57. Ibid.

58. Ibid., 252–53.

59. Ibid.

60. Ibid., 253.

61. Graham Allan, "Being Unfaithful: His and Her Affairs," in *The State of Affairs: Explorations in Infidelity and Commitment*, eds. Jean Duncombe, Kaeren Harrison, Graham Allan, and Dennis Marsden (Mahwah: Lawrence Erlbaum Associates, 2004), 121–40 (129–30).

62. Allan, "Being Unfaithful," 130.

63. Ibid.

6. Born to Bond: The Seduction of Similarity

1. Pamela M. Anderson, Karin K. Coyle, Anisha Johnson, and Jill Denner, "An Exploratory Study of Adolescent Pimping Relationships," *Journal of Primary Prevention* 35 (2014): 113–17 (114–15), doi: 10.1007/s10935-014-0338-3.

2. Anderson et al., "An Exploratory Study," 116.

3. R. Matthew Montoya and Robert S. Horton, "A Meta-Analytic Investigation of the Processes Underlying the Similarity-Attraction Effect," *Journal of Social and Personal Relationships* 30, no. 1 (2012): 64–94, doi: 10.1177/0265407512452989.

4. Ap Dijksterhuis and Ad van Knippenberg, "The Relation Between Perception and Behavior, or How to Win a Game of Trivial Pursuit," in *Social Cognition: Key Readings*, ed. David L. Hamilton (New York: Psychology Press, 2005), 266–82 (280).

5. Miller McPherson, Lynn Smith-Lovin and James M. Cook, "Birds of a Feather: Homophily in Social Networks," *Annual Review of Sociology* 27 (2001): 415–44 (416).

6. This general rule has exceptions. See, e.g., Elizabeth E. Umphress, Kristin Smith-Crowe, Arthur P. Brief, Joerg Dietz, and Marla Baskerville Watkins, "When Birds of a Feather Flock Together and When They Do Not: Status Composition, Social Dominance Orientation, and Organizational Attractiveness," *Journal of Applied Psychology* 92, no. 2 (2007): 396–409.

7. Swami and Furnham, *The Psychology of Physical Attraction*, 141.

8. Sarah Trenholm, *Persuasion and Social Influence* (Englewood Cliffs: Prentice Hall, 1989), 11.

9. Dijksterhuis and Van Knippenberg, "The Relation Between Perception and Behavior," 280.

10. Schneider et al., *Applied Social Psychology*, 86.

11. Adler et al., *Interplay*, 278.

12. Elliot Aronson, Timothy D. Wilson, and Robin M. Akert, *Social Psychology*, 6th ed. (Upper Saddle River: Pearson Prentice Hall, 2007), 312.

13. Adler et al., *Interplay*, 277.

14. Aronson et al., *Social Psychology*, 312.

15. Fitness et al., "Interpersonal Attraction," 259.

16. McPherson et al., "Birds of a Feather," 415.

17. Owen Hargie and David Dickson, *Skilled Interpersonal Communication: Research, Theory and Practice*, 4th ed. (London: Routledge, 2004), 345. Even negative gossip solidifies social bonding through validating group norms and membership. Sally D. Farley, Diane R. Timme, and Jason W. Hart, "On Coffee Talk and Break-Room Chatter: Perceptions of Women Who Gossip in the Workplace," *The Journal of Social Psychology* 150, no. 4 (2010): 361–68 (362).

18. See, e.g., Cook et al., *Cooperation Without Trust?* 67 (seeking interaction with trusted others, many people restrict associations to individuals within their ethnic or social group).

19. Mark Schaller, "Evolutionary Bases of First Impressions," in *First Impressions*, eds. Nalini Ambady and John J. Skowronski (New York: The Guilford Press, 2008), 15–34 (23). Facial similarity does not, however, appear to increase sexual attraction. Schaller, "Evolutionary Bases," 23.

20. Zebrowitz and Montepare, "First Impressions," 188 (citing DeBruine, 2002).

21. Cialdini and Sagarin, "Principles of Interpersonal Influence," 156 (citing Emswiller, Deaux, and Willits, 1971).

22. Cialdini and Sagarin, "Principles of Interpersonal Influence," 156–57 (citing Suedfeld, Bochner, and Matas, 1971).

23. Simone Kuhn, Barbara C. N. Muller, Rick B. van Baaren, Anne Wietzker, Ap Dijksterhuis, and Marcel Brass, "Why Do I Like You When You Behave Like Me? Neural Mechanisms Mediating Positive Consequences of Observing Someone Being Imitated," *Social Neuroscience* 5, no. 4 (2010): 384–92 (384–85).

24. Nicolas Gueguen, Angelique Martin, and Sebastien Meineri, "Similarity and Social Interaction: When Similarity Fosters Implicit Behavior Toward a Stranger," *The Journal of Social Psychology* 151, no. 6 (2011): 671–73 (672).

25. John T. Jones, Brett W. Pelham, Mauricio Carvallo, and Matthew C. Mirenberg, "How Do I Love Thee? Let Me Count the Js: Implicit Egotism and Interpersonal Attraction," *Journal of Personality and Social Psychology* 87, no. 5 (2004): 665–83.

26. Burger, "Fleeting Attraction," 160.

27. Pratkanis, "Social Influence Analysis," 34.

28. Jerry M. Burger, Nicole Messian, Shebani Patel, Alicia del Prado, and Carmen Anderson, "What a Coincidence! The Effects of Incidental Similarity on Compliance," *Personality and Social Psychology Bulletin* 30, no. 1 (January, 2004): 35–43.

29. Wallace V. Schmidt, Roger N. Conaway, Susan S. Easton, and William J. Wardrope, *Communicating Globally: Intercultural Communication and International Business* (Los Angeles: SAGE Publications, 2007), 69.

30. Lanning, *Child Molesters: A Behavioral Analysis*, 56.

31. Sanderson, *The Seduction of Children*, 173.

32. Van Dam, *Identifying Child Molesters*, 108.

33. Ibid., 96.

34. Babiak and Hare, *Snakes in Suits*, 79.

35. Ibid., 76.

36. Ibid.

37. Ibid.

38. Ibid.

39. Ibid., 86–87.

40. Bud Allen and Diana Bosta, *Games Criminals Play: How You Can Profit by Knowing Them* (Sacramento: Ray John Publishers, 1981), 36–37.

41. Ibid.

42. McKenna, "MySpace or Your Place," 238–39.

43. Vazire and Gosling, "E-Perceptions," 124.

44. McKenna, "MySpace or Your Place," 241–42.

45. Bredow et al., "Have We Met Before?" 8.

46. Michael H. Kernis and Brian M. Goldman, "A Multicomponent Conceptualization of

Authenticity: Theory and Research," *Advances in Experimental Psychology* 38 (2006): 283–357 (300). See also Michael H. Kernis and Brian M. Goldman, "From Thought and Experience to Behavior and Interpersonal Relationships: A Multicomponent Conceptualization of Authenticity," in *On Building, Defending and Regulating the Self: A Psychological Perspective*, eds. Abraham Tesser, Joanne V. Wood, and Diederik A. Stapel (New York: Psychology Press, 2005), 31–52 (34).

47. Kernis and Goldman, "From Thought and Experience to Behavior," 45.

48. Frederick G. Lopez and Kenneth G. Rice, "Preliminary Development and Validation of a Measure of Relationship Authenticity," *Journal of Counseling Psychology* 53, no. 3 (2006): 362–71 (363).

49. Henri Tajfel, "Social Psychology of Intergroup Relations," *Annual Review of Psychology* 33 (1982): 1–39 (24).

50. Tasuku Igarashi, Yoshihisa Kashima, Emiko S. Kashima, Tomas Farsides, Uichol Kim, Fritz Strack, Lioba Werth, and Masaki Yuki, "Culture, Trust, and Social Networks," *Asian Journal of Social Psychology* 11 (2008): 88–101 (88).

51. Robert B. Lount, Jr. "The Impact of Positive Mood on Trust in Interpersonal and Intergroup Interactions," *Journal of Personality and Social Psychology* 98, no. 3 (2010): 420–33 (421).

52. Babiak and Hare, *Snakes in Suits*, 90.

53. Ibid.

54. Salter, *Predators*, 35–36.

55. Richard Storey, *The Art of Persuasive Communication* (Hampshire: Gower, 1997), 91–92.

56. Daniel Goleman, *Social Intelligence: The New Science of Human Relationship*. (New York: Bantam Books, 2006), 30–31.

57. Tanya L. Chartrand and John A. Bargh, "The Chameleon Effect: The Perception-Behavior Link and Social Interaction," *Journal of Personality and Social Psychology*, 76, no. 6 (1999): 893–910 (893).

58. Chartrand and Bargh, "The Chameleon Effect," 893–910 (893).

59. Marianne Sonnby-Borgstrom, Peter Jonsson, and Owe Svensson, "Emotional Empathy as Related to Mimicry Reactions at Different Levels of Information Processing," *Journal of Nonverbal Behavior* 27, no. 1 (2003): 3–23.

60. Wai and Tiliopoulos, "The Affective and Cognitive," 794.

61. Joel T. Johnson, Emilie B. Mitchell, and Michael D. Robinson, "Inferences About the Authentic Self: When Do Actions Say More Than Mental States?" *Journal of Personality and Social Psychology* 87, no. 5 (2004): 615–30 (628).

62. Margaret S. Clark and Ian Brissette, "Relationship Beliefs and Emotion: Reciprocal Effects," in *Emotions and Beliefs: How Feelings Influence Thoughts*, eds. Nico H. Frijda, Antony S. R. Manstead, and Sacha Bem (Cambridge: Cambridge University Press, 2000), 212–40 (233–34).

63. Clark et al., "Some Thoughts and Findings," 266–67.

64. Goleman, *Social Intelligence*, 22 (citing Jean Decety and Thierry Chaminade, "Neural Correlates of Feeling Sympathy," *Neuropsychologia* 41 (2003): 127–38).

65. Horberg et al., "Pride Displays," 24.

66. Wai and Tiliopoulos, "The Affective and Cognitive," 797 (referring to *primary* psychopaths, who engage in planned behavior enabled by lack of morals, as opposed to *secondary* psychopaths, who are more unstable and impulsive). Wai and Tiliopoulos, "The Affective and Cognitive," 795.

67. Ibid.

7. The Ax Murderer Next Door: Familiarity Breeds Contentment

1. Fitness et al., "Interpersonal Attraction," 259.
2. Adler et al., *Interplay*, 277.
3. See, e.g., Harry T. Reis, Michael R. Maniaci, Peter A. Capariello, Paul W. Eastwick, and Eli J. Finkel, "Familiarity Does Indeed Promote Attraction in Live Interaction," *Journal of Personality and Social Psychology* 101, no. 3 (2011): 557–70.
4. Burger, "Fleeting Attraction," 157.
5. Schneider et al., *Applied Social Psychology*. Schneider et al. describe "environmental spoiling," which holds that repeated contact with a disliked person increases aversion. Schneider et al., *Applied Social Psychology*, 80.
6. Schneider et al., *Applied Social Psychology*, 81. Familiarity can lead to contempt when dealing with others we find aversive. Reis et al., "Familiarity Does Indeed Promote Attraction," 558–59.
7. Ibid., 80–81.
8. Anthony C. Little, Lisa M. DeBruine, and Benedict C. Jones, "Sex Differences in Attraction to Familiar and Unfamiliar Opposite-Sex Faces: Men Prefer Novelty and Women Prefer Familiarity," *Arch Sex Behavior*, doi: 10.1007/s10508-013-0120-2. Note, however, that this study showed that men preferred novelty over familiarity in judging the attractiveness of female faces. Little et al., "Sex Differences in Attraction."
9. Guerrero and Floyd, *Nonverbal Communication*, 183.
10. McKenna, "MySpace or Your Place," 237 (citing Rubin, 1975).
11. Babiak and Hare, *Snakes in Suits*, 48–49.
12. Bredow et al., "Have We Met Before?" 17.
13. Derlega et al., "Self-Disclosure," 156.
14. McKenna, "MySpace or Your Place," 240.
15. Ibid., 240–41.
16. Ibid., 241.
17. Research reveals that within intimate relationships, love can be both blind and realistic. See, e.g., Garth J. O. Fletcher and Patrick S. G. Kerr, "Through the Eyes of Love: Reality and Illusion in Intimate Relationships," *Psychological Bulletin* 136, no. 4 (2010): 627–58.
18. Sandra L. Murray, John G. Holmes, and Dale W. Griffin, "The Benefits of Positive Illusions: Idealization and the Construction of Satisfaction in Close Relationships," *Journal of Personality and Social Psychology* 70, no. 1 (1996): 79–98; Sandra L. Murray, John G. Holmes, and Dale W. Griffin, "The Self-Fulfilling Nature of Positive Illusions in Romantic Relationships: Love is Not Blind, but Prescient," *Journal of Personality and Social Psychology* 71, no. 6 (1996): 1155–80.
19. Paul J. E. Miller, Sylvia Niehuis, and Ted L. Huston, "Positive Illusions in Marital Relationships: A 13-Year Longitudinal Study," *Personality and Social Psychology Bulletin* 32, no. 12 (December 2006): 1579–94, doi: 10.10.1177/0146167206292691.
20. Miller et al., "Positive Illusions," 1580.
21. Ibid.
22. Ibid.
23. James K. McNulty, Erin M. O'Mara, and Benjamin R. Karney, "Benevolent Cognitions as a Strategy of Relationship Maintenance: 'Don't Sweat the Small Stuff' . . . But It Is Not All Small Stuff," *Journal of Personality and Social Psychology* 94, no. 4 (2008): 631–46 (643), doi: 10.1037/0022-3514.94.4.631.

24. Edward P. Lemay, Jr. and Angela M. Neal, "The Wishful Memory of Interpersonal Responsiveness," *Journal of Personality and Social Psychology* 104, no. 4 (2013): 653–72, doi: 10.1037/a0030422

25. Lemay, Jr. and Neal, "The Wishful Memory," 654.

26. Sandra L. Murray and John G. Holmes, "Seeing Virtues in Faults: Negativity and the Transformation of Interpersonal Narratives in Close Relationships," *Journal of Personality and Social Psychology* 65, no. 4 (1993): 707–22.

27. Murray and Holmes, "Seeing Virtues in Faults," 719.

28. Ibid., 707.

29. Ibid., 719.

30. Ibid.

31. Ibid.

32. Kate Sweeny, Darya Melnyk, Wendi Miller, and James A. Shepperd, "Information Avoidance: Who, What, When, and Why," *Review of General Psychology* 14, no. 4 (2010): 340–53, doi: 10.1037/a0021288.

33. Sweeny et al., "Information Avoidance," 340.

34. Ibid., 343.

35. Ibid., 342–44.

36. Ibid., 344.

37. Ibid., 346.

38. Schneider et al., *Applied Social Psychology,* 80.

39. Ibid. (citing Festinger, Schachter, and Back, 1950).

40. Swami and Furnham, *The Psychology of Physical Attraction,* 138–39.

41. Ibid., 139.

42. Ibid.

43. Jones et al., "How Do I Love Thee?" 665–83 (665) (citing Bossard, 1932, Festinger, Schachter, and Back, 1950).

44. Josh Levs, Phil Gast, and Steve Almasy, "Charles Ramsey: I'm No Hero in Freeing of Captive Women," CNN (May 9, 2013); http://www.cnn.com/2013/05/07/us/ohio-cleveland-ramsey/index.html.

45. Alex Perez, Matthew Jaffe, Steven Portnoy, and Alyssa Newcomb, "Cleveland Kidnapping Suspect Ariel Castro Hid a Dark Side, His Uncle Says," (May 7, 2012); http://abcnews.go.com/US/cleveland-kidnap-suspect-charismatic-guy-ashamed-neighbor/story?id=19122845.

46. Perez et al., "Cleveland Kidnapping Suspect."

47. Laurie Segall, Erica Fink, and Ben Brumfield, "'He Is Dead to Me,' Daughter of Ohio Suspect Says in CNN Exclusive," *CNN.com*, (May 10, 2013); http://www.cnn.com/2013/05/09/us/ohio-suspect-daughter.

48. Segall, et al. "'He Is Dead to Me.'"

49. Ibid.

50. Ibid.

51. Ibid.

52. Ibid.

53. Ibid.

54. Jon Swaine, "Ohio Abductions: Ariel Castro Threatened to Kill Wife and Daughters," *The Telegraph*, May 7, 2013; http://www.telegraph.co.uk/news/worldnews/northamerica/usa/10042926/Ohio-abductions-Ariel-Castro-threatened-to-kill-wife-and-daughters.html.

55. Terry R. Bacon, *The Elements of Power: Lessons on Leadership and Influence*. New York: AMACOM, 2011, 71–76.

56. Bacon, *The Elements of Power*, 79.

8. Craving Excitement: The Call of the Wild

1. See, e.g., Bredow et al., "Have We Met Before?" 16.

2. Marvin Zuckerman, *Sensation Seeking and Risky Behavior* (Washington D.C.: American Psychological Association, 2007), 77.

3. Michael J. Apter, *Danger: Our Quest for Excitement* (Oxford: Oneworld Publications, 2007), 44–45.

4. Zuckerman, *Sensation Seeking*, 88.

5. Apter, *Danger*, 41–52.

6. Zuckerman, *Sensation Seeking*, 105.

7. Ibid.

8. See also Mervyn K. Wagner, "Behavioral Characteristics Related to Substance Abuse and Risk-Taking, Sensation-Seeking, Anxiety Sensitivity, and Self-Reinforcement," *Addictive Behaviors* 26 (2001): 115–20.

9. Shmuel Lissek, Johanna M. P. Baas, Daniel S. Pine, Kaebah Orme, Sharone Dvir, Emily Rosenberger, and Christian Grillon, "Sensation Seeking and the Aversive Motivational System," *Emotion* 5, no. 4 (2005): 396–407 (396), doi: 10.1037/1528-3542.5.4.396.

10. Wagner, "Behavioral Characteristics," 119.

11. Zuckerman, *Sensation Seeking*, 94.

12. Peter J. Rentfrow and Samuel D. Gosling, "The Do Re Mi's of Everyday Life: The Structure and Personality Correlates of Music Preferences," *Journal of Personality and Social Psychology* 84, no. 6 (2003): 1236–56 (1237), doi: 10.1037/0022-3514.84.6.1236 (citing McNamara and Ballard, 1999).

13. Chantal den Daas, Michael Hafner, and John de Wit, "Out of Sight, Out of Mind: Cognitive States Alter the Focus of Attention," *Experimental Psychology* 60, no. 5 (2013): 313–23, doi: 10.1027/1618-3169/a000201.

14. Den Daas et al., "Out of Sight, Out of Mind," 313.

15. Ibid., 321.

16. Laura C. Crysel, Benjamin S. Crosier, and Gregory D. Webster, "The Dark Triad and Risk Behavior," *Personality and Individual Differences* 54 (2013): 35–40 (35), http://dx.doi.org/10.1016/j.paid.2012.07.029.

17. Crysel et al., "The Dark Triad and Risk Behavior," 35.

18. Crysel et al., "The Dark Triad and Risk Behavior," 35; Carter et al., "The Dark Triad: Beyond a 'Male' Mating Strategy," 160. Psychopaths are more likely to be impulsive, while Machiavellians practice impulse control in pursuit of success. Jones and Paulhus, "Differentiating the Dark Triad," 254–55.

19. Babiak and Hare, *Snakes in Suits*, 38.

20. Hare, *Without Conscience*, 34.

21. Theodore Millon and Roger Davis, "Ten Subtypes of Psychopathy," in *Psychopathy: Antisocial, Criminal, and Violent Behavior* (New York: The Guilford Press, 1998), 161–70 (164).

22. Visser et al., "Status-Driven Risk Taking."

23. Ibid., 2.

24. Hare, *Without Conscience*, 34.

25. Carter et al., "The Dark Triad: Beyond a 'Male' Mating Strategy," 160.

26. Charles A. Pierce, Donn Byrne, and Herman Aguinis, "Attraction in Organizations: A Model of Workplace Romance," *Journal of Organizational Behavior* 17 (1996): 5–32 (14).

27. Pierce et al., "Attraction in Organizations," 14.

28. Ibid. The authors propose that these findings may be able to explain romantic attraction in the workplace. Pierce et al., "Attraction in Organizations," 14.

29. Donald G. Dutton and Arthur P. Aron, "Some Evidence for Heightened Sexual Attraction Under Conditions of High Anxiety," *Journal of Personality and Social Psychology* 30, no. 4 (1974): 510–17.

30. Dutton and Aron, "Some Evidence," 511.

31. Ibid.

32. Ibid., 512.

33. Gregory L. White, Sanford Fishbein, and Jeffrey Rutstein, "Passionate Love and the Misattribution of Arousal," *Journal of Personality and Social Psychology* 41, no. 1 (1981): 56–62 (57).

34. White et al., "Passionate Love," 57–58

35. Ibid., 60.

36. Ibid., 59.

37. Ibid., 60–62.

38. Erica B. Slotter and Wendi L. Gardner, "The Dangers of Dating the 'Bad Boy' (or Girl): When Does Romantic Desire Encourage Us to Take on the Negative Qualities of Potential Partners" *Journal of Experimental Social Psychology* 48 (2012): 1173–78, doi: 10.1016/j.jesp.2012.05.007.

39. Slotter and Gardner, "The Dangers," 1173.

40. Ibid., 1177.

41. Ibid.

42. Williamson and Cluse-Tolar, "Pimp-Controlled Prostitution," 1080.

43. Swami et al., "More Than Just Skin Deep? Personality Information," 629.

44. Daniel N. Jones and Delroy L. Paulhus, "The Role of Impulsivity in the Dark Triad of Personality," *Personality and Individual Differences* 51 (2011): 679–82 (679).

45. Daniel Nettle, "An Evolutionary Approach to the Extraversion Continuum," *Evolution and Human Behavior* 26 (2005): 363–73 (370), doi: 10.1016/j.evolhumbehav.2004.12.004.

46. Nettle, "An Evolutionary Approach."

47. Jonason et al., "The Dark Triad: Facilitating a Short-Term Mating Strategy in Men," 7.

48. Ibid.

49. Nettle, "An Evolutionary Approach," 370

50. Carter et al., "The Dark Triad: Beyond a 'Male' Mating Strategy," 160.

51. Brittany Gentile, "Celebrity and Narcissism," in *The Handbook of Narcissism and Narcissistic Personality Disorder: Theoretical Approaches, Empirical Findings, and Treatments*, eds. W. Keith Campbell and Joshua D. Miller (Hoboken: John Wiley & Sons, Inc., 2011), 403–9 (404).

52. Back et al., "Why are Narcissists so Charming at First Sight?" 133.

53. Jones and Paulhus, "The Role of Impulsivity," 680.

54. Ibid., 681.

55. Back et al., "Narcissistic Admiration and Rivalry," 1013.

56. Twenge and Campbell, *The Narcissism Epidemic*, 217.

57. Nicholas S. Holtzman, Simine Vazier, and Matthias R. Mehl, "Sounds Like a Narcissist: Behavioral Manifestations of Narcissism in Everyday Life," *Journal of Research in Personality* 44 (2010): 478–84, doi: 10.1016/j.jrp.2010.06.001.

58. Holtzman et al., "Sounds Like a Narcissist," 482–483. They also found that narcissists who exhibited the characteristics of entitlement and exploitativeness were more likely to skip class. Holtzman et al., "Sounds Like a Narcissist," 482.

59. McHoskey, "Machiavellianism and Sexuality," 780.

60. Jonason et al., "The Dark Triad: Facilitating a Short-Term Mating Strategy in Men," 7.

61. McHoskey, "Machiavellianism and Sexuality," 779.

62. Wai and Tiliopoulos, "The Affective and Cognitive," 794.

63. Boddy, *Corporate Psychopaths*, 64.

64. See generally, Peter K. Jonason and David M. Buss, "Avoiding Entangling Commitments: Tactics for Implementing a Short-Term Mating Strategy," *Personality and Individual Differences* 52 (2012): 606–10 (610), doi: 10.1016/j.paid.2011.12.015.

65. Jonason and Buss, "Avoiding Entangling Commitments," 610.

66. Xianchi Dai, Ping Dong, and Jayson S. Jia, "When Does Playing Hard to Get Increase Romantic Attraction?" *Journal of Experimental Psychology: General* (2013): 1–6 (1).

67. Erin R. Whitchurch, Timothy D. Wilson, and Daniel T. Gilbert, "'He Loves Me, He Loves Me Not . . .': Uncertainty Can Increase Romantic Attraction," *Psychological Science* 22, no. 2 (2011): 172–75.

68. Whitchurch et al., "'He Loves Me, He Loves Me Not . . .'" 173.

69. Little et al., "Sex Differences in Attraction," Note that men found familiar male faces to be more attractive. Little et al., "Sex Differences in Attraction."

70. Ibid.

71. Rowland S. Miller, "We Always Hurt the Ones We Love: Aversive Interactions in Close Relationships," in Robin M. Kowalski, ed., *Aversive Interpersonal Behaviors* (New York: Plenum Press, 1997) 11–29 (18) (citing Dewsbury, 1981).

72. Miller, "We Always Hurt the Ones We Love," 18.

73. Garth Fletcher, Jeffry A. Simpson, Lorne Campbell, and Nickola C. Overall, *The Science of Intimate Relationships* (Malden: Wiley-Blackwell, 2013), 143 (citing Schmitt et al., 2003).

74. Fletcher et al., *The Science of Intimate Relationships*, 143 (citing a study done by Russell Clark and Elaine Hatfield in 1978 and repeated in 1982).

75. Jonason and Buss, "Avoiding Entangling Commitments," 610.

76. Jonason et al., "Mate-Selection," 761–62.

77. Peter K. Jonason, Victor X. Luevano, and Heather M. Adams, "How the Dark Triad Traits Predict Relationship Choices," *Personality and Individual Differences* 53 (2012): 180–84.

78. Peter K. Jonason, Norman P. Li, Gregory D. Webster, and David P. Schmitt, "The Dark Triad: Facilitating a Short-Term Mating Strategy in Men," *European Journal of Personality* 23 (2009): 5–18 (7).

79. Peter K. Jonason and Phillip Kavanaugh, "The Dark Side of Love: Love Styles and the Dark Triad," *Personality and Individual Differences*, 2010, Vol. 49, 606–10.

80. Peter K. Jonason, Norman P. Li, and David M. Buss, "The Costs and Benefits of the Dark Triad: Implications for Mate Poaching and Mate Retention Tactics," *Personality and Individual Differences* 48 (2010): 373–78.

81. Jonason et al., "The Dark Triad: Facilitating a Short-Term Mating Strategy in Men," 6–7.

82. S. Mark Young and Drew Pinsky, "Narcissism and Celebrity," *Journal of Research in Personality* 40 (2006): 463–71 (463–464).

83. Young and Pinsky, "Narcissism and Celebrity," 464.

84. Gentile, "Celebrity and Narcissism," 406.

85. Young and Pinsky, "Narcissism and Celebrity," 463–64. The authors caution that this research was designed to detect narcissistic traits, not narcissistic personality disorder. Young and Pinsky, "Narcissism and Celebrity," 465.

86. Ibid., 469.

87. Gentile, "Celebrity and Narcissism," 407.

88. Ibid., 407–408 (citing Horton et al., 2010).

89. Young and Pinsky, "Narcissism and Celebrity." Within each celebrity subtype, Reality TV personalities scored highest on self-sufficiency and vanity, while comedians scored highest on exploitativeness, exhibitionism, and superiority, among other traits. Young and Pinsky, "Narcissism and Celebrity," 469.

90. Ibid., 470.

91. See, e.g., Bredow et al., "Have We Met Before? 16.

92. Diane H. Felmlee, "From Appealing to Appalling: Disenchantment with a Romantic Partner," *Sociological Perspectives* 44, no. 3 (2001): 263–80 (270).

93. Felmlee, "From Appealing to Appalling," 264.

94. Ibid., 266.

95. Ibid.

96. Susan Sprecher and Diane Felmlee, "Insider Perspectives on Attraction," in *Handbook of Relationship Initiation*, eds. Susan Sprecher, Amy Wenzel, and John Harvey (New York: Psychology Press, 2008), 297–313 (308).

97. Sprecher and Felmlee, "Insider Perspectives," 308.

98. Swann and Bosson, "Identity Negotiation," 455.

99. Ibid.

9. Forbidden Fruit: The Temptation of Taboo

1. Jack Katz, *Seductions of Crime: Moral and Sensual Attractions in Doing Evil* (New York: Basic Books, Inc., 1988), 52.

2. Katz, *Seductions of Crime*, 52.

3. Apter, *Danger,*150–51.

4. B. J. Rye and Glenn J. Meaney, "Voyeurism: It Is Good as Long as We Do Not Get Caught," *International Journal of Sexual Health* 19, no. 1 (2007): 47–56, doi: 10.1300/J514v19n01_06.

5. Rye and Meaney, "Voyeurism," 52–53.

6. Mark Hedley, "The Geometry of Gendered Conflict in Popular Film: 1986–2000," *Sex Roles* 47, nos. 5–6 (September 2002): 201–17.

7. Esther Jansen, Sandra Mulkens, Yvette Emond, and Anita Jansen, "From the Garden of Eden to the Land of Plenty: Restriction of Fruit and Sweets Intake Leads to Increased Fruits and Sweets Consumption in Children," *Appetite* 51 (2008): 570–75.

8. Brad J. Bushman and Angela D. Stack, "Forbidden Fruit Versus Tainted Fruit: Effects of Warning Labels on Attraction to Television Violence," *Journal of Experimental Psychology: Applied* 2, no. 3 (1996): 207–26.

9. Marije Nije Bijvank, Elly A. Konijn, Brad J. Bushman, and Peter H. M. P. Roelofsma, "Age and Violent-Content Labels Make Video Games Forbidden Fruits for Youth," *Pediatrics* (2008): 870–76, doi: 10.1542/peds.2008-0601.

10. Steve Sussman, Rachel Grana, Pallav Pokhrel, Louise A. Rohrbach, and Ping Sun, "Forbidden Fruit and the Prediction of Cigarette Smoking," *Substance Use & Misuse* 45 (2010): 1683–93, doi: 10.3109/0826081003682230.

11. Esther K. Papies, Wolfgang Stroebe, and Henk Aarts, "The Allure of Forbidden Food: On the Role of Attention in Self-Regulation," *Journal of Experimental Social Psychology* 44 (2008): 1283–92.

12. Papies et al., "The Allure of Forbidden Food," 1290.

13. Ibid.

14. Ibid.

15. Bushman and Stack, "Forbidden Fruit," 217.

16. Bijvank et al., "Age and Violent-Content Labels," 874.

17. Sussman et al., "Forbidden Fruit," 1684.

18. See generally, Jansen et al., "From the Garden of Eden to the Land of Plenty."

19. Bushman and Stack, "Forbidden Fruit," 208.

20. Ibid. Note that hard-to-get partners are not always viewed as most coveted. See Elaine Walster, G. William Walster, Jane Piliavin, and Lynn Schmidt, "'Playing Hard to Get' Understanding an Elusive Phenomenon," *Journal of Personality and Social Psychology* 26, no. 1 (1973): 113–21.

21. Loes Keijsers, Susan Branje, Skyler T. Hawk, Seth J. Schwartz, Tom Frijns, Hans M. Koot, Pol van Lier, and Wim Meeus, "Forbidden Friends as Forbidden Fruit: Parental Supervision of Friendships, Contact with Deviant Peers, and Adolescent Delinquency," *Child Development* 83, no. 2 (March/April 2012): 651–66, doi: 10.1111/j.1467-8624.2011.01701.x.

22. Keijsers et al., "Forbidden Friends," 661.

23. Ibid., 662.

24. Richard Driscoll, Keith E. Davis, and Milton E. Lipetz, "Parental Interference and Romantic Love: The Romeo and Juliet Effect," *Journal of Personality and Social Psychology* 24, no. 1 (1972): 1–10 (2).

25. Driscoll et al., "Parental Interference."

26. C. Nathan DeWall, Jon K. Maner, Timothy Deckman, and D. Aaron Rouby, "Forbidden Fruit: Inattention to Attractive Alternatives Provokes Implicit Relationship Reactance," *Journal of Personality and Social Psychology* 100, no. 4 (2011): 621–29, doi: 10.1037/a0021749.

27. DeWall et al., "Forbidden Fruit," 623.

28. Ibid., 624.

29. Ibid., 625.

30. Lise VanderVoort and Steve Duck, "Sex, Lies, and . . . Transformation," in *The State of Affairs: Explorations in Infidelity and Commitment*, eds. Jean Duncombe, Kaeren Harrison, Graham Allan, and Dennis Marsden (Mahwah: Lawrence Erlbaum Associates, 2004), 1–13 (5).

31. Katherine Tarbox, *A Girl's Life Online* (New York: Plume, 2000), 61.

32. Tarbox, *A Girl's Life Online*, 132.

33. Alexis Singer, *Alexis: My True Story of Being Seduced by an Online Predator* (Deerfield Beach: Health Communications, Inc., 2010), 60–62.

34. Ibid., 60–61.

35. Ibid., 62–63.

36. Ibid., 72.
37. Daniel M. Wegner, Julie D. Lane, and Sara Dimitri, "The Allure of Secret Relationships," *Journal of Personality and Social Psychology* 66 (2005): 287–300.
38. Reuben A. Lang and Roy R. Frenzel, "How Sex Offenders Lure Children," *Annals of Sex Research* 1 (1988): 303–17 (312).
39. Wegner et al., "The Allure of Secret Relationships," 287. More recent research indicates that secrecy may decrease the quality of ongoing romantic relationships due to situational difficulties. Craig A. Foster and W. Keith Campbell, "The Adversity of Secret Relationships," *Personal Relationships* 12 (2005), 125–43.
40. Foster and Campbell, "The Adversity of Secret Relationships," at 126; Wegner et al., "The Allure of Secret Relationships," 288; Daniel M. Wegner, Joann W. Shortt, Anne W. Blake, and Michelle S. Page, "The Suppression of Exciting Thoughts," *Journal of Personality and Social Psychology* 58 (1990): 409–18.
41. Gian C. Gonzaga, Martie G. Haselton, Julie Smurda, Mari sian Davies, and Joshua C. Poore, "Love, Desire, and the Suppression of Thoughts of Romantic Alternatives," *Evolution and Human Behavior* 29 (2008): 119–26 (120), doi: 10.1016/j.evolhumanbehav.2007.11.003.
42. Gonzaga et al., "Love, Desire, and the Suppression of Thoughts," 120. This effect can even apply to thoughts about past relationships. Daniel M. Wegner and Daniel B. Gold, "Fanning Old Flames: Emotional and Cognitive Effects of Suppressing Thoughts of a Past Relationship," *Journal of Personality and Social Psychology* 68, no. 5 (1995): 782–92.
43. Wegner et al., "The Suppression of Exciting Thoughts." 409.
44. Ibid., 413–14.
45. Babiak and Hare, *Snakes in Suits*, 27.
46. Widiger and Lynam, "Psychopathy and the Five-Factor Model," 175.
47. Brown, *Women Who Love Psychopaths*, 52.
48. Ibid.
49. Babiak and Hare, *Snakes in Suits*, 27.
50. Ibid., 46.
51. Salter, *Predators*, 141–43.
52. Ibid., 141.
53. Ibid.
54. Robert M. Worley, Richard Tewksbury, and Durant Frantzen, "Preventing Fatal Attractions: Lessons Learned From Inmate Boundary Violators in a Southern Penitentiary System," *Criminal Justice Studies* 23, no. 4 (December, 2010): 347–60 (348) (citing Beck and Harrison, 2008), doi: 10.1080/1478601X.2010.516532.
55. See, e.g., NewsOne, "14 More Correctional Officers Charged in Baltimore Black Guerilla Family Jail Sex Scandal," November 25, 2013, http://atlantadailyworld.com/2013/11/25/14-more-correctional-officers-charged-in-baltimore-black-guerilla-family-jail-sex-scandal/; Mitchel Maddux, Larry Celona, and Dan Mangan, "Jail Guard Pregnant With Cop-Killer's Child," *New York Post*, February 6, 2013; www.nypost.com/p/news/local/brooklyn/jailer_carries_monster_baby_hTZACrgVZHanbKc5PIbF8J.

10. Seeking the Wolf: When Dangerous Is Desirable

1. Isenberg, *Women Who Love Men Who Kill*, 154.
2. Ibid., 155.

3. Ibid., 100.
4. Ibid.
5. Hare, *Without Conscience*, 149.
6. Ibid.
7. Jonason et al., "The Antihero in Popular Culture." The authors adopt the definition of "antihero" as for example, "a protagonist whose character is conspicuously contrary to an archetypal hero." Jonason et al., "The Antihero in Popular Culture," 192.
8. Daniel J. Kruger, Maryanne Fisher, and Ian Jobling, "Proper and Dark Heroes as Dads and Cads," *Human Nature* 14, no. 3 (2003): 305–17.
9. Isenberg, *Women Who Love Men Who Kill*, 138.
10. Ibid.
11. Ibid., 138–40.
12. Jonason et al., "Mate-Selection," 762.
13. Ibid.
14. Moscovici, *Dangerous Liaisons*, 82–84.
15. Ibid., 85–86.
16. Carter et al., "The Dark Triad Personality," 57–61.
17. Ibid., 60.
18. Ibid.
19. Jessica L. Tracy and Alec T. Beall, "Happy Guys Finish Last: The Impact of Emotion Expressions on Sexual Attraction," *Emotion* 11, no. 6 (2011): 1379–87, doi: 10.1037/a0022902.
20. Tracy and Beall, "Happy Guys." The results were opposite for women—with happiness judged to be the most attractive female expression, and pride the least attractive. Tracy and Beall, "Happy Guys," 1385.
21. Ibid.
22. Ibid.
23. See, e.g., Susan Forward and Joan Torres, *Men Who Hate Women and the Women Who Love Them* (Toronto: Bantam Books, 1986).
24. Forward and Torres, *Men Who Hate Women*, 23–30.
25. Sally A. Lloyd and Beth C. Emery, "The Context and Dynamics of Intimate Aggression Against Women," *Journal of Social and Personal Relationships* 17, nos. 4–5 (2000): 503–21 (503).
26. Lloyd and Emery, "The Context and Dynamics," 503.
27. Ibid., 505.
28. Ibid.
29. McNulty et al., "Benevolent Cognitions," 632.
30. Lloyd and Emery, "The Context and Dynamics," 505.
31. Edward P. Lemay, Jr., and Margaret S. Clark, "How the Head Liberates the Heart: Projection of Communal Responsiveness Guides Relationship Promotion," *Journal of Personality and Social Psychology* 94, no. 4 (2008): 647–71 (668), doi: 10.1037/0022-3514.94.4.647.
32. McNulty et al., "Benevolent Cognitions," 632.
33. Kristina Coop Gordon, Shacunda Burton, and Laura Porter, "Predicting the Intentions of Women in Domestic Violence Shelters to Return to Partners: Does Forgiveness Play a Role?" *Journal of Family Psychology* 18 (2004): 331–38 (332), doi: 10/1037/0893-3200.18.2.331.
34. Moscovici, *Dangerous Liaisons*, 85.
35. Ibid.
36. Lloyd and Emery, "The Context and Dynamics," 512.

37. Zuckerman, *Sensation Seeking*, 94.

38. Ibid., 102.

39. Ibid., 94.

40. Gregory Louis Carter, Anne C. Campbell, and Steven Muncer, "The Dark Triad: Beyond a 'Male' Mating Strategy," *Personality and Individual Differences* 56 (2014): 159–64 (160).

41. Isenberg, *Women Who Love Men Who Kill*.

42. Ibid., 48–49.

43. Ibid., 207.

44. Ibid., 224.

45. Ibid., 225.

46. Ibid., 49.

47. Isenberg, *Women Who Love Men Who Kill*, 53. This is true even though some of these women argue that their men are innocent, or that their killing was justified under the circumstances. Isenberg, *Women Who Love Men Who Kill*, 52–53.

48. Elizabeth A. Gurian, "Explanations of Mixed-Sex Partnered Homicide: A Review of Sociological and Psychological Theory," *Aggression and Violent Behavior* 18 (2013): 520–26 (523), http://dx.doi.org/10.1016/javb.2013.07.007.

49. Gurian, "Explanations of Mixed-Sex Partnered Homicide," 522–23.

50. Hare, *Without Conscience*, 149–50.

51. Ibid., 150.

52. Isenberg, *Women Who Love Men Who Kill*, 57.

53. Ibid., 206.

54. Ibid.

55. Ibid., 206–207.

56. Hare, *Without Conscience*, 150.

57. Ogas and Gaddam, *A Billion Wicked Thoughts*.

58. Ibid., 22.

59. Ibid.

60. Ibid., 213–15.

61. Ibid., 220–25.

62. Jonason et al., "The Antihero," 192.

63. Ibid., 196.

64. Ibid., 194.

65. Felmlee, "From Appealing to Appalling," 278.

66. Ibid.

Green Lights: When What Looks Good Really Is

1. McKenna et al., "MySpace or Your Place," 245.

2. Burgoon et al., *Nonverbal Communication*, 87.

3. James M. Honeycutt and Suzette P. Bryan, *Scripts and Communication for Relationships* (New York: Peter Lang, 2011), 12–13.

4. Kelly Fudge Albada, Mark L. Knapp, and Katheryn E. Theune, "Interaction Appearance Theory: Changing Perceptions of Physical Attractiveness Through Social Interaction," *Communication Theory* 12, no. 1 (2002): 8–40.

5. Albada et al., "Interaction Appearance Theory," 9–10.
6. Susan S. Hendrick and Clyde Hendrick, "Satisfaction, Love, and Respect in the Initiation of Romantic Relationships," in *Handbook of Relationship Initiation*, eds. Susan Sprecher, Amy Wenzel, and John Harvey (New York: Psychology Press, 2008), 337–71 (345).
7. Hendrick and Hendrick, "Satisfaction, Love, and Respect," 345.
8. Sosik et al., "The Value of Virtue," 377.
9. Ibid.
10. Bacon, *The Elements of Power*, 90–91.
11. Ibid., 91–92.
12. Raven, "The Bases of Power," 3.
13. Robert P. Vecchio, "Power, Politics, and Influence," in *Leadership: Understanding the Dynamics of Power and Influence in Organizations*, ed. Robert P. Vecchio (Notre Dame: University of Notre Dame Press, 2007), 69–95 (72–73).
14. Raven, "The Bases of Power," 2.
15. Bacon, *The Elements of Power*, 113–27.
16. Ibid., 113.
17. Ibid., 113–14.
18. Andersen and Guerrero, "The Bright Side," 311.
19. Swann and Pelham, "The Truth About Illusions," 367.
20. Belle Rose Ragins and John L. Cotton, "Mentor Functions and Outcomes: A Comparison of Men and Women in Formal and Informal Mentoring Relationships," *Journal of Applied Psychology* 84, no. 4 (1999): 529–50 (530).
21. Ruth H. V. Sealy and Val Singh, "The Importance of Role Models and Demographic Context for Senior Women's Work Identity Development," *International Journal of Management Reviews* 12, no. 3 (2009): 284–300 (285–286).

Final Thoughts: A Life Well Perceived

1. Matthew 7:15–20.

Bibliography

Adler, Ronald B., Lawrence B. Rosenfeld, and Russell F. Proctor II. *Interplay: The Process of Interpersonal Communication*. Oxford: Oxford University Press, 2010.

Albada, Kelly Fudge, Mark L. Knapp, and Katheryn E. Theune. "Interaction Appearance Theory: Changing Perceptions of Physical Attractiveness Through Social Interaction." *Communication Theory* 12, No. 1 (2002) 8–40.

Ali, Farah, Ines Sousa Amorim, and Tomas Chamorro-Premuzic. "Empathy Deficits and Trait Emotional Intelligence in Psychopathy and Machiavellianism." *Personality and Individual Differences* 47 (2009): 758–62, doi: 10.1016/j.paid.2009.06.016.

Allan, Graham. "Being Unfaithful: His and Her Affairs." In *The State of Affairs: Explorations in Infidelity and Commitment*, edited by Jean Duncombe, Kaeren Harrison, Graham Allan, and Dennis Marsden, 121–40. Mahwah: Lawrence Erlbaum Associates, 2004.

Allen, Bud, and Diana Bosta. *Games Criminals Play: How You Can Profit by Knowing Them*. Sacramento: Ray John Publishers, 1981.

Andersen, Peter A. "Influential Actions." In *Perspectives on Persuasion, Social Influence, and Compliance Gaining*, edited by John S. Seiter and Robert H. Gass, 165–80. Boston: Pearson Education Inc., 2004.

Andersen, Peter A., and Laura K. Guerrero. "The Bright Side of Relational Communication: Interpersonal Warmth as a Social Emotion." In *Handbook of Communication and Emotion: Research, Theory, Applications, and Contexts*, edited by Peter A. Andersen and Laura K. Guerrero, 303–29. San Diego: Academic Press, 1998.

Anderson, Pamela M., Karin K. Coyle, Anisha Johnson, and Jill Denner. "An Exploratory Study of Adolescent Pimping Relationships." *Journal of Primary Prevention* 35 (2014): 113–17, doi: 10.1007/s10935-014-0338-3.

Apter, Michael J. *Danger: Our Quest for Excitement*. Oxford: Oneworld Publications, 2007.

Aron, Raphael. *Cults, Terror, and Mind Control*. Point Richmond: Bay Tree Publishing, LLC, 2009.

Aronson, Elliot. "The Power of Self-Persuasion." *American Psychologist*. November: 875–84, 1999.

Aronson, Elliot, Timothy D. Wilson, and Robin M. Akert. *Social Psychology*. 6th ed. Upper Saddle River: Pearson Prentice Hall, 2007.

Austin, Elizabeth J., Daniel Farrelly, Carolyn Black, and Helen Moore. "Emotional Intelligence, Machiavellianism and Emotional Manipulation: Does EI Have a Dark Side?" *Personality and Individual Differences* 43 (2007): 179–89, doi: 10.1016/j.paid.2006.11.019.

Babiak, Paul, "From Darkness into the Light: Psychopathy in Industrial and Organizational Psychology." In *The Psychopath: Theory, Research, and Practice*, edited by Hugues Herve and John C. Yuille, 411–28. Mahway: Lawrence Erlbaum Associates: 2007.

Babiak, Paul, and Robert Hare. *Snakes in Suits: When Psychopaths Go to Work*. New York: Regan Books, 2006.

Babiak, Paul, Craig S. Neumann, and Robert D. Hare. "Corporate Psychopathy: Talking the Walk." *Behavioral Sciences and the Law* 28 (2010): 174–93, doi: 10.1002/bsl.925.

Back, Mitja D., Albrecht C. P. Kufner, Tanja M. Gerlach, Michael Dufner, John F. Rauthmann, and Jaap J. A. Denissen. "Narcissistic Admiration and Rivalry: Disentangling the Bright and Dark Sides of Narcissism." *Journal of Personality and Social Psychology* 105, No. 6 (2013): 1013–37, doi: 10.1037/a0034431.

Back, Mitja D., Stefan C. Schmukle, and Boris Egloff. "Why are Narcissists so Charming at First Sight? Decoding the Narcissism-Popularity Link at Zero Acquaintance." *Journal of Personality and Social Psychology* 98, No. 1 (2010): 132–45.

Bacon, Terry R. *The Elements of Power: Lessons on Leadership and Influence*. New York: AMACOM, 2011.

Barrick, Murray R., Jonathan A. Shaffer, and Sandra W. DeGrassi. "What You See May Not Be What You Get: Relationships Among Self-Presentation Tactics and Ratings of Interview and Job Performance." *Journal of Applied Psychology* 94, No. 6 (2009): 1394–1411, doi: 10.1037/a0016532.

Bauer, Jack J., and Dan P. McAdams. "Growth Goals, Maturity, and Well-Being." *Developmental Psychology* 40, No. 1 (2004): 114–27, doi: 10.1037/0012-1649.40.1.114.

Beauregard, Eric, Jean Proulx, Kim Rossmo, Benoit Leclerc, and Jean-Francois Allaire. "Script Analysis of the Hunting Process of Serial Sex Offenders," *Criminal Justice and Behavior* 34, No. 8 (August, 2007): 1069–84.

Bereczkei, Tamas, Bela Birkas, and Zsuzsanna Kerekes. "The Presence of Others, Prosocial Traits, Machiavellianism: A Personality x Situation Approach." *Social Psychology* 41, No. 4 (2010): 238–45, doi: 10.1027/1864-9335/a000032.

Bereczkei, Tamas, Bela Birkas, and Zsuzsanna Kerekes. "Public Charity Offer as a Proximate Factor of Evolved Reputation-Building Strategy: An Experimental Analysis of a Real-Life Situation." *Evolution and Human Behavior* 28, No. 4 (2007): 277–84.

Bijvank, Marije Nije, Elly A. Konijn, Brad J. Bushman, and Peter H. M. P. Roelofsma. "Age and Violent-Content Labels Make Video Games Forbidden Fruits for Youth." *Pediatrics* (2008): 870–876, doi: 10.1542/peds.2008-0601.

Black, Pamela J., Michael Woodworth, and Stephen Porter. "The Big Bad Wolf? The Relation Between the Dark Triad and the Interpersonal Assessment of Vulnerability." *Personality and Individual Differences* (in press) (2013): 1–5, http://dx.doi.org/10.1016/j.paid.2013.10.026.

Blau, Peter M. *Exchange and Power in Social Life*. Oxford: Transaction Books, 1986.

Bleidorn, Wiebke, Christian Kandler, Ute R. Hulsheger, Rainer Riemann, Alois Angleitner, and Frank M. Spinath. "Nature and Nurture of the Interplay Between Personality Traits and Major Life Goals." *Journal of Personality and Social Psychology* 99, No. 2 (2010): 366–79, doi: 10.1037/a0019982.

Boddy, Clive R. "Corporate Psychopaths, Bullying and Unfair Supervision in the Workplace." *Journal of Business Ethics* 100 (2011): 367–79, doi: 10.1007/s10551-010-0689-5.

Boddy, Clive R. *Corporate Psychopaths: Organizational Destroyers.* New York: Palgrave Macmillan, 2011.

Booth-Butterfield, Melanie, and Michael R. Trotta. "Attributional Patterns for Expressions of Love." *Communication Reports* 7, No. 2 (Summer 1994): 119–29.

Brand, Rebecca J., Abigail Bonatsos, Rebecca D'Orazio, and Hilary DeShong. "What is Beautiful is Good, Even Online: Correlations Between Photo Attractiveness and Text Attractiveness in Men's Online Dating Profiles." *Computers in Human Behavior* 28 (2012): 166–70.

Brauer, Markus, and Richard Y. Bourhis. "Social Power." *European Journal of Social Psychology* 36 (2006): 601–616.

Bredow, Carrie A., Rodney M. Cate, and Ted L. Huston. "Have We Met Before? A Conceptual Model of First Romantic Encounters." In *Handbook of Relationship Initiation*, edited by Susan Sprecher, Amy Wenzel, and John Harvey, 3–28. New York: Psychology Press, 2008.

Briggs, Peter, Walter T. Simon, and Stacy Simonsen. "An Exploratory Study of Internet-Initiated Sexual Offenses and the Chat Room Offender: Has the Internet Enabled a New Typology of Sex Offender?" *Sexual Abuse: A Journal of Research and Treatment* 23, No. 1 (2011): 72–91.

Brown, Sandra L. *Women Who Love Psychopaths: Inside the Relationships of Inevitable Harm with Psychopaths, Sociopaths, and Narcissists.* 2nd ed. Penrose: Mask Publishing, 2009.

Brunell, Amy B., and W. Keith Campbell. "Narcissism and Romantic Relationships: Understanding the Paradox." In *The Handbook of Narcissism and Narcissistic Personality Disorder: Theoretical Approaches, Empirical Findings, and Treatments*, edited by W. Keith Campbell and Joshua D. Miller, 344–50. Hoboken: John Wiley & Sons, Inc., 2011.

Bryan, Angela D., Gregory D. Webster, and Amanda L. Mahaffey. "The Big, the Rich, and the Powerful: Physical, Financial, and Social Dimensions of Dominance in Mating and Attraction." *Personality and Social Psychology Bulletin* 37, No. 3 (2011): 365–82.

Burger, Jerry M. "Fleeting Attraction and Compliance with Requests." In *The Science of Social Influence: Advances and Future Progress*, edited by Anthony R. Pratkanis, 155–66. New York: Psychology Press, 2007.

Burger, Jerry M., Nicole Messian, Shebani Patel, Alicia del Prado, and Carmen Anderson. "What a Coincidence! The Effects of Incidental Similarity on Compliance." *Personality and Social Psychology Bulletin* 30, No. 1 (January, 2004): 35–43.

Burgoon, Judee K., Laura K. Guerrero, and Kory Floyd. *Nonverbal Communication.* Boston: Allyn and Bacon, 2010.

Burgoon, Judee K., and Aaron E. Bacue. "Nonverbal Communication Skills." In *Handbook of Communication and Social Interaction Skills*, edited by John O. Greene and Brant R. Burleson, 179–219. New York: Lawrence Erlbaum Associates, 2003.

Bushman, Brad J., and Angela D. Stack. "Forbidden Fruit Versus Tainted Fruit: Effects of Warning Labels on Attraction to Television Violence." *Journal of Experimental Psychology: Applied* 2, No. 3 (1996): 207–26.

Campbell, W. Keith. "Narcissism and Romantic Attraction." *Journal of Personality and Social Psychology* 77, No. 6 (1999): 1254–70.

Campbell, W. Keith, and Craig A. Foster. "Narcissism and Commitment in Romantic Relationships: An Investment Model Analysis." *Personality and Social Psychology Bulletin* 28, No. 4 (2002): 484–95.

Carter, Gregory Louis, Anne C. Campbell, and Steven Muncer. "The Dark Triad: Beyond a 'Male' Mating Strategy." *Personality and Individual Differences* 56 (2014): 159–64.

Carter, Gregory Louis, Anne C. Campbell, and Steven Muncer. "The Dark Triad Personality: Attractiveness to Women." *Personality and Individual Differences* 56 (2014): 57–61.

Chan, Elaine, and Jaideep Sengupta. "Insincere Flattery Actually Works: A Dual Attitudes Perspective." *Journal of Marketing Research* 47 (February 2010): 122–33.

Chartrand, Tanya L., and John A. Bargh. "The Chameleon Effect: The Perception-Behavior Link and Social Interaction." *Journal of Personality and Social Psychology* 76, No. 6 (1999): 893–910.

Cheng, Joey T., Jessica L. Tracy, Alan Kingstone, Tom Foulsham, and Joseph Henrich. "Two Ways to the Top: Evidence that Dominance and Prestige Are Distinct Yet Viable Avenues to Social Rank and Influence." *Journal of Personality and Social Psychology* 104, No. 1 (2013): 103–25.

Cherulnik, Paul. D., Kristina A. Donley, Tay Sha R. Wiewel, and Susan R. Miller. "Charisma is Contagious: The Effect of Leaders' Charisma on Observers' Affect." *Journal of Applied Social Psychology* 31 (2001): 2149–59.

Cialdini, Robert B., and Brad J. Sagarin. "Principles of Interpersonal Influence." In *Persuasion: Psychological Insights and Perspectives.* 2nd ed. Edited by Timothy C. Brock and Melanie C. Green, 143–69. Thousand Oaks: SAGE Publications, 2005.

Clark, Margaret S., and Ian Brissette. "Relationship Beliefs and Emotion: Reciprocal Effects." In *Emotions and Beliefs: How Feelings Influence Thoughts,* edited by Nico H. Frijda, Antony S. R. Manstead, and Sacha Bem, 212–40. Cambridge: Cambridge University Press, 2000.

Clark, Margaret S., Sherri P. Pataki, and Valerie H. Carver. "Some Thoughts and Findings on Self-Presentation of Emotions in Relationships." In *Knowledge Structures in Close Relationships: A Social Psychological Approach,* edited by Garth J. O. Fletcher and Julie Fitness, 247–74. Mahwah: Lawrence Erlbaum Associates, 1996.

Cleckley, Hervey. *The Mask of Sanity.* New York: New American Library, 1982.

Collins, David R., and Arthur A. Stukas. "Narcissism and Self-Presentation: The Moderating Effects of Accountability and Contingencies of Self-Worth." *Journal of Research in Personality* 42 (2008): 1629–34.

Collins, Nancy L., Maire B. Ford, and Brooke C. Feeney. "An Attachment-Theory Perspective on Social Support in Close Relationships." In *Handbook of Interpersonal Psychology: Theory, Research, Assessment, and Therapeutic Interventions,* edited by Leonard M. Horowitz and Stephen Strack, 209–31. Hoboken: John Wiley & Sons, 2011.

Cook, Karen S., Russell Hardin, and Margaret Levi. *Cooperation Without Trust?* New York: Russell Sage Foundation, 2005.

Crocker, L., L. Clare, and K. Evans. "Giving Up or Finding a Solution? The Experience of Attempted Suicide in Later Life." *Aging & Mental Health* 10, No. 6 (November 2006): 638–47.

Crysel, Laura C., Benjamin S. Crosier, and Gregory D. Webster. "The Dark Triad and Risk Behavior." *Personality and Individual Differences* 54 (2013): 35–40, http://dx.doi.org/10.1016/j.paid.2012.07.029.

Cunningham, Michael R., and Anita P. Barbee. "Prelude to a Kiss: Nonverbal Flirting, Opening Gambits, and Other Communication Dynamics in the Initiation of Romantic Relationships." In *Handbook of Relationship Initiation,* edited by Susan Sprecher, Amy Wenzel, and John Harvey, 97–120. New York: Psychology Press, 2008.

Dai, Xianchi, Ping Dong, and Jayson S. Jia, "When Does Playing Hard to Get Increase Romantic Attraction?" *Journal of Experimental Psychology: General* (2013): 1–6.

De Kwaadsteniet, Erik W., and Erik van Dijk. "Social Status as a Cue for Tacit Coordination." *Journal of Experimental Social Psychology* 46 (2010): 515–24.

DeWall, C. Nathan, Jon K. Maner, Timothy Deckman, and D. Aaron Rouby. "Forbidden Fruit: Inattention to Attractive Alternatives Provokes Implicit Relationship Reactance." *Journal of Personality and Social Psychology* 100, No. 4 (2011): 621–29, doi: 10.1037/a0021749.

Demarais, Ann, and Valerie White. *First Impressions*. New York: Bantam Books, 2004.

Demir, Meliksah, and Metin Ozdemir. "Friendship, Need Satisfaction and Happiness." *Journal of Happiness Studies* 11 (2010): 243–59.

Den Daas, Chantal, Michael Hafner, and John de Wit. "Out of Sight, Out of Mind: Cognitive States Alter the Focus of Attention." *Experimental Psychology* 60, No. 5 (2013): 313–23, doi: 10.1027/1618-3169/a000201.

Derber, Charles. *The Pursuit of Attention: Power and Ego in Everyday Life*. 2nd ed. Oxford: Oxford University Press, 2000.

Derlega, Valerian J., Barbara A. Winstead, and Kathryn Greene. "Self-Disclosure and Starting a Close Relationship." In *Handbook of Relationship Initiation*, edited by Susan Sprecher, Amy Wenzel, and John Harvey, 153–74. New York: Psychology Press, 2008.

Diagnostic and Statistical Manual of Mental Disorders. 5th ed. Washington D.C.: American Psychiatric Publishing, 2013.

Dijksterhuis, Ap, and Ad van Knippenberg. "The Relation Between Perception and Behavior, or How to Win a Game of Trivial Pursuit." In *Social Cognition: Key Readings*, edited by David L. Hamilton, 266–82. New York: Psychology Press, 2005.

Dimitrius, Jo-Ellan, and Wendy Patrick Mazzarella. *Reading People; How to Understand People and Predict Their Behavior—Anytime, Anyplace* (revision). New York: Random House, 2008.

Dombrowski, Stefan C., John W. LeMasney, C. Emmanuel Ahia, and Shannon A. Dickson. "Protecting Children From Online Sexual Predators: Technological, Psychoeducational, and Legal Considerations." *Professional Psychology: Research and Practice* 35, No. 1 (2004): 65–73.

Driscoll, Richard, Keith E. Davis, and Milton E. Lipetz. "Parental Interference and Romantic Love: The Romeo and Juliet Effect." *Journal of Personality and Social Psychology* 24, No. 1 (1972): 1–10.

Duck, Steve. *Friends, for Life: The Psychology of Close Relationships*. Brighton, Sussex: The Harvester Press Limited, 1983.

Dumas, Rafaele, and Benoit Teste. "The Influence of Criminal Facial Stereotypes on Juridic Judgments." *Swiss Journal of Psychology* 65, No. 4 (2006): 237–44.

Dutton, Donald G., and Arthur P. Aron. "Some Evidence for Heightened Sexual Attraction Under Conditions of High Anxiety." *Journal of Personality and Social Psychology* 30, No. 4 (1974): 510–17.

Dutton, Kevin. *The Wisdom of Psychopaths: What Saints, Spies, and Serial Killers Can Teach Us About Success*. New York: Scientific American/ Farrar, Straus and Giroux, 2012.

Eastwick, Paul W., Eli J. Finkel, Daniel Mochon, and Dan Ariely. "Selective Versus Unselective Romantic Desire." *Psychological Science* 18, No. 4 (2007): 317–19.

Eastwick, Paul W., Brian M. Wilkey, Eli J. Finkel, Nathaniel M. Lambert, Grainne M. Fitzsimons, Preston C. Brown, and Frank D. Fincham. "Act With Authority: Romantic Desire at the Nexus of Power Possessed and Power Perceived." *Journal of Experimental Social Psychology* 49 (2013): 267–71, http://dx.doi.org/10.1016/jesp.2012.10.019.

Ehrensperger, Kathy. *Paul and the Dynamics of Power: Communication and Interaction in the Early Christ-Movement*. London, New York: T&T Clark International, 2009.

Elliot, Andrew J., Tobias Greitemeyer, Richard H. Gramzow, Daniela Niesta Kayser, Stephanie Lichtenfeld, Markus A. Maier, and Huijun Liu. "Red, Rank, and Romance in Women Viewing Men." *Journal of Experimental Psychology: General* 139, No. 3 (2010): 399–417.

Elliot, Andrew J., and Daniela Niesta. "Romantic Red: Red Enhances Men's Attraction to Women." *Journal of Personality and Social Psychology* 95, No. 5 (2008): 1150–64.

Farley, Sally D., Diane R. Timme, and Jason W. Hart. "On Coffee Talk and Break-Room Chatter: Perceptions of Women Who Gossip in the Workplace." *The Journal of Social Psychology* 150, No. 4 (2010): 361–68.

Felmlee, Diane H. "From Appealing to Appalling: Disenchantment with a Romantic Partner." *Sociological Perspectives* 44, No. 3 (2001): 263–80.

Fine, Mark A., Tina A. Coffelt, and Loreen N. Olson, "Romantic Relationship Initiation Following Relationship Dissolution." In *Handbook of Relationship Initiation*, edited by Susan Sprecher, Amy Wenzel, and John Harvey, 391–407. New York: Psychology Press, 2008.

Fletcher, Garth J. O., and Patrick S. G. Kerr. "Through the Eyes of Love: Reality and Illusion in Intimate Relationships." *Psychological Bulletin* 136, No. 4 (2010): 627–58.

Fletcher, Garth, Jeffry A. Simpson, Lorne Campbell, and Nickola C. Overall. *The Science of Intimate Relationships*. Malden: Wiley-Blackwell, 2013.

Floyd, Kory. *Communicating Affection: Interpersonal Behavior and Social Context*. Cambridge: Cambridge University Press, 2006.

Floyd, Kory, and Perry M. Pauley. "Affectionate Communication Is Good, Except When It Isn't: On the Dark Side of Expressing Affection." In *The Dark Side of Close Relationships II*, edited by William R. Cupach and Brian H. Spitzberg, 145–73. New York: Routledge, 2011.

Forward, Susan, and Joan Torres. *Men Who Hate Women and the Women Who Love Them*. Toronto: Bantam Books, 1986.

Foster, Craig A., and W. Keith Campbell. "The Adversity of Secret Relationships." *Personal Relationships* 12 (2005), 125–43.

Fragale, Alison R., Jennifer R. Overbeck, and Margaret A. Neale. "Resources Versus Respect: Social Judgments Based on Targets' Power and Status Positions." *Journal of Experimental Social Psychology* 47 (2011): 767–75.

Furnham, Adrian, Steven C. Richards, and Delroy L. Paulhus. "The Dark Triad of Personality: A 10 Year Review." *Social and Personality Psychology Compass* 7 No. 3 (2013): 199–216, doi: 10.1111/spc3.12018.

Ganim, Sarah. "Jerry Sandusky, Former Penn State Football Staffer, Subject of Grand Jury Investigation." *The Patriot-News* (March, 31, 2011), http://www.pennlive.com/midstate/index.ssf/2011/03/jerry_sandusky_former_penn_sta.html.

Ganim, Sarah. "Report: Former Coach Jerry Sandusky Used Charity to Molest Kids." *The Patriot News* (November 6, 2011), http://www.pennlive.com/midstate/index.ssf/2011/11/report_former_coach_jerry_sand.html.

Gaspar, Roger, and Peter Bibby. "How Rings Work," in *Organized Abuse: The Current Debate*, edited by Peter C. Bibby, 49–58. Aldershot, Hants: 1996.

Gass, Robert H. and John S. Seiter. *Persuasion, Social Influence, and Compliance Gaining*. 4th ed. Boston: Allyn & Bacon, 2011.

Gayle, Barbara May, and Raymond W. Preiss. "An Overview of Dyadic Processes in Interpersonal Communication." In *Interpersonal Communication Research: Advances Through Meta-Analysis*, edited by Mike Allen, Raymond W. Preiss, Barbara Mae Gayle, and Nancy A. Burrell, 111–23. Mahway: Lawrence Erlbaum Associates, 2002.

Gentile, Brittany. "Celebrity and Narcissism." In *The Handbook of Narcissism and Narcissistic Personality Disorder: Theoretical Approaches, Empirical Findings, and Treatments*, edited by W. Keith Campbell and Joshua D. Miller, 403–409. Hoboken: John Wiley & Sons, Inc., 2011.

Goldblatt Grace, Lisa. "Understanding the Commercial Sexual Exploitation of Children." *The Link* 7, No. 2 (Fall 2008/ Winter 2009): 1, 3–6.

Goleman, Daniel. *Social Intelligence: The New Science of Human Relationships*. New York: Bantam Books, 2006.

Gonzaga, Gian C., Martie G. Haselton, Julie Smurda, Mari sian Davies, and Joshua C. Poore. "Love, Desire, and the Suppression of Thoughts of Romantic Alternatives." *Evolution and Human Behavior* 29 (2008): 119–26, doi: 10.1016/j.evolhumanbehav.2007.11.003.

Gordon, Kristina Coop, Shacunda Burton, and Laura Porter. "Predicting the Intentions of Women in Domestic Violence Shelters to Return to Partners: Does Forgiveness Play a Role?" *Journal of Family Psychology* 18 (2004): 331–38, doi: 10/1037/0893-3200.18.2.331.

Grant, Adam M., and Francesca Gino. "A Little Thanks Goes a Long Way: Explaining Why Gratitude Expressions Motivate Prosocial Behavior." *Journal of Personality and Social Psychology* 98, No. 6 (2010): 946–55.

Graziano, William G., and Jennifer Weisho Bruce, "Attraction and the Initiation of Relationships: A Review of the Empirical Literature." In *Handbook of Relationship Initiation*, edited by Susan Sprecher, Amy Wenzel, and John Harvey, 269–95. New York: Psychology Press, 2008.

Greer, Arlette E., and David M. Buss. "Tactics for Promoting Sexual Encounters." *The Journal of Sex Research* 31, No. 3 (1994): 185–201.

Gueguen, Nicolas, and Lubomir Lamy. "Short Research Note: Men's Social Status and Attractiveness: Women's Receptivity to Men's Date Requests." *Swiss Journal of Psychology* 71, No. 3 (2012): 157–60, doi: 10.1024/1421-0185/a000083.

Gueguen, Nicolas, Angelique Martin, and Sebastien Meineri. "Similarity and Social Interaction: When Similarity Fosters Implicit Behavior Toward a Stranger." *The Journal of Social Psychology* 151, No. 6 (2011): 671–73.

Guerrero, Laura K., and Kory Floyd. *Nonverbal Communication in Close Relationships*. Mahwah: Lawrence Erlbaum Associates, 2006.

Guerrero, Laura K., Peter A. Andersen, and Walid A. Afifi. *Close Encounters: Communication in Relationships*. 2nd ed. Los Angeles: SAGE Publications, 2007.

Gurian, Elizabeth A. "Explanations of Mixed-Sex Partnered Homicide: A Review of Sociological and Psychological Theory." *Aggression and Violent Behavior* 18 (2013): 520–26, http://dx.doi.org/10.1016/javb.2013.07.007.

Hackathorn, Jana, and Amanda Brantley. "To Know You Is (Not) to Want You: Mediators Between Sociosexual Orientation and Romantic Commitment." *Current Psychology* (January 10, 2014) doi: 10.1007/s12144-013-9199-9.

Hakim, Catherine. *Erotic Capital: The Power of Attraction in the Boardroom and the Bedroom*. New York: Basic Books, 2011.

Hall, Jason R., and Stephen D. Benning. "The 'Successful' Psychopath: Adaptive and Subclinical Manifestations of Psychopathy in the General Population." In *Handbook of Psychopathy*, edited by Christopher J. Patrick, 459–78. New York: The Guilford Press, 2006.

Hare, Robert D. *Without Conscience: The Disturbing World of the Psychopaths Among Us*. New York: The Guilford Press, 1993.

Hargie, Owen, and David Dickson. *Skilled Interpersonal Communication: Research, Theory and Practice*. 4th ed. London: Routledge, 2004.

Harris, Monica J., and Christopher P. Garris. "You Never Get a Second Chance to Make a First Impression: Behavioral Consequences of First Impressions." In *First Impressions*, edited by Nalini Ambady and John J. Skowronski, 147–68. New York: The Guilford Press, 2008.

Hartsock, Nancy C. M. *Money, Sex, and Power: Toward a Feminist Historical Materialism*. New York: Longman, 1983.

Hassan, Steven. *Combating Cult Mind Control*. Rochester: Park Street Press, 1988.

Hedley, Mark. "The Geometry of Gendered Conflict in Popular Film: 1986–2000." *Sex Roles* 47, Nos. 5–6 (September 2002): 201–17.

Helmreich, Robert, Elliot Aronson, and James LeFan. "To Err is Humanizing—Sometimes: Effects of Self-Esteem, Competence, and a Pratfall on Interpersonal Attraction." *Journal of Personality and Social Psychology* 16, No. 2 (1970): 259–64.

Hendrick, Susan S., and Clyde Hendrick. "Satisfaction, Love, and Respect in the Initiation of Romantic Relationships." In *Handbook of Relationship Initiation*, edited by Susan Sprecher, Amy Wenzel, and John Harvey, 337–71. New York: Psychology Press, 2008.

Holtzman, Nicholas S. "Facing a Psychopath: Detecting the Dark Triad From Emotionally-Neutral Faces, Using Prototypes From the Personality Faceaurus." *Journal of Research in Personality* 45 (2011): 648–54.

Holtzman, Nicholas S., and Michael J. Strube. "People with Dark Personalities Tend to Create a Physically Attractive Veneer." *Social Psychological and Personality Science* 4, No. 4 (2012): 461–67.

Holtzman, Nicholas S., and Michael J. Strube. "The Intertwined Evolution of Narcissism and Short-Term Mating: An Emerging Hypothesis." In *The Handbook of Narcissism and Narcissistic Personality Disorder: Theoretical Approaches, Empirical Findings, and Treatments*, edited by W. Keith Campbell and Joshua D. Miller, 210–20. Hoboken: John Wiley & Sons, Inc., 2011.

Holtzman, Nicholas S., Simine Vazier, and Matthias R. Mehl. "Sounds Like a Narcissist: Behavioral Manifestations of Narcissism in Everyday Life." *Journal of Research in Personality* 44 (2010): 478–84, doi: 10.1016/j.jrp.2010.06.001.

Honekopp, Johannes. "Once More: Is Beauty in the Eye of the Beholder? Relative Contributions of Private and Shared Taste to Judgments of Facial Attractiveness." *Journal of Experimental Psychology* 32, No. 2 (2006): 199–209, doi: 10.1037/0096-1523.32.2.199.

Honeycutt, James M., and Suzette P. Bryan. *Scripts and Communication for Relationships*. New York: Peter Lang, 2011.

Horberg, E . J., Dacher Keltner, and Michael W. Kraus. "Pride Displays Communicate Self-Interest and Support for Meritocracy." *Journal of Personality and Social Psychology* 105, No. 1 (2013): 24–37, doi: 10.1037/a0032849.

Hortulanus, Roelof, Anja Machielse, and Ludwien Meeuwesen. *Social Isolation in Modern Society*. London: Routledge, 2006.

Howard, Daniel J., Charles Gengler, and Ambuj Jain. "What's in a Name? A Complimentary Means of Persuasion." *Journal of Consumer Research* 22 (September, 1995): 200–11.

Hughes, David John, Moss Rowe, Mark Batey, and Andrew Lee. "A Tale of Two Sites: Twitter vs. Facebook and the Personality Predictors of Social Media Usage." *Computers in Human Behavior* 28 (2012): 561–69, doi: 10.1016/j.chb.2011.11.001.

Igarashi, Tasuku, Yoshihisa Kashima, Emiko S. Kashima, Tomas Farsides, Uichol Kim, Fritz Strack, Lioba Werth, and Masaki Yuki. "Culture, Trust, and Social Networks." *Asian Journal of Social Psychology* 11 (2008): 88–101.

Isenberg, Sheila. *Women Who Love Men Who Kill*. New York: Simon & Schuster, 1991.

Jacobson, Marsha B. "Effects of Victim's and Defendant's Physical Attractiveness on Subjects' Judgments in a Rape Case." *Sex Roles* 7, No. 3 (1981): 247–55.

Jakobwitz, Sharon, and Vincent Egan. "The Dark Triad and Normal Personality Traits." *Personality and Individual Differences* 40 (2006): 331–39, doi: 10.1016/j.paid.2005.07.006.

Jansen, Esther, Sandra Mulkens, Yvette Emond, and Anita Jansen. "From the Garden of Eden to the Land of Plenty: Restriction of Fruit and Sweets Intake Leads to Increased Fruits and Sweets Consumption in Children." *Appetite* 51 (2008): 570–75.

Johnson, Joel T., Emilie B. Mitchell, and Michael D. Robinson. "Inferences About the Authentic Self: When Do Actions Say More Than Mental States?" *Journal of Personality and Social Psychology* 87, No. 5 (2004): 615–30.

Jonason, Peter K., and David M. Buss. "Avoiding Entangling Commitments: Tactics for Implementing a Short-Term Mating Strategy." *Personality and Individual Differences* 52 (2012): 606–610, doi: 10.1016/j.paid.2011.12.015.

Jonason, Peter K., and Phillip Kavanaugh. "The Dark Side of Love: Love Styles and the Dark Triad." *Personality and Individual Differences* 49 (2010): 606–10.

Jonason, Peter K., and Gregory Webster. "A Protean Approach to Social Influence: Dark Triad Personalities and Social Influence Tactics." *Personality and Individual Differences* 52 (2012): 521–26, doi: 10.1016/j.paid.2011.11.023.

Jonason, Peter K., Norman P. Li, and David M. Buss. "The Costs and Benefits of the Dark Triad: Implications for Mate Poaching and Mate Retention Tactics." *Personality and Individual Differences* 48 (2010): 373–78.

Jonason, Peter K, Norman P. Li, Gregory D. Webster, and David P. Schmitt. "The Dark Triad: Facilitating a Short-Term Mating Strategy in Men." *European Journal of Personality* 23 (2009): 5–18.

Jonason, Peter K., Norman P. Li, and Emily A. Teicher. "Who is James Bond? The Dark Triad as an Agentic Social Style." *Individual Differences Research* 8, No. 2 (2010): 111–20.

Jonason, Peter K., Victor X. Luevano, and Heather M. Adams. "How the Dark Triad Traits Predict Relationship Choices." *Personality and Individual Differences* 53 (2012): 180–84.

Jonason, Peter K, David P. Schmitt, Gregory D. Webster, Norman P. Li, and Laura Crysel. "The Antihero in Popular Culture: Life History Theory and the Dark Triad Personality Traits." *Review of General Psychology* 16, No. 2 (2012): 192–99.

Jonason, Peter K., Sarah Slomski, and Jamie Partyka. "The Dark Triad at Work: How *Toxic* Employees Get Their Way." *Personality and Individual Differences* 52 (2012): 449–53, doi:10.1016 /j.paid.2011.11.008.

Jonason, Peter K., Katherine A. Valentine, Norman P. Li, and Carmelita L. Harbeson. "Mate-Selection and the Dark Triad: Facilitating a Short-Term Mating Strategy and Creating a Volatile Environment." *Personality and Individual Differences* 51 (2011): 759–63, doi: 10.1016/j .paid.2011.06.025.

Jones, Daniel N., and Delroy L. Paulhus. "The Role of Impulsivity in the Dark Triad of Personality." *Personality and Individual Differences* 51 (2011): 679–82.

Jones, Daniel N., and Delroy L. Paulhus, "Differentiating the Dark Triad Within the Interpersonal Circumplex." In *Handbook of Interpersonal Psychology: Theory, Research, Assessment, and Therapeutic Interventions*, edited by Leonard M. Horowitz and Stephen Strack, 249–67. Hoboken: John Wiley & Sons, 2011.

Jones, John T., Brett W. Pelham, Mauricio Carvallo, and Matthew C. Mirenberg. "How Do I Love Thee? Let Me Count the Js: Implicit Egotism and Interpersonal Attraction." *Journal of Personality and Social Psychology* 87, No. 5 (2004): 665–83.

Katz, Jack. *Seductions of Crime: Moral and Sensual Attractions in Doing Evil*. New York: Basic Books, Inc., 1988.

Keijsers, Loes, Susan Branje, Skyler T. Hawk, Seth J. Schwartz, Tom Frijns, Hans M. Koot, Pol van Lier, and Wim Meeus. "Forbidden Friends as Forbidden Fruit: Parental Supervision of

Friendships, Contact with Deviant Peers, and Adolescent Delinquency." *Child Development* 83, No. 2 (March/April 2012): 651–66, doi: 10.1111/j.1467-8624.2011.01701.x.

Keltner, Dacher, Deborah H. Gruenfeld, and Cameron Anderson. "Power, Approach, and Inhibition." *Psychological Review* 110, No. 2 (2003): 265–84.

Kernis, Michael H., and Brian M. Goldman. "A Multicomponent Conceptualization of Authenticity: Theory and Research." *Advances in Experimental Psychology* 38 (2006): 283–357.

Kernis, Michael H., and Brian M. Goldman. "From Thought and Experience to Behavior and Interpersonal Relationships: A Multicomponent Conceptualization of Authenticity." In *On Building, Defending and Regulating the Self: A Psychological Perspective*, edited by Abraham Tesser, Joanne V. Wood, and Diederik A. Stapel, 31–52. New York: Psychology Press, 2005.

Kniffin, Kevin M., and David Sloan Wilson. "The Effect of Nonphysical Traits on the Perception of Physical Attractiveness: Three Naturalistic Studies." *Evolution and Human Behavior* 25 (2004): 88–101.

Knoll, James. "Teacher Sexual Misconduct: Grooming Patterns and Female Offenders." *Journal of Child Sexual Abuse* 19 (2010): 371–86.

Kruger, Daniel J., Maryanne Fisher, and Ian Jobling. "Proper and Dark Heroes as Dads and Cads." *Human Nature* 14, No. 3 (2003): 305–17.

Kuhn, Kristine M., Timothy R. Johnson, and Douglas Miller. "Applicant Desirability Influences Reactions to Discovered Resume Embellishments." *International Journal of Selection and Assessment* 21, No. 1 (2013): 111–20.

Kuhn, Simone, Barbara C. N. Muller, Rick B. van Baaren, Anne Wietzker, Ap Dijksterhuis, and Marcel Brass. "Why Do I Like You When You Behave Like Me? Neural Mechanisms Mediating Positive Consequences of Observing Someone Being Imitated." *Social Neuroscience* 5, No. 4 (2010): 384–92.

Kunstman, Jonathan W., and Jon K. Maner. "Sexual Overperception: Power, Mating Motives, and Biases in Social Judgment." *Journal of Personality and Social Psychology* 100, No. 2 (2010): 282–294 (282), doi: 10.1037/a0021135.

Lang, Reuben A., and Roy R. Frenzel "How Sex Offenders Lure Children." *Annals of Sex Research* 1 (1988): 303–17.

Langlois, Judith H., Lisa Kalakanis, Adam J. Rubenstein, Andrea Larson, Monica Hallam, and Monica Smoot. "Maxims or Myths of Beauty? A Meta-Analytic and Theoretical Review." *Psychological Bulletin* 126, No. 3 (2000): 390–423.

Lanning, Kenneth V. *Child Molesters: A Behavioral Analysis: For Law-Enforcement Officers Investigating the Sexual Exploitation of Children by Acquaintance Molesters.* 4th ed. Alexandria: National Center for Missing and Exploited Children, 2001.

Lawson, Louanne. "Isolation, Gratification, Justification: Offenders' Explanations of Child Molesting." *Issues in Mental Health Nursing* 24 (2003): 695–705.

Leberg, Eric. *Understanding Child Molesters: Taking Charge.* Thousand Oaks: SAGE Publications, 1997.

Leclerc, Benoit, Jean Proulx, Patrick Lussier, and Jean-Francois Allaire. "Offender-Victim Interaction and Crime Event Outcomes: Modus Operandi and Victim Effects on the Risk of Intrusive Sexual Offenses Against Children." *Criminology* 47, No. 2 (2009): 595–618.

Lee, Seung Yun, Aiden P. Gregg, and Seong Hoon Park. "The Person in the Purchase: Narcissistic Consumers Prefer Products that Positively Distinguish Them." *Journal of Personality and Social Psychology* 105, No. 2 (2013): 335–352. doi: 10.1037/a0032703.

Lemay, Edward P., Jr., and Margaret S. Clark. "How the Head Liberates the Heart: Projection of Communal Responsiveness Guides Relationship Promotion." *Journal of Personality and Social Psychology* 94, No. 4 (2008): 647–71, doi: 10.1037/0022-3514.94.4.647.

Lemay, Edward P., Jr., and Angela M. Neal. "The Wishful Memory of Interpersonal Responsiveness." *Journal of Personality and Social Psychology* 104, No. 4 (2013): 653–72, doi: 10.1037/a0030422.

Lemay, Edward P., Jr., Margarite A. Bechis, Jessamine Martin, Angela M. Neal, and Christine Coyne. "Concealing Negative Evaluations of a Romantic Partner's Physical Attractiveness." *Personal Relationships* 20 (2013): 669–89. doi: 10.1111/pere.12007.

Levine, Robert. *The Power of Persuasion: How We're Bought and Sold.* Hoboken: John Wiley and Sons, 2003.

Levs, Josh, Phil Gast, and Steve Almasy. "Charles Ramsey: I'm No Hero in Freeing of Captive Women," CNN May 9, 2013; http://www.cnn.com/2013/05/07/us/ohio-cleveland-ramsey/index.html.

Lewis, David M. G., Judith A. Easton, Cari D. Goetz, and David M. Buss. "Exploitative Male Mating Strategies: Personality, Mating Orientation, and Relationship Status." *Personality and Individual Differences* 52 (2012): 139–43, doi: 10.1016/j.paid.2011.09.017.

Lilienfeld, Scott O., Irwin D. Waldman, Kristin Landfield, Ashley L. Watts, Steven Rubenzer, and Thomas R. Faschingbauer. "Fearless Dominance and the U.S. Presidency: Implications of Psychopathic Personality Traits for Successful and Unsuccessful Political Leadership." *Journal of Personality and Social Psychology* 103, No. 3 (2012): 489–505, doi: 10.1037/a0029392.

Lissek, Shmuel, Johanna M. P. Baas, Daniel S. Pine, Kaebah Orme, Sharone Dvir, Emily Rosenberger, and Christian Grillon. "Sensation Seeking and the Aversive Motivational System." *Emotion* 5, No. 4 (2005): 396–407 (396), doi: 10.1037/1528-3542.5.4.396.

Little, Anthony C., Lisa M. DeBruine, and Benedict C. Jones. "Sex Differences in Attraction to Familiar and Unfamiliar Opposite-Sex Faces: Men Prefer Novelty and Women Prefer Familiarity." *Arch Sex Behavior* (June 6, 2013), doi: 10.1007/s10508-013-0120-2.

Littlejohn, Stephen W. *Theories of Human Communication.* 7th ed. Belmont: Wadsworth/ Thompson Learning, 2002.

Lloyd, Sally A., and Beth C. Emery. "The Context and Dynamics of Intimate Aggression Against Women." *Journal of Social and Personal Relationships* 17, nos. 4–5 (2000): 503–521.

Lopez, Frederick G., and Kenneth G. Rice. "Preliminary Development and Validation of a Measure of Relationship Authenticity." *Journal of Counseling Psychology* 53, No. 3 (2006): 362–71.

Lount, Robert B., Jr. "The Impact of Positive Mood on Trust in Interpersonal and Intergroup Interactions." *Journal of Personality and Social Psychology* 98, No. 3 (2010): 420–33.

Lykken, David T. "Psychopathic Personality: The Scope of the Problem." In *Handbook of Psychopathy*, edited by Christopher J. Patrick, 3–13. New York: The Guilford Press, 2006.

Maddux, Mitchel, Larry Celona, and Dan Mangan. "Jail Guard Pregnant with Cop-Killer's Child." *New York Post*, February 6, 2013; http://www.nypost.com/p/news/local/brooklyn/jailer_carries_monster_baby_hTZACrgVZHanbKc5PIbF8J.

Maner, Jon K., Matthew T. Gailliot, D. Aaron Rouby, and Saul L. Miller. "Can't Take My Eyes Off You: Attentional Adhesion to Mates and Rivals." *Journal of Personality and Social Psychology* 93, No. 3 (2007): 389–401, doi: 10.1037/0022-3514.93.3.389.

Marchand, Miquelle A. G., and Roos Vonk. "The Process of Becoming Suspicious of Ulterior Motives." *Social Cognition* 23, No. 3 (2005): 242–56.

Martin, John Levi. "Is Power Sexy?" *American Journal of Sociology* 111, No. 2 (September 2005): 408–446, http://www.jstor.org/stable/10.1086/432781.

Maslow, Abraham H. *Motivation and Personality*. 3rd ed. New York: HarperCollins Publishers, 1987.

Maslow, A. H. "A Theory of Human Motivation." *Psychological Review* 50, No. 4 (1943): 370–96.

Mathes, Eugene W., and Linda L. Edwards. "Physical Attractiveness as an Input in Social Exchanges." *The Journal of Psychology* 98 (1978): 267–75.

McCabe, Kira O., Nico W. Van Yperen, Andrew J. Elliot, and Marc Verbraak. "Big Five Personality Profiles of Context-Specific Achievement Goals." *Journal of Research in Personality* 47 (2013): 698–707.

McHoskey, John W. "Machiavellianism and Sexuality: On the Moderating Role of Biological Sex." *Personality and Individual Differences* 31 (2001): 779–89.

McKenna, Katelyn Y. A. (Yael Kaynan). "MySpace or Your Place: Relationship Initiation and Development in the Wired and Wireless World." In *Handbook of Relationship Initiation*, edited by Susan Sprecher, Amy Wenzel, and John Harvey, 235–47. New York: Psychology Press, 2008.

McNulty, James K., Erin M. O'Mara, and Benjamin R. Karney. "Benevolent Cognitions as a Strategy of Relationship Maintenance: 'Don't Sweat the Small Stuff' . . . . But It Is Not All Small Stuff." *Journal of Personality and Social Psychology* 94, No. 4 (2008): 631–46, doi: 10.1037/0022-3514.94.4.631.

McPherson, Miller, Lynn Smith-Lovin, and James M. Cook. "Birds of a Feather: Homophily in Social Networks." *Annual Review of Sociology* 27 (2001): 415–44.

Meier, Brian P., and Sarah Dionne. "Downright Sexy: Verticality, Implicit Power, and Perceived Physical Attractiveness." *Social Cognition* 27, No. 6 (2009): 883–92.

Metts, Sandra, and Erica Grohskopf. "Impression Management: Goals, Strategies, and Skills." In *Handbook of Communication and Social Interaction Skills*, edited by John O. Greene and Brant R. Burleson, 357–399. Mahway: Lawrence Erlbaum Associates, 2003.

Michniewicz, Kenneth S., and Joseph A. Vandello. "The Attractive Underdog: When Disadvantage Bolsters Attractiveness." *Journal of Social and Personal Relationships* 30, No. 7 (2013): 942–52.

Milgram, Stanley. "Behavioral Study of Obedience." *Journal of Abnormal and Social Psychology* 67, No. 4 (1963): 371–78.

Miller, Paul J. E., Sylvia Niehuis, and Ted L. Huston. "Positive Illusions in Marital Relationships: A 13-Year Longitudinal Study." *Personality and Social Psychology Bulletin* 32, No. 12 (December 2006): 1579 94, doi: 10.10.1177/0146167206292691.

Miller, Rowland S. "We Always Hurt the Ones We Love: Aversive Interactions in Close Relationships." In *Aversive Interpersonal Behaviors*, edited by Robin M. Kowalski, 11–29. New York: Plenum Press, 1997.

Millon, Theodore, and Roger Davis. "Ten Subtypes of Psychopathy." In *Psychopathy: Antisocial, Criminal, and Violent Behavior* (edited by Theodore Millon et al.), 161–70. New York: The Guilford Press, 1998.

Montoya, R. Matthew, and Robert S. Horton. "A Meta-Analytic Investigation of the Processes Underlying the Similarity-Attraction Effect." *Journal of Social and Personal Relationships* 30, No. 1 (2012): 64–94, doi: 10.1177/0265407512452989.

Mortensen, C. David. *Optimal Human Relations: The Search for a Good Life*. New Brunswick, London: Transaction Publishers, 2008.

Moscovici, Claudia. *Dangerous Liaisons: How to Recognize and Escape from Psychopathic Seduction*. Lanham: Hamilton Books, 2011.

Murray, Sandra L., and John G. Holmes. "Seeing Virtues in Faults: Negativity and the Transformation of Interpersonal Narratives in Close Relationships." *Journal of Personality and Social Psychology* 65, No. 4 (1993): 707–22.

Murray, Sandra L., John G. Holmes, and Dale W. Griffin. "The Benefits of Positive Illusions: Idealization and the Construction of Satisfaction in Close Relationships." *Journal of Personality and Social Psychology* 70, No. 1 (1996): 79–98.

Murray, Sandra L., John G. Holmes, and Dale W. Griffin. "The Self-Fulfilling Nature of Positive Illusions in Romantic Relationships: Love is Not Blind, but Prescient." *Journal of Personality and Social Psychology* 71, No. 6 (1996): 1155–80.

Nettle, Daniel. "An Evolutionary Approach to the Extraversion Continuum." *Evolution and Human Behavior* 26 (2005): 363–73, doi: 10.1016/j.evolhumbehav.2004.12.004.

Nevicka, Barbora, Annebel H. B. De Hoogh, Annelies E. M. Van Vianen, and Femke S. Ten Velden. "Uncertainty Enhances the Preference for Narcissistic Leaders." *European Journal of Social Psychology* 43 (2013): 370–80, doi: 10.1002/ejsp.1943.

NewsOne. "14 More Correctional Officers Charged in Baltimore Black Guerilla Family Jail Sex Scandal." November 25, 2013, http://atlantadailyworld.com/2013/11/25/14-more-correctional-officers-charged-in-baltimore-black-guerilla-family-jail-sex-scandal/.

Nordhall, Ola, and Jens Agerstrom. "Future-Oriented People Show Stronger Moral Concerns." *Current Research in Social Psychology* (2013): 52–59, http://www.uiowa.edu/~grpproc/crisp/crisp.html.

"Nurses Remain Most Trusted Professionals in America, Gallup Survey Says." National News, *Advance Healthcare Network*, December 5, 2012; http://nursing.advanceweb.com/News/National-News/Nurses-Remain-Most-Trusted-Professionals-in-America-Gallup-Survey-Says.aspx.

Ogas, Ogi, and Sai Gaddam. *A Billion Wicked Thoughts: What the World's Largest Experiment Reveals About Human Desire.* New York: Dutton, 2011.

O'Keefe, Daniel J. *Persuasion Theory and Research.* 2nd ed. Thousand Oaks: SAGE Publications, 2002.

Oliner, Samuel P. *The Nature of Good and Evil: Understanding the Many Acts of Moral and Immoral Behavior.* St. Paul: Paragon House, 2011.

Papies, Esther K., Wolfgang Stroebe, and Henk Aarts. "The Allure of Forbidden Food: On the Role of Attention in Self-Regulation." *Journal of Experimental Social Psychology* 44 (2008): 1283–92.

Patrick, Wendy L. *Using the Psychology of Attraction in Christian Outreach: Lessons from the Dark Side.* New York: Peter Lang, 2013.

Paunonen, Sampo V. "You are Honest, Therefore I Like You and Find You Attractive." *Journal of Research in Personality* 40 (2006): 237–49.

Perez, Alex, Matthew Jaffe, Steven Portnoy, and Alyssa Newcomb. "Cleveland Kidnapping Suspect Ariel Castro Hid a Dark Side, His Uncle Says," May 7, 2012; http://abcnews.go.com/US/cleveland-kidnap-suspect-charismatic-guy-ashamed-neighbor/story?id=19122845.

Perloff, Richard M. *The Dynamics of Persuasion: Communication and Attitudes in the 21st Century.* 4th ed. New York: Routledge, 2010.

Pierce, Charles A., Donn Byrne, and Herman Aguinis. "Attraction in Organizations: a Model of Workplace Romance." *Journal of Organizational Behavior* 17 (1996): 5–32.

Pratkanis, Anthony R. "Social Influence Analysis: An Index of Tactics." In *The Science of Social Influence: Advances and Future Progress*, edited by Anthony R. Pratkanis, 17–82. New York: Psychology Press, 2007.

Ragins, Belle Rose, and John L. Cotton. "Mentor Functions and Outcomes: A Comparison of Men and Women in Formal and Informal Mentoring Relationships." *Journal of Applied Psychology* 84, No. 4 (1999): 529–50.

Ramsland, Katherine, and Patrick N. McGrain. *Inside The Minds Of Sexual Predators*. Santa Barbara: Praeger, 2010.

Rauthmann, John F., and Gerald P. Kolar. "How 'Dark' are the Dark Triad Traits? Examining the Perceived Darkness of Narcissism, Machiavellianism, and Psychopathy." *Personality and Individual Differences* 53 (2012): 884–89.

Rauthmann, John F., and Gerald P. Kolar. "The Perceived Attractiveness and Traits of the Dark Triad: Narcissists Are Perceived as Hot, Machiavellians and Psychopaths Not." *Personality and Individual Differences* 54 (2010): 582–86.

Raven, Bertram H. "The Bases of Power and the Power/Interaction Model of Interpersonal Influence." *Analyses of Social Issues and Public Policy* 8, No. 1 (2008): 1–22.

Reddington, Frances P., and Betsy Wright Kreisel. *Sexual Assault: The Victims, the Perpetrators, and the Criminal Justice System*. 2nd ed. Durham: Carolina Academic Press, 2009.

Reeder, Glenn D. "Perceptions of Goals and Motives in Romantic Relationships." In *Handbook of Relationship Initiation*, edited by Susan Sprecher, Amy Wenzel, and John Harvey, 499–514. New York: Psychology Press, 2008.

Reeder, Glenn D., Marla J. Ronk, Roos Vonk, Jaap Ham, and Melissa Lawrence. "Dispositional Attribution: Multiple Inferences About Motive-Related Traits." *Journal of Personality and Social Psychology* 86, No. 4 (2004): 530–44, doi: 10.1037/0022-3514.86.4.530.

Reis, Harry T., Michael R. Maniaci, Peter A. Caprariello, Paul W. Eastwick, and Eli J. Finkel. "Familiarity Does Indeed Promote Attraction in Live Interaction." *Journal of Personality and Social Psychology* 101, No. 3 (2011): 557–70.

Rentfrow, Peter J., and Samuel D. Gosling. "The Do Re Mi's of Everyday Life: The Structure and Personality Correlates of Music Preferences." *Journal of Personality and Social Psychology* 84, No. 6 (2003): 1236–56, doi: 10.1037/0022-3514.84.6.1236.

Riggio, Ronald E., Keith F. Widaman, Joan S. Tucker, and Charles Salinas. "Beauty is More Than Skin Deep: Components of Attractiveness." *Basic and Applied Social Psychology* 12, No. 4 (1991): 423–39.

Romero-Canyas, Rainer, and Geraldine Downey. "What I See When I Think It's About Me: People Low in Rejection-Sensitivity Downplay Cues of Rejection in Self-Relevant Interpersonal Situations." *Emotion* 13, No. 1 (2013): 104–17, doi: 10.1037/a0029786.

Rudman, Laurie A., and Julie E. Phelan. "The Interpersonal Power of Feminism: Is Feminism Good for Romantic Relationships?" *Sex Roles* 57 (2007): 787–99.

Rye, B. J., and Glenn J. Meaney. "Voyeurism: It Is Good as Long as We Do Not Get Caught." *International Journal of Sexual Health* 19, No. 1 (2007): 47–56, doi: 10.1300/J514v19n01_06.

Salter, Anna C. *Predators: Pedophiles, Rapists, and Other Sex Offenders: Who They Are, How They Operate, and How We Can Protect Ourselves and Our Children*. New York: Basic Books, 2003.

Sanderson, Christiane. *The Seduction of Children: Empowering Parents and Teachers to Protect Children from Child Sexual Abuse*. London: Jessica Kingsley Publishers, 2004.

Sandfort, Theo. *Boys on Their Contacts with Men: A Study of Sexually Expressed Friendships*. Elmhurst: Global Academic Publishers, 1987.

"Scarface: The Quotes." http://www.jgeoff.com/scarface/quotes.html.

Schaller, Mark. "Evolutionary Bases of First Impressions." In *First Impressions*, edited by Ambady, Nalini and John J. Skowronski, 15–34. New York: The Guilford Press, 2008.

Schinaia, Cosimo. *On Paedophilia*. London: Karnac, 2010.

Schmidt, Wallace V., Roger N. Conaway, Susan S. Easton, and William J. Wardrope. *Communicating Globally: Intercultural Communication and International Business*. Los Angeles: SAGE Publications, 2007.

Schneider, Frank W., Jamie A. Gruman, and Larry M. Coutts. *Applied Social Psychology: Understanding and Addressing Social and Practical Problems*. Thousand Oaks: SAGE Publications, 2005.

Schultheiss, Oliver C. "Implicit Motives." In *Handbook of Personality: Theory and Research*, 3rd ed. Edited by Oliver P. John, Richard W. Robins, and Lawrence A. Pervin, 603–633. New York: The Guilford Press, 2008.

Sealy, Ruth H. V., and Val Singh. "The Importance of Role Models and Demographic Context for Senior Women's Work Identity Development." *International Journal of Management Reviews* 12, No. 3 (2009): 284–300.

Segall, Laurie, Erica Fink, and Ben Brumfield. "'He is Dead To Me,' Daughter of Ohio Suspect Says in CNN Exclusive," *CNN.com*, May 10, 2013; http://www.cnn.com/2013/05/09/us/ohio-suspect-daughter.

Self, Charles C. "Credibility." In *An Integrated Approach to Communication Theory and Research*. 2nd ed. Edited by Don W. Stacks and Michael B. Salwen, 435–56. New York: Routledge, 2009.

Sigall, Harold, and Nancy Ostrove. "Beautiful but Dangerous: Effects of Offender Attractiveness and Nature of the Crime on Juridic Judgment." *Journal of Personality and Social Psychology* 31, No. 3 (1975): 410–14.

Singer, Alexis. *Alexis: My True Story of Being Seduced by an Online Predator*. Deerfield Beach: Health Communications, Inc., 2010.

Slotter, Erica B., and Wendi L. Gardner. "The Dangers of Dating the 'Bad Boy' (or Girl): When Does Romantic Desire Encourage Us to Take on the Negative Qualities of Potential Partners." *Journal of Experimental Social Psychology* 48 (2012): 1173–78, doi: 10.1016/j.jesp.2012.05.007.

Smith, Sarah Francis, Scott O. Lilienfeld, Karly Coffey, and James M. Dabbs. "Are Psychopaths and Heroes Twigs Off the Same Branch? Evidence from College, Community, and Presidential Samples." *Journal of Research in Personality* 47 (2013): 634–46, http://dx.doi.org/10.1016/j.jrp.2013.05.006.

Sonnby-Borgstrom, Marianne, Peter Jonsson, and Owe Svensson. "Emotional Empathy as Related to Mimicry Reactions at Different Levels of Information Processing." *Journal of Nonverbal Behavior* 27, No. 1 (2003): 3–23.

Sosik, John J., William A. Gentry, and Jae Uk Chun. "The Value of Virtue in the Upper Echelons: A Multisource Examination of Executive Character Strengths and Performance." *The Leadership Quarterly* 23 (2012): 367–82, doi: 10.1016/j.leaqua.2011.08.010.

Spielmann, Stephanie S., Geoff MacDonald, Jessica A. Maxwell, Samantha Joel, Diana Peragine, Amy Muise, and Emily Impett. "Settling for Less Out of Fear of Being Single." *Journal of Personality and Social Psychology* 20 (2013), 1–25.

Sprecher, Susan, and Diane Felmlee, "Insider Perspectives on Attraction." In *Handbook of Relationship Initiation*, edited by Susan Sprecher, Amy Wenzel, and John Harvey, 297–313. New York: Psychology Press, 2008.

Staw, Barry M., Robert I. Sutton, and Lisa H. Pelled. "Employee Positive Emotion and Favorable Outcomes at the Workplace." *Organization Science* 5, No. 1 (1994): 51–71.

Stiff, James B., and Paul A. Mongeau. *Persuasive Communication*. 2nd ed. New York: Guilford Press, 2003.

Storey, Richard. *The Art of Persuasive Communication*. Hampshire: Gower, 1997.

Sussman, Steve, Rachel Grana, Pallav Pokhrel, Louise A. Rohrbach, and Ping Sun. "Forbidden Fruit and the Prediction of Cigarette Smoking." *Substance Use & Misuse* 45 (2010): 1683–93, doi: 10.3109/0826081003682230.

Swaine, Jon. "Ohio Abductions: Ariel Castro Threatened to Kill Wife and Daughters." *The Telegraph*, May 7, 2013; http://www.telegraph.co.uk/news/worldnews/northamerica/usa/10042926/Ohio-abductions-Ariel-Castro-threatened-to-kill-wife-and-daughters.html.

Swami, Viren, and Adrian Furnham. *The Psychology of Physical Attraction*. London: Routledge, 2008.

Swami, Viren, Corina Greven, and Adrian Furnham. "More Than Just Skin-Deep? A Pilot Study Integrating Physical and Non-Physical Factors in the Perception of Physical Attractiveness." *Personality and Individual Differences* 42 (2007): 563–72.

Swami, Viren, Adrian Furnham, Tomas Chamorro-Premuzic, Kanwal Akbar, Natalie Gordon, Tasha Harris, Jo Finch, and Martin J. Tovee. "More Than Just Skin Deep? Personality Information Influences Men's Ratings of the Attractiveness of Women's Body Sizes." *The Journal of Social Psychology* 150, No. 6 (2010): 628–47.

Swami, Viren, Stefan Stieger, Tanja Haubner, Martin Voracek, and Adrian Furnham. "Evaluating the Physical Attractiveness of Oneself and One's Romantic Partner: Individual and Relationship Correlates of the Love-Is-Blind Bias." *Journal of Individual Differences* 30, No. 1 (2009): 35–43, doi: 10.1027/1614-0001.30.1.35.

Swann, Sara. "Helping Girls Involved in 'Prostitution': A Barnardos Experiment." In *Home Truths About Child Sexual Abuse: Influencing Policy and Practice: A Reader*, edited by Catherine Itzin, 277–89. London: Routledge: 2000.

Swann, William B., Jr., and Jennifer K. Bosson. "Identity Negotiation: A Theory of Self and Social Interaction," in *Handbook of Personality: Theory and Research*. 3rd ed. Edited by Oliver P. John, Richard W. Robins, and Lawrence A. Pervin, 448–71. New York: The Guilford Press, 2008.

Swann, William B., and Brett W. Pelham. "The Truth About Illusions: Authenticity and Positivity in Social Relationships." In *Handbook of Positive Psychology*, edited by C. R. Snyder and Shane J. Lopez, 366–81 Oxford: Oxford University Press, 2002.

Sweeny, Kate, Darya Melnyk, Wendi Miller, and James A. Shepperd. "Information Avoidance: Who, What, When, and Why." *Review of General Psychology* 14, No. 4 (2010): 340–53, doi: 10.1037/a0021288.

Tajfel, Henri. "Social Psychology of Intergroup Relations." *Annual Review of Psychology* 33 (1982): 1–39.

Tarbox, Katherine. *A Girl's Life Online*. New York: Plume, 2000.

Ter Borg, Meerten B. "Religion and Power." In *The Oxford Handbook of The Sociology of Religion*, edited by Peter B. Clarke, 195–209. Oxford: Oxford University Press, 2011.

Tracy, Jessica L., and Alec T. Beall. "Happy Guys Finish Last: The Impact of Emotion Expressions on Sexual Attraction." *Emotion* 11, No. 6(2011): 1379–87, doi: 10.1037/a0022902.

Trenholm, Sarah. *Persuasion and Social Influence*. Englewood Cliffs: Prentice Hall, 1989.

Tucker, Eric. "Social Networking Puts the Bite on Defendants." *The Associated Press* (July 22, 2008), http://www.lawtechnologynews.com/id=1202423145595/Social-Networking-Puts-the-Bite-on-Defendants?slreturn=20140230001425.

Turner, John C. "Explaining the Nature of Power: A Three-Process Theory." *European Journal of Social Psychology* 35 (2005): 1–22.

Turton, Jackie. *Child Abuse, Gender and Society*. New York: Routledge, 2008.

Twenge, Jean M., and W. Keith Campbell. *The Narcissism Epidemic: Living in the Age of Entitlement*. New York: Atria, 2013.

Umphress, Elizabeth E., Kristin Smith-Crowe, Arthur P. Brief, Joerg Dietz, and Marla Baskerville Watkins. "When Birds of a Feather Flock Together and When They Do Not: Status

Composition, Social Dominance Orientation, and Organizational Attractiveness." *Journal of Applied Psychology* 92, No. 2 (2007): 396–409.

Van Dam, Carla. *Identifying Child Molesters: Preventing Child Sexual Abuse by Recognizing the Patterns of the Offenders*. New York: The Haworth Maltreatment and Trauma Press, 2001.

Van Leeuwen, Esther, and Susanne Tauber. "The Strategic Side of Out-Group Helping." In *The Psychology of Prosocial Behavior: Group Processes, Intergroup Relations, and Helping*, edited by Stefan Sturmer and Mark Snyder, 81–99. Chichester: John Wiley and Sons, 2010.

VanderVoort, Lise, and Steve Duck. "Sex, Lies, and . . . Transformation." In *The State of Affairs: Explorations in Infidelity and Commitment*, edited by Jean Duncombe, Kaeren Harrison, Graham Allan, and Dennis Marsden, 1–13. Mahwah: Lawrence Erlbaum Associates, 2004.

Vazire, Simine, and Samuel D. Gosling. "E-Perceptions: Personality Impressions Based on Personal Websites." *Journal of Personality and Social Psychology* 87, No. 1 (2004): 123–32, doi: 10.1037/0022-3514.87.1.123.

Vazire, Simine, Laura P. Naumann, Peter J. Rentfrow, and Samuel D. Gosling. "Portrait of a Narcissist: Manifestations of Narcissism in Physical Appearance." *Journal of Research in Personality* 42 (2008): 1439–47.

Vecchio, Robert P. "Power, Politics, and Influence." In *Leadership: Understanding the Dynamics of Power and Influence in Organizations*, edited by Robert P. Vecchio, 69–95. Notre Dame: University of Notre Dame Press, 2007.

Vela-McConnell, James A. *Unlikely Friends: Bridging Ties and Diverse Friendships*. Lanham, Plymouth: Lexington Books, 2011.

Visser, Beth A., and Julie A. Pozzebon. "Who Are You and What Do You Want? Life Aspirations, Personality, and Well-Being." *Personality and Individual Differences* 54 (2013): 266–71, http://dx.doi.org/10.1016/j.paid.2012.09.010.

Visser, Beth A., Julie A. Pozzebon, and Andrea M. Reina-Tamayo. "Status-Driven Risk Taking: Another 'Dark' Personality?" *Canadian Journal of Behavioral Science* (February 10, 2014): 1–12, doi: 10.1037/a0034163.

Vonk, Roosk. "Self-Serving Interpretations of Flattery: Why Ingratiation Works." *Journal of Personality and Social Psychology* 82, No. 4 (2002): 515–26, doi: 10.1037//0022-3514.82.4.515.

Wagner, Mervyn K. "Behavioral Characteristics Related to Substance Abuse and Risk-Taking, Sensation-Seeking, Anxiety Sensitivity, and Self-Reinforcement." *Addictive Behaviors* 26 (2001): 115–20.

Wai, Michael, and Niko Tiliopoulos. "The Affective and Cognitive Empathic Nature of the Dark Triad of Personality." *Personality and Individual Differences* 52 (2012): 794–99, doi: 10.1016/j.paid.2012.01.008.

Walster, Elaine, G. William Walster, Jane Piliavin, and Lynn Schmidt. "'Playing Hard to Get'" Understanding an Elusive Phenomenon." *Journal of Personality and Social Psychology* 26, No. 1 (1973): 113–21.

Wang, Sheng, Edward C. Tomlinson, and Raymond A. Noe. "The Role of Mentor Trust and Protégé Internal Locus of Control in Formal Mentoring Relationships." *Journal of Applied Psychology* 95, No. 2 (2010): 358–67.

Wartenberg, Thomas E. *The Forms of Power: From Domination to Transformation*. Philadelphia: Temple University Press, 1990.

Wegner, Daniel M., and Daniel B. Gold. "Fanning Old Flames: Emotional and Cognitive Effects of Suppressing Thoughts of a Past Relationship." *Journal of Personality and Social Psychology* 68, No. 5 (1995): 782–92.

Wegner, Daniel M., Julie D. Lane, and Sara Dimitri. "The Allure of Secret Relationships." *Journal of Personality and Social Psychology* 66 (2005): 287–300.

Wegner, Daniel M., Joann W. Shortt, Anne W. Blake, and Michelle S. Page. "The Suppression of Exciting Thoughts." *Journal of Personality and Social Psychology* 58 (1990): 409–18.

Whitchurch, Erin R., Timothy D. Wilson, and Daniel T. Gilbert. "'He Loves Me, He Loves Me Not . . .': Uncertainty Can Increase Romantic Attraction." *Psychological Science* 22, No. 2 (2011): 172–75.

White, Gregory L., Sanford Fishbein, and Jeffrey Rutstein. "Passionate Love and the Misattribution of Arousal." *Journal of Personality and Social Psychology* 41, No. 1 (1981): 56–62.

Widiger, Thomas A., and Donald R. Lynam. "Psychopathy and the Five-Factor Model of Personality." In *Psychopathy: Antisocial, Criminal, and Violent Behavior*, edited by Theodore Millon, Erik Simonsen, Morten Birket-Smith, and Roger D. Davis, 171–87. New York: The Guilford Press, 1998.

Williamson, Celia, and Terry Cluse-Tolar. "Pimp-Controlled Prostitution: Still an Integral Part of Street Life." *Violence Against Women* 8, No. 9 (2002): 1074–92.

Willis, Janine, and Alexander Todorov. "First Impressions: Making Up Your Mind After a 100-Ms Exposure to a Face." *Psychological Science* 17, No. 7 (2006): 592–98.

Wojciszke, Bogdan, and Anna Struzynska-Kujalowicz. "Power Influences Self-Esteem." *Social Cognition* 25, No. 4 (2007): 472–94.

Woodward, Gary C., and Robert E. Denton, Jr. *Persuasion and Influence in American Life*. 5th ed. Long Grove: Waveland Press, Inc., 2004.

Worley, Robert M., Richard Tewksbury, and Durant Frantzen. "Preventing Fatal Attractions: Lessons Learned From Inmate Boundary Violators in a Southern Penitentiary System." *Criminal Justice Studies* 23, No. 4 (December, 2010): 347–60. doi: 10.1080/1478601X.2010.516532.

Young, S. Mark, and Drew Pinsky. "Narcissism and Celebrity." *Journal of Research in Personality* 40 (2006): 463–71.

Zebrowitz, Leslie A. and Joann M. Montepare. "First Impressions from Facial Appearance Cues." In *First Impressions*, edited by Nalini Ambady and John J. Skowronski, 171–204. New York: The Guilford Press, 2008.

Zuckerman, Marvin. *Sensation Seeking and Risky Behavior*. Washington D.C.: American Psychological Association, 2007.

Index